3552 - Scholars Bookshelf - 3 pr 16⁸⁵

THE WORLD OF SEX
VOLUME 3: RESPONSIBLE PARENTHOOD

PERSPECTIVES ON JAPAN AND THE WEST

THE WORLD OF SEX

Volume 3
Responsible Parenthood

IWAO HOSHII

PAUL NORBURY PUBLICATIONS LIMITED
Woodchurch, Ashford, Kent.

First published 1987 by
PAUL NORBURY PUBLICATIONS LTD
Woodchurch, Ashford, Kent.

ISBN 0-904404-56-0

British Library C.I.P. Data
Hoshii, Iwao
The world of sex.
Vol. 3: Responsible Parenthood
1.Sex——Philosophy
I. Title
306.7'01   HQ21

ISBN 0-904404-56-0

Set in Bembo 10 on 12 by Visual Typesetting, Harrow.
Printed and bound by A. Wheaton & Co. Ltd, Exeter, England.

Contents

Foreword

NUMEROUS PHENOMENA indicate that children are in trouble: the increase in juvenile delinquency, the high incidence of teenage pregnancy, drug addiction and school violence involving bullying of schoolmates and assaults on teachers. The victimisation of children is appalling; thousands of children disappear, the international traffic in children seems to equal the white slave trade, child abuse is rampant, child prostitution and child pornography seem out of control, and millions of children live in abject poverty and are exploited by child labour. Naturally, the question arises: where are the parents? But the parents are part of the problem. The British public was shocked to learn that every week a child is killed by its parents or guardians and that every other week a child is murdered by other relatives or strangers. Each week, 400 children are made wards of the state because of ill-treatment or neglect. The Jasmine case has highlighted the dismal failure of the welfare services to protect endangered children and the Chicago case reported by Mike Royko has illustrated the shortcomings of the judicial system.

In the Jasmine case, social workers had ignored warnings by the foster parents that the girl's life would be threatened if returned to her mother and stepfather. Jasmine had been taken away from her mother at the age of 18 months when she was treated for a broken thigh and put in the custody of foster parents. A court later returned her to the custody of her mother and stepfather, an amateur boxer. When the 4-year-old girl was battered to death by her stepfather, she weighed just 10.5 kg. Doctors found that she had suffered 40 head injuries and 20 broken bones before her death by four blows that dislodged her brain.

In the Chicago case, a 1-year-old girl was brought to the Cook County Hospital by her grandmother. Her arms were broken in three different places, her face and jaw were bruised and she had a concussion. Her arms showed burn marks and hundreds of what appeared to be pinch marks covered her abdomen. She was in shock, her blood count was dangerously low and she had trouble breathing. In surgery, the doctors found internal bleeding, her liver had lacerations, her pancreas was bruised and bleeding and she had 10 cm of dead bowel. When placed in the intensive care unit after surgery, doctors discovered old fractures on both arms that were beginning to heal.

The doctors reported their findings to the Illinois Department of Children and Family Services. A case worker was sent to the family's home who asked the baby's mother and grandmother what had happened to the child. They denied that anything had happened. The baby just became ill. The hospital discovered a clue as to what had happened when the baby's 3-year-old brother told a doctor that the mother's boyfriend sometimes hit, choked and pinched him. The mother finally admitted that she had left the baby with her boyfriend when she had gone out for a few hours before the baby was brought to the hospital. And when the boyfriend came to the hospital with the mother, the baby became hysterical at the sight of him.

The Department of Children and Family Services took the case to the Cook County Juvenile Court and asked for temporary custody of the child. Judge Ronald Davis, after hearing the testimony of the doctors, mother and grandmother, said that apparently there was an injurious environment in the child's home but no urgent and immediate danger and refused to give temporary custody to the Department of Children and Family Services. Thanks to Mike Royko's column, the case did not end there but it suffices to show that the protection of battered children is not what it should be.

Children have long ceased to be counted as a blessing. Parents may be concerned with the way to raise their children or the costs of bringing them up but before such problems arise, the decision to have children should be preceded by the consideration of what it takes to be father or mother and whether he or she can qualify. It is a disaster if a child just happens and then forces the parents to take notice of its presence. Marriage means commitment, and this commitment must go beyond the partners and their mutual satisfaction to what was once considered the seal of life-long belonging.

Something is terribly wrong if parents regard their children only as a burden and a nuisance, if children fail to experience the warmth of the family and an affectionate home. In many cases, the material prerequisites for a normal family life are just not there.

This book deals with the ethical and legal aspects of the relations between parents and children. In some developed countries, official policies have wrought havoc with the family, parents and children alike. The denunciation of the family as a 'bourgeois' institution of the nineteenth century to be replaced in the era of socialist progress by nurseries, creches, homes and other establishments of the welfare state has been convicted of its absurdity by the catastrophic results of the new education.

The horror of child abuse is shocking but what children do to other children and adults is no less frightening. Society is paying dearly for perverting the functions of so basic an institution as the family. It is preposterous to sacrifice the natural mission of the mother to the postulates of a man-made economic order instead of accommodating economic conditions to the requirements of human nature.

Children must learn to live as human beings, that's the essence of education. While education is no panacea for all the ills in the situation of children, the erosion of the formative function of the family has been responsible for many of the woes of society. The social environment has suffocated the consciousness of parents of their vocation and the demands of parenthood on their behaviour. Today's living patterns contain little to show what a human being should be and contribute almost nothing to the character formation of either parents or children.

Although the country's abortion rate is horrendous, Japan is still a children's paradise at least for pre-school children. They are allowed to behave more or less as they please and discipline is very lax by western standards. Nevertheless, mothers generally care for their children. The nuclear family has nobody to look after the children when the mothers must go out, so mothers usually take their children along. Mothers riding a bicycle with two youngsters, one in front and another in the back, is a common sight. At the age of four or five, most children go to a kindergarten and the mothers accompany them there or to the bus stop and fetch them again in the afternoon. When the children start going to school, many women resume outside work and the children are often left to fend for themselves. The availability of a home with no adult present has encouraged drinking, smoking and sex by teenagers.

The old wisdom of *exempla trahunt* (examples inspire) is not obsolete but parents cannot be content with serving as 'role models'. Through father and mother, children must experience the warmth of human togetherness, the community of human love, the emotional closeness of a life in common. Parents must make their children feel the family as a living unit which they obviously cannot do if they are not united themselves. The disarray in marital relations is responsible for much of the failure in the education of children. I do not believe in the Socratic proposition that knowledge is virtue but I think that parents can do a better job if they have a clear understanding of what it means to be parents, which is the concern of this book.

IWAO HOSHII
December 1986

1

Family and Society

Society's Influence on the Individual

TRADITIONALLY, the family has been regarded as the smallest and most basic social unit. The family is a community, and community life is its real meaning. Since the family forms part of society, its structure and functions come necessarily under the influence of society and the family, in turn, is of importance for society. For the relation of today's Japanese family to today's Japanese society, two trends are of fundamental significance. The first is the 'depersonalisation' or 'dehumanisation' of society, the second the atomisation of the family.

The original meaning of society implies that people are pals or mates —'socii'. In general, the structure and form of society and its organisation become more rigid and complex in the course of its development. It is not impossible that a single person ('leader') impresses his stamp on a society but it is more common that the members of a group become the interchangeable material substratum of a permanent form and that their ability to influence the activities and behaviour of the group is very limited. The individual largely adapts his conduct to the pattern prevalent in a given society and this adaptation frequently does not stop at external behaviour but extends to the thinking, the value system and the emotional involvement of the individual. This is usually the situation in Japan where society does not constitute a structural unity but forms a conglomerate of sometimes cooperating but often competing groups.

In the West, the 'crisis of the family' has been a matter of concern for many years. Traditions, religious convictions, and sentiments, conventional norms, historical patterns and authoritative models have lost their peremptory validity. The influences of other groups or individuals start to weaken or extinguish the identification with the family at an early date. This process is more advanced in the United States than in Europe. The modern Japanese has excluded family and family relations from what he regards as 'society.' Not as if the family were not recognised as a group, but to the big-city Japanese, it is unrelated and irrelevant to society and concerns him only as an individual.

Importance of Family for Social Restraints

As far as Japanese group relations and group consciousness are concerned, the big-city Japanese is no longer aware of the social significance of the family in the sense that he does not appreciate its value and function as a social unit or relate it to other groups. In the old family system, belonging to a family automatically included a certain social position. In feudal Japan, the 'great' families constituted a structural element of society and the family organisation formed an essential factor in its functioning. In today's Japanese society, family relations may play a role in marriage and in finding employment but are generally without significance for a person's social position (the Imperial family is an exception). The family is irrelevant to the groups that now determine the social order and structure — which does not mean that nepotism is not part of patronage in politics, government and business.

In the old Japan, the 'house' formed a counterweight to the other groups making up society, but today the family remains outside the socially influential groups. In other words, the family is isolated and atomised. Just as individuals, families in the large cities are grains of sand without any organic connection with one another, the local community, or the state. The nuclear family is not the nucleus for additional or more comprehensive social relations but closed in itself and limited to itself. The ancestors formed a constitutive element of the old Japanese house of which the memorial tablets *(ihai)* and the family grave were symbols and representations. For the modern Japanese city family, funerals, anniversaries and visits to the cemetery are ephemeral events apart from the ordinary family life.

The nuclear family entertains only tenuous relations with relatives. Relatives are a peripheral, not a structural element in today's family relations which may create occasional disturbances, impose occasional burdens, and provide occasional benefits.

In post-war Japan, the emphasis was on the individual and self-fulfilment, without the old social restraints and uninfluenced by the values of the old social order. Naturally, most of the legal restraints remained but the new controls, such as the restrictions mentioned in the constitution, were largely abstract and without social sanctions. Politicians tainted by corruption may remain in office and continue to wield power. In the atomised society of liberalism and socialism, the individual ends up by thinking only of himself and blaming society, other people and anyone but himself for his personal problems.

In the country, the family retains more significance. It still fulfills an important economic function as an enterprise and production unit and there remain organic connections with other families and the local community.

Japanese custom obliged the eldest son (who under the old family system was the heir) to take care of the parents. This is no longer considered a duty but the parents and the family of the first-born son may live in the same house (the households are often separate) or one of the children may live near the parental home. The grandmother looks after the little children when the mother is busy and the old people do not feel quite so lonely.

Male Dominance in Japanese Society

A further feature of Japanese society is the continuing predominance of the male. What is usually described as group structure and group consciousness involves women only to a very limited extent. Although women make up nearly 40 per cent of the country's labour force, they are outsiders in Japan's business world. Because few women are in leading and management positions, they are without power. The system is male-created, male-directed, and male-dominated. Working women are largely unconcerned about policy decisions because most measures, including promotions and transfers, affect them only marginally. Social contacts connected with business, such as after-hour drinks with associates, golf with business customers, and meetings with old school friends are generally limited to males, but Japan's 'office ladies' are by no means averse to relaxation after finishing the day's work.

The post-war economic progress has made a more affluent life possible but women have never been given credit for their role in effecting this progress. They accept the result and today Japanese business is well aware of the predominant role of women in spending decisions. But outside the field of advertising which is strongly directed to women and children, this awareness has had no practical effect.

Group Consciousness

Basically, the Japanese retain a peasant mentality. They are conservative, prudent, conformist and shrewd. They maintain a close togetherness in their group relations and deviations are frowned upon. Divergence leads to ostracism (the custom of *mura hachibu* — help only for fire and death). Linked to the farmer's mentality is the group consciousness. Group integration is the most conspicuous national trait. The Japanese are said to consider themselves important not as individuals but rather as members of a group. This statement contains a certain truth but should not be pressed too closely. Today's society no longer comprises groups that claim the entire man. The same individual may belong to various groups, and although group loyalty is much stronger than in most western social bodies, it is usually limited to a particular sphere. The individual goes further in subordinating his personal interests to the group than people in the West. He may even sacrifice his personal aims to the aim and reputation of the group, he avoids appearing to dominate the group. He is always ready to apologise; apology is a lubricant to smooth social relations.

If everyone admits his fault in a misunderstanding, conflicts are prevented and explosive situations can be defused. In everyday life, people are supposed to control their emotions ('neither joy nor anger should appear' goes the saying), but on occasion, everybody can let off steam, whether at *saké* parties or at street demonstrations. At such times, the southern element in the Japanese national character reveals itself (the realisation that the Japanese are basically a southern people is essential to understanding them). Although the anonymity essential to urbanisation pervades Japanese society, there are situations to which the Japanese seem reluctant to apply the pattern of purely functional relationships.

Exchange of Gifts

The maintenance of proper relations involves an intricate system of gifts. The exchange of presents takes on stupendous proportions on two occasions, mid-year *(chûgen)* and year-end *(seibo)*. All department stores set up immense 'gift centres' where properly-labelled gifts can be ordered in all price ranges. Gifts are exchanged not only between individuals or families, but also between businesses. Presents are given by inferiors to superiors to express thanks for favours received and lay the foundation for future favours. Superiors give gifts to inferiors as a means of keeping their loyalty. Politicians reward their supporters and try to ensure their cooperation. Enterprises, including banks, give gifts to show their gratitude to customers and attract more business. Gifts and return gifts form part of the proper etiquette for weddings and funerals. When making a visit, a Japanese will always carry a gift.

Minorities in Japan

There is no Japanese 'race', but the Japanese form a very homogeneous society and discrimination against ethnic minorities such as Ainus, Koreans and Chinese and particularly against the so-called *burakumin* is strong. The *burakumin* are descendants of the former untouchables who slaughtered cattle, handled carcasses and were engaged in tanning. An estimated 2-3 million live in 5-6,000 communities in awful slums at the periphery of the large cities. These minorities are greatly handicapped as regards employment prospects and marriage.

Landlords sometimes refuse to rent apartments to foreigners and occasionally bars post signs 'Japanese only.' The vertical mobility characteristic of Japan's post-war society generally excluded minorities.

Finger-Printing

The contempt of minorities found official expression in the controversy over finger-printing. The Alien Registration Law enacted in 1951 required foreign nationals 14 (now 16) years or over who had been granted a period of stay of one year or over to be finger-printed. At the time of the initial registration, foreigners had to affix their finger-prints to three official documents, an original register for filing by local authorities, a registration certificate for the personal possession of the foreigner, and a finger-print register for storage by the central government. Finger-printing is also required each time the registration is renewed (the longest period for which permission of stay is granted is five years.) The certificate has to be carried at all times and shown to police or other officials whenever requested. Aliens who do not have a valid certificate can be deported.

When the peace treaty of San Francisco came into effect in 1952, the Koreans residing in Japan (most of them had been brought to Japan as forced labourers) who, until then, had been Japanese subjects, were unilaterally designated as 'aliens.' Of the 687,135 Koreans residing in Japan at year-end 1984, 85 per cent are second- or third-generation Koreans, born and raised in Japan, who speak only Japanese and have no connection whatever with Korea (there are also 67,895 Chinese).

Many foreigners object to the finger-printing practice as an infringement of human dignity comparing it to the requirements and status of criminals. Since about 1980, resistance against finger-printing has become widespread. Under the law, local governments cannot issue registration certificates to those refusing to be finger-printed and have to notify the police of the refusal. A number of foreigners have been arrested and others have been denied re-entry permits (needed when going abroad). The courts have invariably decided against foreigners objecting to finger-printing. In a case involving an American woman married to a Japanese, Judge Yoshikatsu Uehara of the Yokohama District Court admitted that finger-printing creates the feeling of humiliation and unhappiness and that there exists psychological resistance because finger-prints have customarily been used for criminal investigation. At the trial, local officials testified that municipal offices never used finger-prints for identifying foreign nationals and relied on names and photos. Nevertheless, the court found Kathleen Morikawa guilty and fined her ¥10,000 for violating the Alien Registration Law. Mrs Morikawa appealed the sentence but withdrew her appeal after the first hearing because she realised that she could not get a fair trial.

When South Korean President, Chun Doo Hwan, visited Japan in September 1984, he asked Prime Minister Yasuhiro Nakasone to improve the treatment of Korean residents. Besides the finger-printing issue, the problems of permitting Koreans to qualify as public primary and junior high school teachers and job discrimination against Koreans were on the list of Korean *gravamina*. The way the Japanese reacted to the Korean complaints revealed the deep-seated arrogance and obstinacy as well as the incorrigible stupidity of the Japanese bureaucracy. Officials of the Ministry of Justice, including justice ministers Eisaku Sumi and Hitoshi

Shimasaki, insisted that outside pressure could never sway them to change the law. In response to Korea's request for improvement, the ministry announced a revision of the law in May 1985. Black ink was replaced by a colourless ink, and instead of rolling the index finger on paper records, it was to be pressed flat on non-carbon duplicate paper. At the same time, the ministry issued a special order to mayors, admonishing them to put more pressure on aliens refusing to be finger-printed.

Koreans denounced the 'improvements' as a sham. In a TV interview, Goro Tomita, director of the Foreign Affairs Section of the Osaka prefectural police, remarked that 'foreign residents who do not want to abide by Japanese law should go home' and added, 'Those foreign nationals who were born and have been raised in this country like ordinary Japanese people should be naturalised.' These remarks greatly angered not only Koreans but also other foreigners.

The reasons the government cites for requiring finger-prints are hardly convincing. When the law was enacted, the government contended that finger-printing was necessary for preventing black marketeering, for catching spies and for curbing illegal entry — reasons which have no relation to present-day conditions. Finger-printing, the government maintains, is the only reliable system for identifying a person, but, as a matter of fact, finger-prints have never been used to identify anybody except in criminal investigations.

Most municipalities are reluctant to follow the ministry's instructions and seek police action against foreign residents who refuse to be finger-printed. The local officials have to deal with the persons affected by the government's system while the officials of the Ministry of Justice or the Home Ministry are only concerned with the proverbial shuffling of papers. Already in July 1983, the National Association of City Mayors unanimously adopted a resolution calling for the abolition of the system of finger-printing and the requirement to carry the registration certificate at all times. Over 700 municipal assemblies adopted resolutions to the same effect. Saburo Ito, the mayor of Kawasaki, defied the ministry by not reporting foreigners who refused to be finger-printed and issuing registration certificates without finger-prints. Only three of the 23 Tokyo ward offices followed the ministry's directives and municipalities all over Japan follow the lead of Kawasaki. Chief Cabinet Secretary, Takao Fujinami, upheld the government's stand that a law is a law and must be observed no matter how absurd it is. Since foreigners do not vote, politicians are not interested in the issue and it is very unlikely that the Diet will do anything to change the law.

In July 1983, the Kyoto police mobilised 30 policemen at 5.30 am to arrest Kim Myong Guan who had refused to be finger-printed but not a single policeman appeared when, thereafter, right-wing groups with loudspeakers harassed Mr Kim for days on end until he moved.

Rejection of Outsiders

An illustration of the rejection of outsiders by Japan's rural communities was the opposition of the town of Otone-machi in Saitama Prefecture to the establishment of an orphanage. When the institution opened despite the local resistance, the town refused to register the orphans as residents and both candidates in a mayoral election vowed that they would try to close the orphanage if elected. The prefectural authorities, however, insisted that, under the law, the town office was obliged to register the orphans as town residents. These children, therefore, will be able to enter the local primary school when they grow up which was the main reason behind the opposition to the orphanage. For these children, the natives feared, would have a negative effect on the education of their own children.

Regional sub-cultures are not prominent in Japan but some professional groups (such as *sumo*) preserve distinctive life-styles.

The ordinary Japanese usually disregards the distinction between 'race' and nationality. Only ethnic Japanese are accepted as 'true' Japanese. People of mixed blood ('halfs') are often just as much discriminated against as Koreans and Chinese living in Japan. Westerners who are naturalised Japanese are too few to be of any significance but they have no position in Japan's social order.

Children of Expatriates

A problem peculiar to Japan is the education of children of expatriates. Compared with other countries, the number of Japanese businessmen posted abroad is relatively large, and many companies make it possible for their employees to take their families with them. According to the Japanese Ministry of Education, 36,223 children of primary and junior high school age were living abroad as of 1 May, 1984. Of these children, 15,456 (42.7 per cent) were enrolled in the 76 Japanese schools established by the government in 55 foreign countries, mainly in Asia and Europe. These schools have a full-time curriculum largely identical with that of Japanese schools at home. Of the 20,767 children studying at local schools, 13,329 took additional courses at 102 supplementary schools in 42 countries, mostly in North America and Europe. The supplementary schools provide instruction in Japanese and a few other subjects, such as mathematics.

For many of the young people growing up abroad, the Japanese language becomes a major problem when they return to Japan and their integration into the Japanese society may also prove very difficult. From April 1983 to March 1984, 9,786 children returned from abroad of whom 64.4 per cent were primary school pupils, 23.1 per cent junior and 12.3 per cent senior high school students. Often, their fluency in foreign languages and their understanding of foreign cultures may go to waste. When they enroll in Japanese schools, they are sometimes treated as 'outsiders' and regarded as a threat to a closely-knit society. They feel that there is a wall between themselves and other students and experience that Japan is still a self-contained clan rejecting foreign influences. In all schools, students form groups who talk together, have lunch together, play together and, in the case of girls, go to the lavatory together. The returnees are excluded from these groups. If there are a number of returnees at the same school, they may form their own group.

In English classes, the students who have grown up in English-speaking countries are never asked to recite, to read or to answer questions, for two reasons. The teacher is unsure of his own English and he does not want the other students to feel inferior. When returnees converse among themselves in English, they are told by other students, 'This is Japan — so speak Japanese!' The boys and girls who have become used to the openness with which everything is discussed in western society are taken aback by the reticence, furtiveness and evasiveness of the 'true' Japanese.

Public Officials

Japanese society is a multi-layered mould in which the new co-exists with the old rather than replaces it. The public sector includes politicians and political parties, central and local administration, the judiciary, police and military, the public school system, public health service and the public communication and transportation networks. The total number of public employees amounted to 1.95 million in 1982. All the organs and agencies comprise a multitude of partly hierarchically structured nationwide or local divisions and subdivisions. The different branches of the administration are often engaged in jurisdictional squabbles, asserting the incompatible claims of their clients or other pressure groups.

While many officials are intelligent and well-informed, polite and helpful, there are also prejudiced, narrow-minded, arrogant and self-conceited bureaucrats whose behaviour contradicts their constitutional role of 'servants of the whole community' (Art. 15, Par. 2).

Conflict of Interest

By law, officials leaving the government service are barred for two years from employment with private enterprises closely connected with the agencies to which they belonged in the five years prior to their retirement (National Public Service Law, Art. 103, Par. 2). But the National Personnel Authority can grant exemption from this prohibition, and the assumption of executive posts in private companies by retiring bureaucrats (popularly referred to as *amakudari* — descent from heaven) is an indication of the 'incestuous' relations between business and the bureaucracy. In 1985, 318 government officials with the rank of section chief *(kachô)* and higher were given permission to seek re-employment with private firms. Former officials of the Ministry of Finance topped the list with 60, retirees from the Ministry of International Trade and Industry (MITI) numbered 36 and those from the Ministry of Agriculture, Fisheries and Forestry and from the Ministry of Transportation each came to 29. Numerically, the 318 retirees accounted for 8.8 per cent of the 3,600 high-ranking government employees retiring in 1985 and 0.6 per cent of the total of 51,000 government retirees, but the influence of the Old Boy network should not be underestimated.

The subdivisions of the state do not constitute a true hierarchy but only an administrative organisation whose structure possesses no social reality but represents only a system of competencies. Each administrative organ can deal directly with each citizen and its internal organisation is irrelevant to its orders and decisions. The administrative gradation is not based on the social functions of a certain group of officials but on the order of competency and the chain of command.

The diversity and irreconcilability of interests is also found among politicians to whom the demands of their constituencies and the groups and associations that support them are more important than the fate of their party or the common good.

The same disunity prevails in the private sector in which the mixture of harmony and discord, cooperation and wrangling, agreement and dissension exists between enterprises in the same industrial branch, the various industries, management and workforce, entrepreneurs and labour unions. Then, there are different and sometimes rival organisations, groups and factions in sports, entertainment, arts and sciences, and warring clans of gangsters. In such groups, the influence of personalities may outweigh the importance of the organisation which is also the case in agriculture and fisheries. The bosses of the agricultural cooperatives have close ties with politicians and are able to have the government adopt and maintain policies and measures inimical to the interests of the consumers and compromising the country's foreign relations.

In large corporations, the contest of individuals for the top posts is often accompanied by the formation of factions. Executives hostile to the leading clique may prefer to quit rather than fight and the gang in power usually succeeds in easing its opponents out of influential positions. The in-fighting is aided by two features of Japan's corporate scene. First, the shareholders meeting of Japanese companies is a pure formality stage-managed by the leading members of the board of directors. Secondly, private conduct may be discussed in personal conversation but is rarely brought into the open (except by investigative or mud-raking reporters of the weeklies). Even costly mistakes in the conduct of business are seldom used for forcing out an incompetent executive; he is given an opportunity to retire gracefully with a golden handshake.

Education and Career

Japanese society attaches enormous importance to a person's educational background, an attitude referred to as *gakureki henchô* (overemphasis on formal schooling). Because a diploma says nothing about real ability, large companies restrict their recruitment to graduates from a limited number of institutions. Since it is difficult to fire an employee once he or she is hired, this selectivity provides a certain guarantee against the risk of hiring duds. Education in the sense of having a diploma from a prestigious university is an essential factor for obtaining employment leading to a career with high income and high social status.

Because of the restrictive hiring practices of large enterprises, parents are anxious to have their sons graduate from one of the famous schools preferred by big business. This process now starts with kindergarten. If a boy is admitted into the right kindergarten, he can get on the 'escalator' — the right elementary school, junior and senior high school and university. Graduation from the University of Tokyo *(Tôdai)* is the key to a career in government while in the private sector, some private universities such as Keio and Waseda also open the road to success. Recently, the business magazine, *Shûkan Diamond,* surveyed the educational background of some 30,000 board members of Japanese companies listed on the stock exchanges and came up with the following data. *Tôdai* was top with 4,671 of its graduates holding executive positions, Kyoto University was second with 2,125, followed by Waseda with 1,723, Keio with 1,654 and Hitotsubashi with 1,034. There was, however, a significant shift if the executives were classified by age groups. *Tôdai* graduates accounted for the largest number of the board members over 50, but in the age group from 40 to 49, Keio graduates predominated and the same applied to the lower age brackets.

This situation has created a vicious circle. Because the large companies prefer certain institutions in their recruitment, young people want to get into these institutions; because these institutions attract the best talent, enterprises tend to limit their hiring to the graduates from these institutions.

The situation is different for girls. Prospects of a 'good' marriage overshadow the chances of employment. *Gakushûin,* the former Peers School, used to confer the highest degree of social prestige on its graduates but the formation given young women at the *alma mater* of Crown Princess Michiko, the University of the Sacred Heart, is deemed a special asset for the wives of future government and business leaders.

Limits of Group Consciousness

The above description of Japanese society is meant to clarify the meaning of this term. The Japanese are often labelled group-oriented, success-oriented, and work-oriented; they are said to feel more comfortable at their place of work than at home and to put the interest of their work ahead of that of their families. Such global judgements may be accurate in some respects but too sweeping and far from reality in others. It must be stressed that the group adherence and group consciousness of the Japanese is not related to the abstract 'society' but to a specific group and therefore subject to drastic changes. Belonging to an enterprise or factory may be included in the group consciousness of an employee but the division or section to which he is assigned may dominate his thinking and particularly his feeling so that the human element may be more important than the organisation.

The group consciousness involves human as well as organisational aspects which is one of the reasons why the typical 'organisation' man is rare in Japan. The individual's position in the organisation to which he belongs determines his social standing but does not necessarily define his human relations and the group with which he identifies. People who belong to very different organisations may show very strong similarities. The élite consciousness stemming from the school from which an individual graduated, the organisation with which he is associated and his position may be intense but does not involve segregation into a particular class or caste.

Typical of Japan is that the position within a group which determines the individual's relations to the other members of the group also influence the behaviour of the members of his family to the members of the group and their families.

Social stratification based on birth, education, occupation and wealth remains strong. In manufacturing industries, the advance in technology and the Japanese management system, notably the measures for quality control, have created more contacts between white and blue collar workers, but in large enterprises, an indelible line separates the office staff from the service personnel. In hotels, restaurants and coffee shops, the customer-servant relationship precludes any attempt at 'fraternisation.' Service in Japanese establishments may be impeccable but patrons do not show their appreciation and waiters and waitresses do not expect it (instead of tips, a 10 or 15 per cent service charge is added to the bill).

Assertion of Individuality

Self-assertion is not impossible, and there are many examples of strong leadership, not only in the military, but also in politics, business and above all in religion. But leadership must be in conformity with the individual's position in society. A man must have advanced to the top or have been promoted by the group before he can assert his authority. Very often, mere organisational or paper authority remains ineffective.

Relatively few Japanese have stood apart and defied the group in the name of higher principles. Japan lacks religious and moral values transcending the group. During the war, many intellectuals showed an abject submissiveness; they believed or pretended to believe in the myth that the emperor was a living god and supported militarism. After the war, they bowed before the American occupation authorities to save their positions.

Due to their Confucian tradition, Japanese preferred to listen without voicing their own opinions. Women, in particular, were trained not to raise questions or proffer opinions. It would be impolite to put somebody on the spot by asking difficult questions, and to state an opinion different from that of one's superior would be a challenge to authority. A younger man taking the initiative in a conference might be scolded after the event for being *namaiki* (impertinent) or *deshabari* (presumptuous).

Most people do not belong to a political party or religious organisation. They are not interested in politics or economics 'as such' but in their own personal well-being. They feel a basic insecurity, rely for their views on the mass media, want the 'affluent' society but harbour many unfulfilled aspirations: a home of their own or a better home, more leisure and less stress. They feel a personal allegiance to their company and are generally conservative, but they are outraged by the corruption and venality of the ruling party. However, they know no viable alternative: socialism is no desirable life-style for acquiring greater affluence.

The West often suffered from its inability or unwillingness to take Japan seriously. Foreigners view Japan as a country motivated solely by self-interest without any consideration for larger, more abstract issues or basic principles. Japan shows no positive leadership and merely reacts to strong external pressure.

Public Waste

Democracy as practised in Japan has not the faintest resemblance with what was originally understood by this term. The Japanese élite craves for wealth and power. Politicians evince an undisguised contempt of the common people and a silly predilection for ostentatious and useless prestige projects. The central government, prefectures and municipalities have wasted the taxpayers' money on pretentious office buildings and sumptuous temples of culture while schools, hospitals, orphanages and other social facilities have been neglected. Enormous sums have been squandered because the construction of expressways, railroads and bridges was used for profiteering and political advantage. The construction of the Narita International Airport is an example of incredible miscalculations and atrocious mismanagement but nobody has ever been questioned let alone prosecuted for the enormous waste connected with this project.

Politicians and bureaucrats do not feel the slightest qualm when they increase their own salaries and pensions in utter disregard of probity and justice, rig the tax system and provide for themselves sinecures assuring them of millions of unearned income after retirement. The Dalai Lama's assessment of Mao Zedong may apply to Japan's ruling elite: 'My conclusion is that unbridled materialism leads to lust for power and power ends in arrogance which breeds mistakes and finally destruction.'

Inequality in Electoral System

Japan's election results are deceptive because the cities are under-represented. For many years, the courts turned down suits seeking redress in the unequal allocation of seats but finally, in 1983, the Supreme Court conceded that the disproportion in the 'value' of votes (one vote in a largely rural electoral district had the same 'weight' as four votes in a city district) was 'an unconstitutional state of affairs' but did not invalidate the election.

In July 1985, the Supreme Court ruled that the December 1983 general election had been unconstitutional because the disproportional allocation of seats to the various constituencies contravened the constitutional provision of equality under the law. In the fifth district of Hyogo Prefecture, for example, 82,033 voters were entitled to elect one representative while in Chiba's fourth district, one seat was allocated to 362,041 voters, which means a ratio of 1:4.41. In the actual voting, a candidate in Niigata's third district who received 40,931 votes was successful while the candidate elected with the lowest number of votes in Chiba's fourth district needed 140,966 votes, a ratio of 1:3.44. The court did not invalidate the election holding that the uncertainties created by such an invalidation would be disproportionate to the benefits of such a ruling but one of the judges dissented and asserted that the election should be declared invalid at least in some constituencies.

The conservative party secures the farm vote by absurd agricultural policies which have raised the price of Japan's staple food, rice, to eight times the world market price. The city population is generally dissatisfied on account of high prices and unsatisfactory housing and commuting conditions and has no trust in the political leadership. There is no sympathy for active revolutionaries but resentment of the establishment, politicians, bureaucrats and business leaders, is deep-seated. However, the prevailing political mood of the masses is apathy. Since the Japanese version of the affluent society has made money the sole measure of success, the moral corruption of the political leadership is only castigated in the mud-raking articles of the weeklies.

There is no universal moral system recognised by society and most rules of conduct are concerned with proper etiquette and the appropriate behaviour in specific social situations. More important than principles are human feelings, and respect for social relations has nothing to do with the legitimacy of the social order.

Confucian morality on which many of Japan's social values were based stressed the right social order and the hierarchy of social relations. But the average Japanese holds no firm inner principles and is not greatly restrained by moral taboos. Nothing prevents him from trying and adopting new, convenient, useful and profitable things. The middle class, in particular, is uncommitted and individualistic, but their individualism coexists with their identification with a special group.

Lack of Civic-Mindedness

A sphere in which the Japanese compare poorly with western countries is civic-mindedness. Due to the autocratic traditions of the Tokugawa period and the even more restrictive political climate of the Meiji era, autonomous action of the population was largely confined to innocuous celebrations and festivals organised by local communities and the associations connected with temples and shrines or mutual assistance. In case of natural disasters, the authorities are expected to organise relief and spontaneous self-help is quickly supplanted by government-directed action. The funds raised for the community chest in fiscal 1982 amounted to ¥21.2 billion which, on a per capita basis, came to ¥168, only one-tenth of the per-capita contributions in the United States (¥1,700).

In Europe and the United States, private voluntary organisations play an important part in supporting projects in developing countries but they are of relatively little importance in Japan. Grants provided by Japanese non-governmental organisations in 1981 to developing countries amounted to $27.3 million compared with $1,108.0 million for the United States and $371.1 million for West Germany. In the West, the Christian tradition of charity and neighborly love has been an important factor in the consciousness of human solidarity and the Christian churches have been the main supporters of voluntary charitable work. Even the philanthropy of secular humanism has Christian origins. In Japan, neither Shintoism nor Buddhism ever inspired community spirit and social involvement.

As a result of the relativity of value systems, philosophical tenets or religious dogmas in the mind of the 'ordinary' Japanese, truth, right, law or conscience may mean different things in Japan and in the West. Religion, in particular, is a purely private affair. The Sôka Gakkai (Value-creating Society), a modern adaptation of Nichiren Buddhism, had to form a separate organisation for its political activities, and the attempts of the right wing of the Liberal-Democratic Party to re-establish State Shinto have so far failed.

Higher than truth is sincerity, and if a criminal shows repentance (hansei no iro), his crime seems to lose its anti-social character and he is treated like a prodigal son. It is up to the listener to discover the *'honne'* (actual meaning) in the words that state the *'tatemae'* (principle, premise). This may be an integral part of the system of a society that had to reconcile the constraints of oppressive social relations with the basic instinct for individual survival.

Racial Prejudice

Foreigners are often puzzled by the readiness of the Japanese to disregard common sense if it seems contrary to official 'guidance'. Japanese universities had had foreigners on their staffs since the Meiji era but in 1953, the National Personnel Authority (NPA) ruled that professors at national universities should be Japanese nationals because a professor at these institutions is a civil servant and therefore engaged in the process of forming 'state will' and executing 'state power'.

There is nothing in the law which requires Japanese nationality at state universities and private universities have always appointed many foreigners as professors, but on account of the fatuous interpretation of the NPA, state and public universities have relegated foreigners to the status of part-time lecturers, teaching assistants or visiting professors for the past 30 years. Thirty prefectures have made Japanese citizenship a condition for admission to the teaching certificate examination (a measure intended primarily to exclude Koreans from teaching).

In an ugly demonstration of racial prejudice, the Nagano Prefectual Board of Education cancelled the recruitment of a Korean woman who had twice passed the recruitment test for teachers and had been hired to start teaching in 1985. The woman, Yang Hong Ja, was born to a Korean father and a Japanese mother in Higashi-Osaka; the family moved to Nagano where the girl graduated from the School of Education of Shinshu University and obtained a teacher's licence. She passed the public teacher recruitment examination but was not hired because of her nationality. She took the examination again in 1984 and was notified on 20 November that she would be employed as a primary school teacher in the coming year. But the Ministry of Education called board officials to Tokyo several times and insisted that the board follow the ministry's policy of not hiring foreigners as 'public servants.' The ministry has no legal authority to interfere with the decisions of the local boards of education but the ministry, a citadel of chauvinism, xenophobia and sheer stupidity, has assiduously followed a policy of regaining its domineering pre-war position. Miss Yang was verbally (!) notified of the cancellation of her recruitment on 17 December.

Following public condemnation of the outrageous affair, Miss Yang, in a typically Japanese compromise, was hired as an instructor *(kôshi)*, not as a full-time teacher.

Westernisation

Since the Meiji Restoration, Japan's leaders have been fascinated by the *Fata Morgana* of Japan as a nation accepted and respected as equal by the world's leading powers. The country's modernisation in the form of westernisation was considered essential to reaching this goal, and in this process Japan has run the risk of losing her identity as an Asian nation. She has been attacked by the West for not conforming to western standards and rejected by the East for embracing the cultural atrocities of the West. Because Japan tries hard to behave as a western nation, westerners assume that she believes in western values and blame her for not living up to these values. But most Japanese have only the haziest idea of what western values are and no inclination whatever of conforming to them. Some politicians may profess their faith in fair trade or international cooperation but they are unable to overcome the parochial policies of the bureaucracy.

On the surface, westernisation has greatly affected popular tastes and the people's life-style, but mentally and ideologically, Japan is no nearer to the West than over a 100 years ago when this trend began. The products of western civilisation and western technology, imitated and recreated, have become integral parts of modern Japan. Western dress, food and housing, although referred to in the language as 'western,' are not perceived as un-Japanese and their use does not imply any partiality for the West. Business suits are just as Japanese as are Toyota cars, Nikon cameras or Sony video cassettes, and the super-express is just as Japanese as Nikko's Tôshôgû's shrine. This does not exclude the fact that western fads may enjoy tremendous popularity and that Coca-Cola, McDonald's hamburgers or Stevie Wonder enjoy colossal success.

Foreign Views on Japan

The foreigners' image of Japan, Japanese society and the Japanese people has undergone numerous changes and oscillated between the poles of blind hostility and indulgent sympathy. Japan never was a European colony but attitudes of colonial or imperial superiority towards an 'oriental' people occasionally surface even today. Because westerners felt that they had nothing to learn from Japan, they consistently underestimated the country, failed to understand its course and therefore were frequently caught by surprise. The pre-war image of Japan was, as the title of Ruth Benedict's *The Chrysanthemum and the Sword* (the book was based on material produced under a programme for psychological warfare in the Pacific but published in 1946) indicates, a juxtaposition of the *'Madame Butterfly'* pattern of an exotic Shangri-la depicted in many of Lafcadio Hearn's stories (who, however, was also bitterly disappointed and frustrated) and the fanatical, bellicose and cruel warriors who had defeated China and Russia and achieved infamous notoriety by the sacking of Nanking (1937) with the loss of so many Chinese lives. Japan, therefore, is 'a dreamland and a nightmareland' (Luis A Camales), the Japanese race is aggressive and unaggressive, the Japanese are insolent and polite, rigid and adaptable, loyal and treacherous (Ruth Benedict), lovable and barbaric (Lafcadio Hearn).

Yasukuni Shrine

The atrocities committed by the Japanese army have never become the subject of national soul-searching. The Tokyo War Crime Trials were too much of a put-up job to make a deep impression, and some of those found guilty did not deserve their fate. On the other hand, the pre-war professional soldiers received far too generous treatment after the war but nobody objected. The association of bereaved families which sponsors nationalistic causes wields considerable political clout which it uses above all for increasing the pensions of ex-servicemen and their families. The soft-pedalling of the excesses of the Japanese military by the Ministry of Education is by no means accidental, and the many flagrant violations of human rights in Japan before and during the war by the police (especially the *tokkô-ka,* political police) and the army, above all the infamous *kenpeitai* (military police) have never been investigated by the Japanese.

The Ministry of Health and Welfare belatedly acknowledged that it had violated the constitution by paying for the enshrinement of war dead between 1950 and 1971. The Japanese were baffled by the angry reaction in Korea and China to the 'official' 1985 visit of Prime Minister Yasuhiro Nakasone to Yasukuni Shrine because they do not understand the ideological significance of the shrine. These people were not outraged because the war dead and some war criminals like General Tôjô are enshrined there. Yasukuni Shrine is the symbol of pre-war militarism and chauvinism, the emperor cult and the exaltation of the *kokutai* (national polity), the oppression of the freedom of thought and the torture of dissidents. The symbolic past of the shrine cannot be wiped away by pious protestations of sincere intentions.

War Compensation

A group of Taiwanese who sustained injuries while serving in the Imperial Japanese Army during World War II brought a suit for compensation. A total of 207,183 Taiwanese were conscripted as soldiers or civilian employees during the war of whom 30,300 were killed in action. Former Japanese soldiers who were injured or became sick while on duty and the families of soldiers killed in action are entitled to pensions and allowances, but Taiwanese and Koreans who were drafted into the army automatically lost Japanese nationality after the war. The issue of compensation was settled with South Korea but negotiations with the government of Chiang Kai-shek dragged out and when Japan established relations with the People's Republic of China, no further steps were taken. The Taiwanese lost in the district court in 1982 and the Tokyo High Court upheld the decision in August 1985. The court admitted that the Taiwanese had been discriminated against but asserted that there was no legal foundation for recognising their claim. The fear that North Korea would put forward claims for compensation has been a factor in the Japanese government's failure to take relief measures but basically, the government does not care about human rights.

Japan's Post-War Image

In the post-war period, the sinister image of Japan changed from militaristic totalitarianism to the economic-bureaucratic totalitarianism of Japan, Inc. Japan appeared as an unpredictable and unreliable trading partner, imitating western products, stealing western technology, and engaged in unfair competition and social dumping. Japan was accused of conducting trade wars, utilising cheap labour, polluting the country's overcrowded industrial conglomerations and exporting unemplolyment. In the 1982 American election campaign, Japan-bashing became a favourite electioneering ploy. Some politicians blamed Japan for all the woes besetting the American economy, and particularly for unemployment. Their shrill hypocritical rhetoric and their unvarnished protectionism appealed to ethnic prejudice and dark resentment, and their deliberate disinformation was in the best 'know-nothing' tradition.

Japanese Character

Foreigners are critical of the Japanese for not clearly saying 'yes' or 'no' and expressing negative feelings or opinions only implicitly. Western tact does not include saying something that is not true. To the Japanese, directness means rudeness; it is impossible to be both direct and polite. Japanese tact emphasises making the person feel good over the relative truth of the compliment, places more weight on trying to please than on the actual words used. The Japanese say something because it is the socially acceptable thing to say under the circumstances. Foreigners are sometimes put off by the euphemisms and circumlocutions of Japanese politeness to superiors and strangers and the rudeness to inferiors including, in the old generation, one's wife.   Familiar expressions such as the seemingly meaningless fixed greetings do not shock or upset. They do not require originality or individuality and their triteness makes them appropriate under almost all circumstances. They make a conversation possible if nobody has anything to say and allow to start a conversation that may become unpleasant.

The Japanese can be the most stubborn people in the world. If a Japanese is not convinced, it is virtually impossible to get him to do something, and he will seldom do something on his own unless he is excited about it. He must be convinced on his own terms; otherwise, the difference in terms precludes reaching an agreement on issues and substance. The Japanese humbleness and self-depreciation seems hypocritical to foreigners because the same individual can also be proud and haughty.

The Japanese think that it is impolite to express preferences and avoid indicating personal likes and dislikes. Sometimes, they seem to have no opinion of their own, particularly when they are in a group. However, if there is no obvious group spokesman (somebody much senior than everybody else), no individual wants to voice a view or even say 'yes,' because in doing so, he would make himself the spokesman of the group. To show off one's ability or seize the spotlight is considered impolite and poor form. Japanese avoid contentious subjects and dislike discussing difficult issues. But in a relaxed atmosphere, they greatly enjoy witty repartees, and while they shun ideological confrontation and have no taste for abstract arguments, they appear very inquisitive when it comes to personal questions. Foreigners may consider it an intrusion into a person's privacy to ask questions about a stranger's family and his social or economic status, but a Japanese finds it difficult to start or continue a conversation without background information. Ordinarily, a Japanese can place an individual when he sees his namecard, but this does not work for foreigners.

Favourable Foreign Opinion

Foreign opinion friendly to Japan looks upon the country as a well-organised, neat, clean and functioning society which despite its efficiency has not lost its sense for aesthetic values. People still care in Japan, and have pride in what they are doing. Society is kept together by discipline, hard work and self-respect. Traditions, over-emphasised and distorted during the war, are rediscovered and national identity is again linked to the country's cultural heritage. Foreigners are impressed by the service in Japanese hotels, restaurants, department stores, banks and service stations. People keep their appointments despite horrible traffic conditions. Tokyo's subway system is the envy of many foreign visitors. The precision of the train sequence is exemplary, the cars are neat and clean, the plush seats undamaged and the walls not smeared with graffiti.

Although the Japanese have an almost morbid interest in the opinions of foreigners on everything Japanese, their self-consciousness has hardly been affected by foreign approval or condemnation. Throughout their history, the Japanese have shown a versatile readiness to accept foreign influences while, at the same time, maintaining the firm conviction of their ethnic and national uniqueness. They believe that they are different from all other people in the world and that their system, sentiments and sanctions defy the understanding by non-Japanese.

Demographic Data

As mentioned in Volume 2, society relies more or less as a matter of course on the functions of the family to assure the continuity of the species. As a 'producer of people,' the family supports not only the quantitative growth of society but is equally important for its quality because of the essential role the family plays in education. As in most industrialised countries, the will to have children has weakened considerably in Japan's post-war era. In 1951, the birth rate stood at 25.5 births per 1,000 population. This already was a decline from the 'baby boom' in the years from 1947 to 1949 when the birth rate reached 33 to 34 (Japan's highest rate had been in 1920 when it came to 36.6). In 1966, the rate dropped to a low of 13.7 but rose again in the following years (1973: 19.4) only to decline again. It sank to 12.5 in 1984 and declined to 11.9 in 1985, the first time since 1899 (when the survey started) that the birth rate fell below 12. In the five years from 1975 to 1980, Japan's population increased at an average yearly rate of 0.92 per cent, relatively high compared with other industrial countries, but in the following quinquennium, the average dropped to 0.7 per cent. As of 1 October 1985, Japan's population totaled 121,047,196 (59.5 million men, 61.55 million women), up 3.4 per cent over 1980, the lowest growth rate in the past 40 years.

Reflecting the post-war baby boom, the number of marriages rose sharply in the beginning of the seventies and reached a peak of 1.1 million in 1972, but it fell swiftly thereafter and was down to 735,000 in 1985. Moreover, women marry at a later age. The proportion of unmarried women in the age group from 20 to 24 rose from 69.2 per cent in 1975 to 77.9 per cent in 1980 while in the same period, that of married women dropped from 30.3 per cent to 21.7 per cent. In the 25 to 29 age group, the ratio of unmarried women increased from 20.9 per cent to 23.9 per cent, that of married women declined from 77.8 per cent to 74.7 per cent. Furthermore, birth control is widely practised and about 87 per cent of all married women in the age group from 20 to 29 use contraceptives.

The effects of the post-World War II baby boom also affect the demographic situation in other countries. In the United States, the population aged 25 to 44 increased by 17.8 per cent between 1980 and 1985 and constituted over 30 per cent of the total US population in that year (as of 1 July 1985, the US population numbered 227,061,000, comprising 122,694,000 women and 116,649,000 men). The average age rose from 30 in 1980 to 31.5 in 1985. The relative increase in the higher age groups was far more rapid than the average growth of the population. Compared with a growth rate of 5.4 per cent for the entire population, between 1980 and 1985, the number of people 65 to 74 grew by 9.1 per cent, that of people from 75 to 84 by 14.2 per cent, and the number of people over 85 rose by 21 per cent to 2,711,010.

Although the number of marriages in the United States is high (1983: 2,445,604), the marriage rate is declining; it was 99.3 weddings per 1,000 single women aged 15 to 44 in 1983, the first time that the rate dropped below the 100 level since 1940 when the statistics were first recorded.

Japan's national census reporting the population figures as of 1 October 1985, put the average number of household members at 3.18, down from 3.25 in 1980. According to a five-year survey conducted by the Ministry of Health and Welfare, the average Japanese family had 2.23 children as of June 1982, slightly up from 2.19 in 1977. About 55 per cent of all families had two children, 25 per cent had three and 10 per cent one child. Most couples have their first child within two years after their marriage, and the second child about three years later. All of their children arrive within the first five years of their marriage.

The birth rate differs for the various regions of the country and is somewhat higher in rural areas than in the cities. Consequently, the size of the families is also different. In 1980, the size of the average family was 2.63 persons in Tokyo prefecture as against 3.87 persons in Yamagata prefecture.

In 1982, families comprising both parents with minor children accounted for 41.5 per cent of the 36,243,000 households (down from 43.1 per cent in 1980). The percentages of the other types of households were: singles 18.8 per cent, spouses only 13.7 per cent, one parent and unmarried children 4.4 per cent, three-generation families 16.1 per cent, other 5.6 per cent.

According to the Institute of Population Problems, Japan's population will grow to a peak of 130.6 million in 2006 when people over 60 will account for about 20 per cent of the population. Japan, therefore, is somewhat behind European countries in its march towards depopulation but the tendency towards growing senescence is becoming more pronounced.

Japan's Aging Society

The increase of the proportion of the older age classes in the structure of Japan's population indicates one of the problems of an aging society. As of 1 October 1985, people aged 65 and older numbered 12.39 million, 10.2 per cent of the country's total population (121,047,136). The other age groups were: children below 14, 26.09 million, 21.6 per cent; 15-64: 85.5 million, 68.2 per cent. Average life expectancy of men was 74.54 years, that of women 80.18 years. There were 3.11 million households in which the husband was 65 years and older, the wife 60 years and older, with children under 18. They accounted for 8.4 per cent of all households (38.11 million), double the ratio in 1970 (4 per cent). Of the people over 65, 5.08 million were men and 7.32 million women; of those over 85, 260,000 were men and 530,000 women.

According to a study sponsored by the Ministry of Health and Welfare, of 1.84 million people over 65 living alone in 1985, 440,000 were men and 1.4 million women. The study estimated that people over 65 living alone would number 3.76 million in the year 2000 and 5.54 million in 2025. In that year, of the people over 65 living alone, men would number 1.87 million and women 3.67 million. Japan's total population over 65 would number 27.08 million in 2025 of whom 10.06 million would be bedridden and 1.24 million suffer from senility.

In 1983, husband and wife living together accounted for 17.7 per cent of the people over 65, one or both parents living with unmarried children made up 23.3 per cent and three-generation households included 47.4 per cent of the people aged 65 and older. Of the women over 65, 71.3 per cent lived with their children, of the men, 62.1 per cent.

A 1984 survey of the Ministry of Construction covering 94,000 households found that parents (of either husband or wife) lived with their married children in 21 per cent of these households. The particular live-in situation was as follows. Both parents of the husband were present in 28 per cent of the households and one of the husband's parents in 56 per cent; both of the wife's parents were members of 4 per cent of the households and in 11 per cent, one parent resided with a married daughter. Both sets of parents lived with their married children in 0.5 per cent of the households.

A survey conducted by the Ministry of Health and Welfare in 1984 found that 57.7 per cent of the families answering the poll were three-generation households. The same survey also showed that 57.4 per cent of the respondents wanted three children. The survey covered 4,043 families in the prefectures Akita, Yamanashi, Kagawa and Miyazaki and the city of Osaka. Since these prefectures comprise largely rural areas, housing conditions are less tight than in the cities, affording more room for accommodating elderly people as well as a larger number of children. Furthermore, elderly people can make themselves more useful in rural households than in the cities.

The tradition that children should take care of their parents is still strong. Of the generation over 60 years, 67.8 per cent think that a married son should take care of the surviving parent if one of the parents died, and 63.2 per cent of the generation in their 30s and 40s hold this view. Of the generation over 60, 14.7 per cent think that the surviving parent should live with a married daughter, and this is the opinion of 20.5 per cent of the people in their 30s and 40s.

Of the women over 60 years of age who became sick and had to stay in bed, 41.4 per cent relied on their daughters-in-law for help, 16.7 per cent on their daughters and 10.8 per cent on their husbands. Of the men over 60 years confined to bed, 68.8 per cent relied on their spouses and 10.6 per cent on their daughters-in-law.

The welfare systems devised to take care of every individual 'from the cradle to the grave' seem increasingly incapable of affording old-age protection. On the other hand, a law to force children to look after their parents when they are old as recently proposed by Prime Minister Lee Kuan Yew of Singapore would create insurmountable difficulties. Lee's concern about the breakdown of the traditional three-generation family is understandable, but this system developed under economic and social conditions that have ceased to exist.

The United Nations World Conference on the Problems of Aging (1982) showed that the increase in the proportion of old people in the population is not limited to the industrialised countries. While the entire world population is expected to grow by 70 per cent in the next 20 years, people over 60 will increase by 90 per cent and number almost 600 million out of a total of 6.7 billion in the year 2000. Families comprising five generations will be no rarity. No solutions are in sight for the enormous social and economic problems. If the present economic system is retained, 100 workers will have to sustain 40 old people and 35 children in 2025. How to prevent the sweeping confinement of the aged in homes and particularly how to assure the support of aged single women will present serious difficulties.

Today's three-generation families do not constitute a return to the old family system. Families are more egalitarian than the old 'house' and practical problems such as the difficulty of finding separate housing, the insufficiency of old-age pensions or the need of looking after the children of working mothers may suggest such arrangements. Frequently, the households of the parents and the young couple remain separate although they live under the same roof. 'Communal families' are practically non-existent in Japan.

Decline in Birth Rate

The decline in the birth rate is attributed to three main factors: 1. the change in the population structure (the smaller proportion of young people and the relative increase in the old-age group); 2. the change in the ratio of married people (due to the postponement of marriage); 3. lower fertility of married women.

The birthrate is of great political significance. For over-populated countries, such as the People's Republic of China and India, the greatest possible reduction of the birth rate constitutes the essential goal of their population policy, and these countries have sometimes resorted to measures greatly restricting individual rights. On the other hand, countries in which the decrease in population has reached threatening proportions have been trying to induce people to have more children. General de Gaulle appealed to the women of France to create a population of a hundred million by the end of the twentieth century but the French women (fortunately?) let him down and with a population of 55 million, the country is far away from achieving this goal. The government has tried to promote childbearing by financial incentives. The Socialist government adopted new family allowances payable from six months before birth until the child is three years old. Parents are allowed to take leave of absence for up to two years to raise their children. Similar laws have been in force in East Germany and Czechoslovakia.

Pre-industrial Western Europe maintained a precarious balance of population and resources in which the population was kept down by high infant mortality and calamities such as wars and epidemics — the Black Death in the early fourteenth century reduced the population in some countries by as much as one half. Although there seems to have been little change in fertility, the removal of the restraints of low agricultural productivity and limited resources together with the decline in mortality triggered the population explosion in the nineteenth century.

In Japan, limited resources were a powerful factor influencing social behaviour. In the century-and-a-half prior to the Meiji Restoration, the population remained nearly constant at 28 to 30 million, which may have been the maximum the country could support. In the inefficient agricultural economy, the peasants had to maintain a large parasitical class of nobles and the officialdom of the feudal system. Famines, epidemics, and natural disasters exacted a heavy toll of human lives while abortion and infanticide were practised in all social classes. A strong uptrend in Japan's population started with the Meiji Restoration. By 1935, the population had doubled compared with the beginning of the Meiji era (68.7 million) and it reached 100 million in 1967.

Japan's modernisation in the Meiji period was largely accomplished at the expense of the farming population. At that time, the urban labourers represented an economically weak minority. The burden of the post-war growth, however, fell on the urban masses. Although the standard of living rose sharply, personal living conditions and the infrastructure were neglected for the sake of industrial expansion. To this day, housing, sewerage and public transportation facilities remain inadequate. The situation was aggravated by the personal greed of the ruling élite — politicians, bureaucrats and business managers. Even now, the Japanese consumer is the 'forgotten man' who has to pay for the privileged treatment of special interest groups such as farmers and doctors and the incredible corruption in public life. The high living expenses, the unsatisfactory housing conditions and the inequitable taxation system have been important factors in the shift to the two- or one-child family

In a book entitled *La peste blanche,* two French authors, Pierre Chaunu and Georges Suffert, point out that the refusal to transmit life means the suicide of the peoples of Europe and North America. Their basic assumption is that the preservation of the population level requires a birth rate of 2.2 to 2.3 per cent so that a birth rate of 0.8 or 0.7 guarantees extinction in a quarter of a century. The catastrophic decline in the birth rate is one element in the general spiritual, political, social and economic development. The inability of a society to reproduce itself either biologically or culturally means its slow death called decadence (Pierre Chaunu, *Histoire et Décadence*).

As in late antiquity, today's decrease in births is an indication of the collapse of a system of civilisation. Although individual motives such as disregard of personal and social values, egoism, cynicism, indulgence and indolence play a large role in the diminishing births, the inherent relation of the decline in births to the general situation cannot be denied.

The necessary obverse side of decadence is progress which requires both physical and cultural continuity. The apprehension of the catastrophe of a nuclear war, political disarray and technological upheavals have generated fear. The meaningless of life, monotony, boredom, dejection and resignation mark the mood of society and the feeling of an irreversible downhill slide has engendered the despair which is the most powerful motive inspiring the denial of life.

Family Policy

A report of the United Nations Fund for Population Activities stated that the growth rate of the world population dropped from 1.99 per cent between 1960 and 1965 to 1.72 per cent in the period from 1975 to 1980. As of 1980, programmes to lower or maintain fertility levels had been adopted by 59 developing countries but 21 countries considered their fertility levels too low and had set up programmes to raise them.

In the beginning of 1982, West Germany's population was decreasing at a rate of 1.5 per 1000 population. Its birth rate of 9.4 per 1000 is one of the lowest in the world and lies below the mortality rate. Measures such as child allowances have not been able to stop the trend. Italy has virtually achieved zero population growth with a growth rate of 0.3 per 1000. The Soviet Union greatly increased motherhood allowances; the country's birth rate came to 0.8 per cent in 1980. The birth rate of the ethnic Russians has been declining for a number of years while it has been rising in the Central Asian Soviet republics. The US government estimates that the population of ethnic Russians which stood at 52.4 per cent of the proportion in 1979 will have slipped to 46.7 per cent by the year 2000.

Despite the basic importance of the family for society and the state, its treatment by governments has often revealed a fundamental incomprehension of the family and a growing encroachment on its role.

The replacement of the family by public agencies has been pushed farthest in education, health care and the care for the aged. Instead of helping the family to fulfil its role under the changed social and economic conditions, the tendency has been to deprive it of its rightful functions and make it superfluous by socialising its activities.

In West Germany, the policies of the Socialist governments systematically eroded the position of the family as an institution. The traditional form of marriage and the family as a basic unit of the social order are obstacles to a collectivistic organisation and the attempt to achieve a Marxist reconstruction of society. Relying on bureaucratisation and legalistic interference with the private sphere, governments, particularly those in states with Socialist majorities, tried to reduce the influence of the family and family education by political and administrative measures intended to weaken the personal bonds with the family so as to bring the individual under the direct and undisputed control of the collectivity. School reforms guided by an egalitarian ideology have been important instruments in the destruction of traditional values and norms, but the main blows against the family were the revision of the divorce law and the revision of the law on parental authority (changed into parental care subject to incisive legal restrictions).

Family as Investment Unit

One of the basic misunderstandings of the family is the assumption that it is only a unit of consumption. The fact that the family often remains a unit of production is completely ignored in modern law but above all, the importance of the family as a unit of investment has received no recognition whatever. The investment carried out in the family is the most important of all investments, the investment in the human potential of society. The family performs the function of ensuring the future of the people not only free of cost to the state but is even penalised for this contribution.

Among the inequities of the present tax systems, the uneven burden placed on the family is one of the most unsocial. The tax burden on the family income fails to take sufficiently into account that the income of a family with children must be substantially higher than that of a single person or a family without children in order to achieve a proportionate per capita income. The tax systems do not adequately reflect that the economic capability of a wage earner changes with the number of dependents for whom he is economically responsible. The deductions for spouse and children do not correspond to the real burden. If husband and wife have two independent incomes, they can split their incomes, but for a wife who devotes herself entirely to her family and the education of her children, no equivalent scheme is available. Some time ago, a German politician, Lothar Späth, prime minister of Baden-Württemberg, proposed that separate tax returns should be allowed for all members of a family. If the family income were split among all those who are supported by this income, the tax burden on families with children would be more equitable and probably become lighter.

In West Germany, an epochal law enacted in 1957 tried to ensure that people could continue to enjoy the standard of living they achieved in their years of economic activity throughout old age by what was called the 'dynamisation' of old-age pensions. The provision for old age was to be linked to the general economic development by financing pensions through the contributions of wage earners and raising pensions on the basis of the rise in wages. The basic idea was that the economically active part of the population should share the fruits of their labour with those who had enabled them to become productive. The original concept was perverted by politicians who wanted to create opportunities for manipulation but the most serious shortcoming of the scheme (which became known by the juridically preposterous name 'pact between generations') was its failure to integrate social security for the aged with social justice for the family. As Father Oswald von Nell-Breuning, SJ, has pointed out, an arrangement in which the working-age population supports the old-age population but which does not take into account the third generation, the children, is unjust. If the pensions of those without children or with few children are based on the work of the children reared by other people, the contribution of the families raising children must somehow be compensated.

Personally, I think that the departure from the concept of insurance and financing without the accumulation of reserves is wrong and that the system cannot be maintained if, as forecast for Japan, one pensioner will have to be carried by the contributions of three wage earners in the year 2010. But the raising of children and the work of a mother staying home to care for her children must be recognised in the distribution of the financial burden on the members of society.

Influence of Economic Conditions on Family Life

The family, as explained above, is a community of life in which each member has the right and duty to fulfil his or her role but all rights and duties towards one another are based on the duties towards the family as a community. As a community, the family provides the basic experience of togetherness. It starts the formative process and remains a life-long support and refuge. The attitudes, experiences and value judgements acquired in the family are of lasting significance for life in society even if they are later revised or rejected. For the well-being of the family, the basic problem is how to form the members of a family living together in the same household into a community of life? To put it differently, how do you make a home? Since a house is not a home, the question is: What is a home?

One of the reasons for the disintegration of the modern family is without doubt the lack of the material preconditions for a home. In many large cities, the housing situation is responsible for the fact that the dwelling is nothing more than a place which can be used as a location for the most indispensable requirements of life, for eating and sleeping and storing things. But not only the dwelling itself, but also the neighbourhood has to be considered if one is to 'feel at home.' Naturally, it is impossible to lay down general norms and the same individual may feel differently about the same place in the course of his life.

The strong desire of many Japanese families to acquire their own house despite adverse financial conditions and their readiness to oblige themselves to twenty or thirty years of interest and amortisation payments seem to indicate that permanence and control are of importance, but the congeniality of the material conditions with the physical, particularly the emotional wants of the family may be the really essential element.

Not only in the developing countries, but also in the advanced industrial nations, the economic situation does not provide the conditions for a healthy family life. A 1983 survey of the National Institute of Economic and Social Research found that 7.5 million out of 56 million Britains lived below the poverty line. Over 7 million had to go without food at some time during the year preceding the survey for lack of money, and 700,000 suffered from extreme poverty; 7.5 million were without essential clothing, 3.25 million did not have reasonable heating and 1.1 million had no bath. The most vulnerable groups were the unemployed, the elderly and some 900,000 single-parent families.

The US Bureau of the Census reported that in 1982, 34.4 million Americans lived in poverty. They constituted 15 per cent of the population, the highest percentage since 1965. Poverty was most prevalent among blacks (of whom 35.6 per cent were poor) and Hispanics (29.9 per cent); households headed by women made up the largest single category of poor families and accounted for 36.3 per cent of the poverty population. Not surprisingly, more than twice as many inner-city residents than suburbanites were below the poverty line. The poverty rate which had risen to 15.2 per cent in 1983, fell to 14.4 per cent in 1984 when the number of Americans below the poverty level declined by 1.8 million. The poverty threshold for a family of four was $10,609.

In his book 'Marriage and the Sex Problem,' Friedrich Wilhelm Foerster, a German pedagogue, warned against the spiritual pitfalls of a self-centred family. In family life lies a source of the finest human feeling, but it also brings the danger of family egoism, the destruction of all higher caritas and all higher spiritual endeavour. Commenting on the separation of St Elizabeth (wife of Landgrave Ludwig of Thuringia) from her children (in which she followed the injudicious advice of her incompetent confessor), Foerster writes: 'The spirit which animated the great saints was one of pure devotion to God. With the penetrating gaze of the purified soul, they saw that a family life not based upon anything higher than earthly love may be no more than a species of extended self-interest; they perceived that blunting of all higher needs which so often accompanies the mere worship of motherhood, that naïve self-reflection in the offspring, that character-destroying exaggeration of outward care, that growing indifference to everything except the welfare of one's own circle, that idolatrous cult of the work of human propagation, without any true and consistent worship of God. They knew, too, that children thus loved and thus brought up, in spite of all outer baptism, would never possess the true baptism; they are reared in the flesh and not in the spirit, and therefore they will be ruled by the flesh and not by the higher life of the spirit.'

The togetherness of the family is an expansion of the togetherness of husband and wife and partakes of the quality of that togetherness. Two elements are of particular significance for the spirit of the family, the structure of the household and the relations between parents and children.

Work and Family,

In today's society, the main problem for the family as a social unit, a community of love and affection, and a cooperative group based on the solidarity of its members comes from the economic system which usually makes it necessary for either husband or wife to work outside the home. Even apart from the complications created by today's economic conditions, the nuclear family comprising only parents and small children implies severe limitations on the activities of the parents. Unless they take their children along or get a baby-sitter, the parents cannot go out together. A mother pregnant with her second child and left alone with a three-year-old boy may find it impossible to cope with the situation. The ebullient energy of growing children clashes with the narrowness of the home, but it may be dangerous to let the children play outside without supervision.

As long as the place of work is near the home, the disruption of family life remains tolerable. This is still the case in many small towns in the West as well as in Japan, and in most Asian towns, the link between occupation and residence seems the dominant pattern. There are occupations in which the worker is away from home for weeks or months on end, such as seamen or fishermen, and often the same conditions exists for seasonal workers. For instance, farmers, particularly from northern Japan, used to take up construction work in the off-season.

For the Japanese male, the system creates a conflict between his solicitude for his family and his commitment to his work and his work group. This conflict is not just a matter of time; it is even more a matter of interest, emotional involvement and the priority of values. If a Japanese chooses to assign the first priority to getting ahead in the company, he will have to become an organisation man — in the Japanese version of this type. If he wants to have a happy family life, he will probably have to give up any idea of getting to the top. If he 'belongs' to a large company, his work demands that he spend not only his regular working hours at his office or place of work, but also a large part of the evening. If he moves up to a relatively important position, he may have to attend meetings and play golf on Saturdays and Sundays. He may have to travel, not only inside Japan but also abroad. Naturally, the situation is not the same for ordinary workers or employees, but the custom of having a drink with one's colleagues or a game of *mah-jongg* on the way home is fairly common. The more successful an executive, the greater the danger of becoming a stranger to his family because his snowballing social engagements (from which his wife is usually excluded) will demand more and more of his time. In the large cities, the housing problem worsens an already bad situation. Employees commuting to work may have to leave home early in the morning and can return only late at night, leaving them little time to be together with their families.

In a comparative study of work attitudes, about one-half of the Japanese workers considered working highly important and 45 per cent agreed with the statement 'My work is the most important part of my life.' Of the American workers, 25 per cent regarded work as very important and 23 per cent attributed to it the highest priority. But 55 per cent of the American workers valued the family as the most important part of their lives while only 39 per cent of the Japanese workers expressed this view.

On the other hand, the five-day work week partially adopted by large Japanese corporations has created psychological problems for husbands as well as wives. The two-day weekend has worsened the Monday blues of the men and caused what has been called Friday dumbs for their wives. 'The thought of having their spouse lolling about the house doing nothing on Saturdays and Sundays is a depressing perspective for wives,' a doctor said. They become nervous when they think about having to keep company with a husband who does not know what to do with his leisure time (a family saddled with payments on housing loans can hardly afford to go out every weekend). The wife's psychological upsets take on a variety of forms and range from a tendency to break into tears at the slightest provocation to headaches, insomnia, loss of memory even to a period of fugue. Some women turn to eating in excess, even more to drinking, and in one case, a housewife developed a 'kitchen allergy' on Fridays. She suffered violent headaches and had difficulties in breathing when faced with pots and pans.

It also happens that the wife spends much of her time outside the home, even if she does not have an outside job. Women attend a great variety of courses, some of immediate usefulness for home-making such as cooking or sewing, some for personal enjoyment, for culture or physical training. There are numerous circles, clubs, associations and societies catering to women and women are usually more involved than men with PTA, religious activities, and charitable, environmental or neighbourhood causes.

On account of the involvement of the male with his job, Japanese wives get almost no help from their husbands in managing the home and bringing up the children. The husband sometimes does not know or does not care what is going on. For the wife, this situation means loneliness and alienation. Because she has nothing else to live for, she starts living through her children, pressing them for success and trying to give her own life meaning and direction by devoting her energy and attention to over-protecting and over-encouraging her children. This type of mother, called *kyôiku mama* ('education mamma') is said to be a major cause of child suicide.

In large Japanese firms, the rather frequent transfers are a particularly difficult problem for married employees. Such transfers may separate a family from relatives or old friends and acquaintainces, make it difficult to take firm roots in a neighbourhood, and create loneliness and an emotional void particularly for the housewives affected by these relocations.

'Tanshin Funin'

The hardest problems concern housing and education. An employee who has acquired his own house does not want to sell it and start all over again at a location where he will stay only a few years. Parents whose children have succeeded in passing the entrance examination to a 'good' school do not want to jeopardise the future life of their offspring. If the wife works, she will have to give up her job. These and other considerations have led to a custom called *'tanshin funin'* (to proceed to one's post alone). The employee leaves his family behind and takes up his new assignment alone. He may live in a company dormitory if the company has one at his new duty station, or he may rent a room or a small apartment. As many as 400,000 employees are said to be living away from their families on account of such transfers. The majority of these employees would have preferred to take their families along but resigned themselves to go alone as inevitable. According to a survey carried out by a business magazine and covering the transfers of 144 major firms in 1984, 51.38 per cent of the companies decided on personnel transfers on the basis of the firm's needs, 42.36 per cent gave employees an opportunity to state their preferences but made the decision in line with their own priorities, and only 6.25 per cent decided on transfers by considering the private affairs of their employees. While 18.2 per cent did not approve of *tanshin funin,* 36.4 per cent stated that it was up to the employee whether to take his family along or go alone, and 43.2 per cent of the firms considered the situation in every case.

Another survey found that the children's education, above all their admission to a higher school, was the major reason for 77.6 per cent of the separations. Parents were unwilling to have their children change schools when they were going to an 'élite' school, if the reputation of the schools at the new post was inferior, or if it would be difficult to arrange a transfer to a public school. Moving to a new place may be postponed if children are only a short time away from graduation, or if they have passed the entrance examination and examinations at the new location are already over. Another major reason for temporary separations is the unwillingness to sell the house.

In a 1985 survey, 68.2 per cent of the employees living away from their families stated that relocating their families would have caused educational problems for their children, 57.3 per cent did not want to sell their house, and 20.3 per cent did not know how to take care of their aged parents. 39 per cent of the husbands and 43 per cent of the wives thought their ties with their spouses had remained strong, but 22 per cent of the husbands and 20 per cent of the wives feared that their marital relations had weakened. Of the transferees 42 per cent felt that their ties with their children had not suffered but 42 per cent of the husbands and about one-third of the wives expressed misgivings about the impact of the separation on the father's relation with the children.

Things that employees living alone find most troublesome are meals, laundry and cleaning. About half try to find lodgings providing room and board, and many get used to doing their own household chores. Middle-aged men find it difficult to cope with their health problems. If distances are not too great, employees may go home for the weekend or have their families visit them. In addition to the physical inconveniences, hardships may result from emotional problems, above all the feeling of loneliness, the lack of the warmth of the family, and the stress of separation. Many realise for the first time the importance of the family; they feel their responsibility for their children and become aware of how fortunate they are in having a wife. They find it more difficult to enjoy their leisure time and may have nothing better to do than to sleep.

The strains imposed on the wife by the separation are no less severe. She has to bear the entire responsibility for the household and the education of the children and is deprived of the togetherness of marital life. Recently, a 36-year-old housewife took her own life after she had quarrelled with her husband who had come home for a visit over his working away from his family. The couple had bought a condominium just two year ago, and when the husband was transferred to a different city, the wife and the two children stayed behind. She complained of her loneliness to her husband who told her to stick it out.

A housewife whose family had to move seven times because of the husband's transfers, described the resulting dislocations as follows: 'Moving, for a family, means starting again from scratch. The life that you have built over the years suddenly crumbles. You have to part from all the acquaintances that you have made, on whom you have to depend because there are no relatives around. You have to leave the people with whom you have grown so close and then build new bonds of friendship all over again.'

Had it not been for her husband's transfers, she wrote, she would have served as a teacher for more than 20 years, qualified for a pension and been economically well off.

Financially, living apart may be a heavy burden and involve extra expenses amounting to ¥500,000 to ¥1.5 million a year. At least 70 per cent of the large enterprises pay 'living apart' allowances which, in 1981, came to an average of ¥19.377 a month for general employees, ¥24,725 for section chiefs, and ¥27,638 for executive personnel.

In 1985, the government changed the method of implementing the tax law so that allowances paid to employees posted away from their families would not be taxed as income (as they have been until now) but treated as business expenses of the enterprise to the extent that trips home could be regarded as related to business.

Nagasakiya, a clothing manufacturer, has devised a system to avoid the frequent transfers which disrupt family life, interfere with education, and prevent the family from settling down. Employees wishing to avoid transfers must apply to the personnel department for 'transferless status.' Such status is granted to a maximum of 180 out of 5,010 employees and does not apply to upper management such as store managers. Those who are exempt from transfers must accept lower pay hikes and slower promotion.

In July 1986, the Supreme Court reversed the decisions of the Osaka District Court and the Osaka High Court and ruled that a company had the right to dismiss a salaried worker who had refused to be transferred. The employee, Toru Yoshida, had joined Toa Paint Co in April 1965 and was first assigned to the Osaka office. He worked two years at the Osaka office of an affiliated firm and was transferred to Kobe in 1971. In 1973, the company assigned Yoshida to its Hiroshima office and when he refused, the transfer was changed to Nagoya. But Yoshida rejected this assignment, too, and he was fired. He claimed that he would have to live away from his wife who was working at a nursing school, and from his mother who was dependent on him. The lower courts sided with Yoshida and held the dismissal invalid but the Supreme Court thought that the disadvantage of the transfer was not unbearable and that the company was justified in firing Yoshida. There was no stipulation in the employment contract limiting the place of work to Osaka, and frequent transfers between the company's ten sales offices were an accepted practice. Only in three cases, the Supreme Court said, would a transfer be unlawful: 1. when there was no business need for the transfer; 2. when the employer had another motive for the transfer than business needs; 3. when the transfer would cause an unacceptable disadvantage to the employee.

A particularly difficult situation arises when employees are posted abroad. Enterprises and the government provide much assistance, especially for housing and education, and businessmen enjoy many perks, a better house, higher income, and more free time. In South-East Asia, families can afford household help they cannot even think of in Japan. It sometimes happens, therefore, that wives become dissatisfied when they come back to Japan and a less affluent life-style, and the dissatisfaction may lead to quarrels.

Recently, a Japanese court rejected the claim of a wife for damages from her husband's company alleging that the firm was responsible for the break-up of her marriage. Her husband had been transferred to the United States and refused to take his family along. He later obtained a divorce in the United States.

Unemployment and Family

Family life experiences an extraordinary strain when the head of the family is out of work. While the material impact is generally cushioned by unemployment compensation and relief, the psychological impact may be fatal. Contrary to the usual assumption that the family provides moral support to the unemployed, conflicts in the family tend to become more frequent and more severe. Following the loss of his job, the unemployed may initially experience a feeling of euphoria as if he were enjoying a welcome vacation, but if his enforced idleness enters the fourth or fifth month, a stage of exhaustion starts which changes to despair, dejection and prostration in the sixth month.

Joblessness is a serious threat to personal health and the quality of family and community life. Unemployed husbands have increased symptoms of anxiety, depression, hostility and psychosomatic conditions. Middle-aged heads of households with young dependents feel more strain than younger single workers.

Psychologically, people find it impossible to get accustomed to prolonged involuntary idleness, and the growing nervousness increases the possibility of family quarrels. The result is the vicious circle of the loss of a job, feeling of guilt, loss of self-confidence, loss of the will to act and, therefore, loss of the ability to regain control of one's life. The collapse of the unemployed's personality has a disastrous effect on his (or her) family.

It goes without saying that the responsibility for family life, the management of the household and the upbringing of the children is the joint duty of husband and wife and that the children share the responsibility for the common life of the family to the extent they are capable when they grow up. Recently, an American housewife went on strike because her husband and her teenage children did not help with the housework. Father and mother play different but equally important roles in the education of their children. It is up to the free decision of the individuals concerned to found a family, but once they are united in a family, they cannot disclaim their duties for the common life. It has been said facetiously that the family is a bunch of people you are stuck with for life. This may not be absolutely true today but it remains true that the members of a family are kept together despite conflicts, misunderstandings, quarrels and disputes.

A Japanese survey found that, in 1984, the wife was mainly taking care of pre-school children in 83 per cent of all families, husband and wife together in 12 per cent, and other family members in 4 per cent. There were no responses to the rubric 'mainly husband.' In the families in which the wife was mainly in charge of the small children, the husband was giving almost no help in 27 per cent, he helped somewhat in 39 per cent, and he helped to a certain extent in 18 per cent of the families.

Generation Gap in Japan

There is, however, a remarkable difference between the generations. People who grew up in the sixties are very different from the old generations almost everywhere in the western world. Women have changed a lot; they have discovered their rights and men, voluntarily or under protest, are changing their attitudes. Men do more work at home. They are learning to do the dishes, shop for groceries, cook, take care of the kids, clean the house and do the laundry. Fathers have come to take a more active role in child rearing and do better than just act as a figure of authority and mete out punishment. With the disappearance of the patriarchal role of the father, the family works better as a system of checks and balances, making it possible for every member of the family to fulfil the part in the family demanded by his or her position.

Nevertheless, the generation gap remains one of the most untractable factors responsible for the disintegration of the family. Along with broken homes resulting from the discord between husband and wife, the lack of harmony between parents and children occasionally escalates into the murder of children by their parents or of parents by their children. The generation gap, therefore, is a major symptom of the instability of today's family. In Japan, there are actually two different gaps, the first between the pre-war or 'Meiji' generation and the post-war generation; the second between the generation that grew up in the war years and the period immediately after the war on the one side and the generation born in the sixties and thereafter on the other. The Meiji generation largely retained the pre-war values and their ideas of family relations are based on Confucianism in which the relations between husband and wife, parents and children, and elder brother and younger brother are essential aspects of the patriarchal system. The partnership marriage based on the equality of the sexes and even more the emancipation of women are alien to the thinking of the Meiji generation. The generation that has experienced the war and the post-war chaos in its youth is probably the least secure segment of the population, They had not absorbed the pre-war ideology and the fight for survival may have been the most impressive experience of their formative years. It is not surprising that they do not have deep-seated beliefs or convictions. The generation born into the incipient affluent society takes the material well-being very much for granted and lacks the discipline that privation gave to the preceding generation. They consider the good life as something due to them without a corresponding effort on their part and are most receptive to the entitlement thinking of the welfare state.

The differences in experience, thought and attitudes result in different social behaviour. Even outside the family, the contrast between the conservatism, politeness and good sense of the old generation and the self-assurance of the young is often striking and it is hardly surprising that these differences create strains and conflicts inside the family.

Children and Parental Conflicts

Children may have completely different relations with each of their parents for reasons that have nothing to do with the Oedipus complex. Children react to differences in personality, character, behaviour and appearance, so to speak, instinctively.

The break-up of family life, particularly the growing number of divorces, has greatly increased the number of children living in one-parent homes. In the US, 12.6 million youngsters under the age of 18 out of a total of 63 million, which means one out of every five, lived with only one parent. In Japan, 55 per cent of the children of working mothers are cared for away from home.

Often children are drawn into the marital battle of the sexes — a battle in which no victor can emerge; they are propositioned as allies by both sides and corrupted. Children have unfailing egoistic instincts and better nerves than their elders; they take advantage of the situation for their own interests and strengthen their own position. In a society in which the fight is no longer for food and survival, the fight is for power. The point of contention is who dominates whom and who exploits whom.

Even if the family breaks up, the parent opposed to the party given parental rights remains a powerful ally of the youngsters although he or she may have no direct contact with them.

The situation is most advantageous for the children living with their fathers. The girls because they are usually spoiled by their father and can easily take care of him. Even a two-year old girl succeeds in turning daddy round her little finger. Men in love — and, as a rule, every man is in love with his daughters — submit to female domination without resistance.

Boys have a more difficult job to assert themselves against their fathers. The combat is more brutal and less sophisticated than in the case of the girls, but eventually the boys will triumph. Many boys avoid using the word 'father' when speaking about their dad and they don't use it when they address him. Contrary to popular belief, girls are somewhat more inclined than boys to say that they have a better relationship with their mum than with their dad, and boys as well as girls are more likely to get on better with their mother than with their father. The age of teenagers, boys and girls, does not appear to be a factor in how well they get on with their parents or whether they get on better with their mother or their father.

While the factors responsible for the disintegration of the family are serious, they are not universal and in many instances, the members of the family themselves can cope with the problems. External factors that cause the weakening and dissolution of the family such as those involved in today's social conditions and particularly in the modern economic organisation are far more difficult to neutralise. Nobody considers it abnormal that the breadwinner is away from home for the best part of the day and sometimes for weeks or months, but this situation can hardly pass as ideal or healthy for the family. If working mothers are blamed for the deterioration of the family, why not working fathers? A system in which the nuclear family cannot function without being subject to disintegration cannot be termed desirable. A rotten society involving the decay of the family is far costlier than a system of jobs for men as well as women that would leave the basic functions of the family intact.

2

Parents and Children

Childless Families

A TYPICAL FAMILY is thought to consist of parents and children; nevertheless, over one-tenth of all families have no children. That children are always a joy and consolation for their parents is a fable, and there are indications that parents whose children have grown up and left the parental home are happier or at least more content than parents still occupied with rearing their children. For many couples, the time of the empty nest turns out to be a time of fulfilment.

Marriages are not necessarily concluded for the procreation of children and the community of marital togetherness constitutes a perfectly legitimate purpose of marriage. The presence or absence of children is less important in itself than in relation to the couple's desire for children. Children can contribute to marital happiness but can also be a source of parental distress. Chances of divorce are greater for childless couples than for those with children largely because parents with children are more reluctant to break up their relationship. Parents of unwanted children show the poorest adjustment, followed by those who have no children and desire none. Divorced or separated people are often unhappy and so are widows. Being single involves greater psychological costs than being married and bachelors or spinsters usually have less satisfaction in life than married people.

If a couple is childless, it makes an important difference whether the childlessness is voluntary or involuntary. Childlessness can be a heart-breaking ordeal for couples who want children. Both spouses may feel distress and frustration at being unable to have offspring, and if the infertility of either husband or wife is ascertained as the reason for the childlessness, feelings of inadequacy, guilt and self-reproach may aggravate the emotional burden. Although in the West's present culture, infertility is no ground for divorce and does not entitle the husband to take a second wife, the condition may affect the relations between the spouses and create coolness and even estrangement. The situation is not helped by the disappointment of the prospective grandparents if the expected grandchild does not arrive or by the embarrassing questions of acquaintances.

Involuntary childlessness is an experience which tests the ability of the partners to find strength and comfort in their togetherness and think of their life in common as giving sufficient meaning to their marriage. Parenthood has both its costs and its rewards. During the years of raising small children, the costs are very substantial; the parents of young children undergo a great deal of stress, both personal and economic. This subsides in later years. After the children are grown and the parents are alone again, their general contentment is high because companionship and mutual understanding is stronger than before.

Burden on Mother

The person most profoundly affected by the decision to have children is the mother. For many women, motherhood is not a healthy experience and maternal mortality has by no means become negligible with the progress in protective measures and ante-natal care. Maternal mortality has a direct relationship to the age of the mother. The safest time for childbearing is between the ages of twenty and twenty-four; the mortality rate is very high for young mothers (who include many unmarried mothers) and mothers over forty. The physical and psychological burdens of pregnancy, childbirth, nursing and taking care of children is hardly compensated by the sense of satisfaction from being needed and the excitement from the children's growth. Motherhood involves more sacrifice than pleasure, and the care of children is a much greater cause of fatigue for women than the care of the house or the preparation of food. That women are impelled by a maternal instinct to become mothers is a fiction, and the decision to have children, if it is made at all, is often a mixture of personal wish and cultural pressure.

Unwanted Children

In too many cases, pregnancy just happens unintentionally as the result of sex in marriage as well as pre-marital or extra-marital sex. It often occurs against the intention of the sex partners because of the failure or neglect of contraceptive measures. More than half of all pregnancies in the United States are unintended and nearly half of these end in abortion. The motives for not wanting children in pre-marital or extra-marital sex are generally simple; they are somewhat more complex in marriage. Married couples may not want children at all or not at a particular time, for example, soon after marriage, because the wife wants to continue working without the burden of having to care for a child.

In the United States, the ascendancy of psychoanalysis with its stress on the deterministic influence of childhood experiences on the entire life has deterred people from having children. They feel unable to shoulder the responsibility involved in being parents.

Children in Racially-Mixed Marriages

A special problem may come up in racially-mixed marriages. A western woman married to a Japanese man may not want children because she is apprehensive of the fate of children of mixed blood. Others feel that they are not really integrated into Japanese society and fear that their children will also remain outsiders. Language may constitute another difficulty; if the mother does not speak Japanese, how will her children be affected when they are assimilated into Japanese culture.

Singapore's Family Policies

Prime Minister Lee Kuan Yew of Singapore created a stir when he told a 1983 National Day rally that the island state faced the danger of losing its reserve of talent because of the declining birth-rate among well-educated women. Uneducated Singaporean women, he said, produced twice as many children as educated, creating the danger of a decline in competence. He bemoaned the tendency among career women to remain single or to give birth to only one child after marriage while conceding that some of his policies, notably the creation of equal employment opportunities for women, strict family planning ('two is enough') and the ban on polygamy had contributed to the imbalance.

In order to promote childbearing by educated women, the prime minister promised a 30 per cent tax rebate to a mother who was a university graduate and gave birth to her third child. Moreover, the children would be entitled to enrol in Singapore's best schools. But in 1985, the government scrapped the policy of giving priority in school admission to children of graduate mothers because it was generally blamed for a drastic decline in the votes garnered by the People's Action Party in the elections in December 1984. In order to limit the proliferation of the poor, women up to the age of 30 with no more than an elementary school education whose monthly family income does not exceed 1,500 Singapore dollars receive a premium of 10,000 Singapore dollars if they undergo sterilisation after the birth of their first or second child. The money is meant to be used as down-payment for the purchase of an apartment. If the family which received the premium thereafter has another child, the money must be repaid with 10 per cent interest.

The Singapore government has set up a special unit to promote contacts between unmarried male and female university graduates in the civil service. The 'Social Development Unit' organises educational seminars and special briefings on the importance of marriage and childbearing.

Dr Linda Y. C. Lim, writing in the *Far Eastern Economic Review*. asserted that the concern that there were too many women in professions such as law, medicine, business management, banking and the foreign service had led to *de facto* quotas or other limitations on the number of women admitted into professional courses of study and into employment in these fields. She thinks that 'the lack of a clear economic rationale for maintaining or reinforcing women's traditional role suggests that it is still ideology — particularly the ideology of Confucian patriarchy — which dominates top political thinking on decision-making on the position of women, all of which is done by men' (5 January, 1984, p. 38).

Critics of the prime minister's views attacked his élitism as well as his stress on the productive function of women. Career women protested the attempt to turn them into 'baby machines' and Lee's political opponents charged that he was trying to perpetuate an élitist rule. The prime minister, relying on a study of the University of Minnesota on identical twins, asserted that the importance of inherited determinants was 80 per cent while that of the environment was only 20 per cent. It seems doubtful that the nature versus nurture controversy admits of such a simple summation. The prime minister ordered a study of matchmaking in Japan, in particular, the marriage bureaux using computers for identifying likely partners and the *mi-ai* marriages.

Fertility Rates

According to a French study, female fertility drops sharply after women reach the age of 30 which means that women who postpone marriage and childbirth while they establish a career may be significantly less able to become pregnant. The study which was based on the capacity for becoming pregnant of women who had sterile husbands and received artificial insemination for a year at eleven French fertility centres arrived at the following fertility rates: women under 25 years of age, 73 per cent; between the ages of 26 and 30, 74 per cent; between 31 and 35, 67 per cent; over 35, 54 per cent.

The results of this study have been dismissed as greatly exaggerated if applied to the general population by the American Population Council, and a study sponsored by the council and based on figures from the national survey of family growth set the percentage of female infertility at 9.4 per cent between the ages of 30 and 34 and at 19.7 per cent between 35 and 39. Other studies put the infertility rate at 6 per cent for the 20-24 age group, 9 per cent for 25-29, 15 per cent for 30-34, 30 per cent for 35-39, and 64 per cent for 40-44. In the United States, the total fertility rate (number of births of women aged 15 to 44) came to 3.7 in 1957 but has been 1.8 in recent years.

In Western Europe, the fertility rate has been dropping dramatically, resulting in a relative shrinkage of the young population and a corresponding increase in the higher age groups. In much of Europe, it is below the rate of 2.1 children per woman needed for the population to replace itself, and in some countries, such as West Germany, Austria,

Belgium, Luxembourg and Denmark, the population has already begun to decline. West Germany, with 1.4 children per woman, has the lowest fertility rate among the European countries as well as the lowest rate of people under 15 years of age (15.5 per cent) and the highest rate of people in the retirement age. But below replacement fertility rates prevail also in France, Britain, Italy, the Scandinavian countries, Switzerland, Austria, Belgium and Holland. Even in Spain, the rate declined to 1.79 children per woman in 1983. Ireland has the highest birth rate in all of Europe (about three children per woman) and one of the youngest populations, but the fertility rate is sinking.

Childbirth and Age of Mother

A study released by the Population Reference Bureau in November 1984, stated that over the past decade, American women tended to marry later and wait longer to have children. Only about half of the women get married by age 24, compared with three-quarters a generation ago, and while 19 per cent of the first births were to women 25 or older, it was 36 per cent by 1982. Among the reasons are the large entry of women into the labour force, increased education for women, the availability of contraceptives and the unstable economic conditions. Many women work after their first child is born and they go back to work sooner after giving birth. In 1950, 12 per cent of married women with children under six were in the labour force; it was 52 per cent in 1984.

In Japan, the birth-rate has been going up for women in the higher age groups. The number of births per 1,000 women 20 to 24 years old declined from 115.5 in 1974 to 70.8 in 1983 while the rate for women in the 25 to 29 age group rose from 180.6 in 1981 to 185 in 1983. For women in their early 30s, the rate was 79 in 1983 and it was 16.3 for those in their late 30s. The upward trend was due mainly to two factors. The average marriage age of women has risen from 22.9 years in 1949 to 25.3 years in 1983, and an increasing number of women have jobs and have their first baby at a higher age than before. In 1983, the average Japanese mother gave birth to her first child at the age of 26.5 years; she was 29.0 when she had her second child and 31.2 when she had a third child. Because many women resume work after childbirth, children are no longer brought up exclusively in the home. While 94.5 per cent of the newborn babies are cared for at home, the percentage of infants remaining at home all day long (that is not being taken to a child-care centre or kindergarten) drops to 90.8 per cent for the 1-year-olds, 86.8 per cent for the 2-year-olds, 67.0 per cent for the 3-year-olds, 33.8 per cent for the 4-year-olds, and 10.7 per cent for children of 5 or 6 years.

The number of children per family was 1.81 in 1984, slightly up from 1.74 in 1981. As of 1 April, 1985, the total number of children aged 15 or younger was estimated at 25.76 million, of whom 13.2 million were boys. Children in the 12 to 13 age bracket constituted the largest group, 4.11 million; they represented the second 'baby boom' generation. Their parents were born in the first boom shortly after World War II. Infants below the age of one year numbered 1.43 million, the lowest level in the last 40 years. The ratio of children aged 15 and below to the total population was 21.2 per cent; it used to be 35 or 36 per cent before the war. Proportionally, Okinawa had the highest child population with 28.5 per cent and Tokyo the lowest with 17.2 per cent. Japan's percentage was about the same as that in the United States (22.0 per cent), Canada (21.9 per cent) and France (21.6 per cent); the percentage was significantly lower in West Germany (15.9 per cent) and Sweden (18.2 per cent).

Difficulties in delivery do not seem to be a major problem for women under 35. Birth defects, including minor ones, are one in 1,000 births for women under 35, three per 1,000 for women between 35 and 39, and 16 per 1,000 births for those between 40 and 44.

Based on data from Sweden's birth registry, researchers claim that the risk of a stillbirth increases with age from 20 years on and climbs very rapidly after 35. Women between the ages of 35 and 39 face twice the risk of delivering premature babies or offspring with unusually low weight than women giving birth in their early twenties.

Number of Desired Children

The question of how many children are desired in a family is rather complex. African mothers are said to consider an average of seven children per family appropriate; the desired average seemed 4.7 children in the Middle East, 4.3 children in Latin America, and 4 children in Asia. In Japan, a survey answered by 4,043 couples showed that 57.4 per cent of the couples wanted three children and 34.1 per cent wanted two. Four children were considered desirable by 7.2 per cent while 1.2 per cent opted for one child. Of the couples with one child, 51 per cent wanted a second child and 41.2 per cent hoped for two more. Families with two children wanting another child accounted for 45.4 per cent of such families. In the industrial countries of the West, the trend is no longer from large to small families but from the two-child to the one-child or no-child family. This development reflects the fact that children cost money and that a large family involves economic disadvantages. But people not only shun the economic burden of a large family but also shy away from the trouble and responsibility of parenthood. Today's society is not greatly interested in children and may even be said to be antagonistic towards them. This hostility lurks behind the difficulty families with children have in finding a home. Children are a nuisance to the neighbourhood because they cry and laugh and play; they not only make noise but also damage doors and windows and deface walls. In many countries, a family with a dog can find a home much easier than a family with a child.

Baby Shock

The so-called 'baby shock,' the unexpected burdens imposed by the arrival of the first child, may result in the refusal to have any more children. There often is a discrepancy between the reasons people give for not having children and their real motives. A child seems to threaten the living standard and even more the manner of living to which people have become accustomed, in particular, the enjoyment of life. Financial reasons are cited by over half of the women in West Germany for not wanting children or not wanting more children. 'We cannot afford a child,' has become a conversational stereotype. Cramped living quarters, inconvenience, the wish to pursue a career and the problems of education figure among the reasons for refusing children.

Reasons for Avoiding Children

Couples with two children may think that their offspring is already too numerous and avoid having more children. Fear of bearing defective children is another reason for eschewing or terminating pregnancy. The fear of giving birth to a Mongoloid child is particularly strong. (Mongolism, now called Dow's Syndrome, is thought to be caused by an extra 21st chromosome or a translocation — part of a chromosome breaking off and attaching itself to another — of the 21st chromosome.) The risk of having a mongoloid baby increases with the age of the mother. For a woman over 45, the probability is more than one in 60, compared with one in 1,000 for a woman under 30.

Popular supersitution also plays a role in the choice of motherhood. In Japan, for example, the birth-rate dropped abruptly in 1966 which, according to the old Chinese sexagesimal cycle (a pair of each of the five elements combined with the twelve signs of the zodiac) was the year *hinoe uma* (elder brother of fire — horse) which is considered an unlucky year for baby girls (they will kill their husbands when they become wives) and girls born in that year have trouble finding a spouse. There are also people who think that the world is already overpopulated and who don't want to add to the number of human beings living on the planet.

Parents have the natural right to procreate children, but only if all the requisite conditions are fulfilled. The right to have children is not absolute. Because parents are responsible for begetting children, they are also responsible for the children's genetic endowment. Parents cannot choose the hereditary mass which will be transmitted to their children but they must understand that the children's genetic constitution will be within the parameters of the parents' genes.

Duty Not to Have Children

If the spouses are sure that their offspring will suffer from serious genetic defects and will be a heavy and painful burden on themselves and on others all their lives, they cannot assert their right to procreation. If the spouses live in such physical and material misery that they are unable to maintain the life they generate or if psychologically and pedagogically they are absolutely unfit to lead the child to maturity so that the child would be exposed to wretchedness and become a burden on others, procreation would no longer be a right but a misuse of their generative power.

The duty of spouses not to produce offspring is particularly serious if there is a well-founded probability that the children will be mentally defective. Eugenic laws providing for compulsory measures such as the eugenic protection laws of the Nazis may constitute an unwarranted interference with personal freedom but the personal responsibility of spouses not to procreate children who would be bodily and mentally handicapped for life and would also be socially disadvantaged cannot be too strongly emphasised. There may be good reasons to recommend such couples to undergo voluntary sterilisation.   .

Why Should Man be Obliged to Live?

The right to produce offspring and the duty to abstain from reproduction indicate a problem that has particularly intrigued the philosophers of pessimism. Why should man live or be obliged to live since he has come into existence without his consent? One of the remarks most frequently uttered by children in squabbles with their parents is the complaint, if this is the right word, that they were brought into this world without their will, without being consulted, and that they had no say in choosing their parents.

Schopenhauer, who has made this thought one of the pillars of his doctrine of the negation of the will to live, wrote in his *The World as Will and Representation:* 'Man has his existence and essence either with his will, that is, his consent, or without it; in the latter case, such an existence, embittered by manifold and inescapable sufferings, would be crying injustice. The ancients, above all the Stoics, but also the Peripatetics and Academics, endeavoured vainly to demonstrate that virtue was sufficient to make life happy. Experience, however, loudly disclaimed this. What actually underlay the endeavour of those philosophers, although not clearly perceived, was the supposed justice of the matter: he who was innocent should also be free of suffering, therefore happy. But the serious and deep solution of the problem lies in the Christian doctrine that works do not justify; hence, even though a man has fulfilled all justice and love of man, thereby the 'good,' the 'virtuous,' and nevertheless is not, as Cicero thought, *culpa omni carens* (free of all guilt) but *el delito mayor del hombre es haber nacido'* (the greatest guilt of man is to have been born), as, illuminated by Christianity, said the poet Calderon in a deeper insight than that of those sages. That man comes into this world already burdened with guilt, therefore, can only appear as nonsensical to somebody who considers him just now made out of nothing and as the work of somebody else.'

What Schopenhauer refers to in this passage is the Christian doctrine of the fall and original sin. By the fall, man lost his original innocence and the happiness of an existence without suffering and pain, and as children of Adam, all men are deprived of the state of grace (according to Catholic doctrine, supernatural grace makes men children of God) and the freedom from physical disabilities. But the doctrine that all men in as much as they are men (as Schopenhauer expressed it, 'just made out of nothing') belong to a fallen human race does not solve the problem indicated above, that is to say, why man must live although he has been born without his will. Philosophically, there is no satisfactory solution to this problem. The existence of the world and therewith the existence of man is a fact that involves no sufficient reason for this existence and therefore is not explicable by itself (the basis of the so-called cosmological proof of the existence of God).

A 'perfect' world is impossible (because no limited being can be perfect) but despite this imperfection, the world is not nonsensical and, at least to a certain degree, rational. Philosophy, however, is unable to give a last answer to the problem of the meaning of life, the meaning of adversity, and the possibility of evil. These are problems to which religion is expected to give an answer. From a theistic point of view, the answer is based on the belief in God as the Creator of the universe. The entire order of things has been ordained by God whose wisdom has planned the world and everything in it and whose providence directs the course of creation. That the individual has no choice in coming into existence is one of the many limitations man has to accept with his nature and his environment. It is a basic fact of life which cannot be changed by the individual's like or dislike. These limitations which religion interprets as the conditions of a created being constitute also the basic challenges in man's existence. Man cannot change the facts of nature and the facts of life but man can use or overcome his limitations instead of being frustrated and overpowered by them.

The fact of being the child of particular parents is linked to man's inherent capabilities which, as explained above, constitute a limitation with regard to all human possibilities but also form the potential of his development. It is a question of approach. In his relations with other human beings as well as things, man can stress the negative aspects and rivet his attention on the burdens and restraints, but he can also give more importance to the positive sides and the opportunities presented by a given situation. To develop this 'philosophy of positive thinking' is one of the basic tasks of education.

Effect of Arrival of Child on Parents

Many fathers experience fear when told that their wives are pregnant. They fear for the health of wife and baby. Although childbirth deaths have bcome fewer, much attention has been drawn to birth defects and congenital diseases. Fathers become more concerned about their own safety because they feel the greater responsibility for the family. A special concern of expectant fathers is their ability to meet the financial needs resulting from the increase in the family.

The arrival of a child, may have a shock effect on the parents. Jack Nicklaus, the imperturbable golfer, actually fainted when being shown not only his first but also his subsequent children. The newborn may upset the relations between husband and wife. Until the birth of a child, the husband had the full attention of his wife; now, the wife's duties as mother take most of her time and energy and the child may become the centre of her affections. Much if not most of the conversation between husband and wife turns on the child, and the emotional involvement of the mother with her child collides with the possessive tendencies of the husband who may feel an unacknowledged jealousy. There may be a complete change in the family atmosphere and the husband-wife relationship, and both partners may have to adjust their feelings and their life-style to the new situation.

Why Have Children?

The motivation for begetting children is extremely varied. Most religions consider children a sign and pledge of divine blessing (Gen 22, 17 and passim in the Old Testament). The idea that children mean wealth and that many children are a status symbol may not be unrelated to this belief. The continuation of the family is naturally linked to the desire to have an heir and a successor to take over the family business. People may want children so as to be taken care of in old age, a calculation which nowadays often goes wrong. In many developing countries and particularly in agricultural societies, children constitute an addition to the productive capacity of the family and therefore economic assets. A United Nations study estimated that one-third of the children aged 12 to 15 have to work and put the number of children at work at 145 million. Children are used as labourers in family farming, craftswork, seasonal labour outside the home, in small wage-earning jobs and in apprenticeships. Unfortunately, child labour is often identical with exploitation.

There are various psychological reasons for desiring children, selfish as well as unselfish motives. Ego gratification may be behind the wish to have children and this may also be involved in the intention to perpetuate the family name. Parents expect children to achieve their own unfulfilled ambitions which may lead to tragic mistakes in forcing children into occupations, careers and marriages for which they are unfit or which they dislike. The desire that 'children should have it better' may lead to the emotional exploitation of children. In former times, people wanted to have children for patriotic reasons, to make the country strong, but such an attitude is alien to the present generation. On the contrary, when, in the nineteen sixties, to have babies went out of fashion, the refusal to supply 'cannon fodder' to the state was an important motive.

Surrogate Mothers

A modern development is to have children for others. There are several versions of the 'hired womb.' Newspaper advertisements seeking surrogate mothers for a fee (US$10,000 — 15,000) are no longer uncommon. A couple wanting a child but unable to have a child because the wife cannot conceive may look for a surrogate mother who will be impregnated by artificial insemination with the husband's sperm. A bachelor wanted a child of his own but did not want to get married or adopt a child. He found a surrogate mother (a divorcee with two children) who was willing to carry and bear a child conceived by artificial insemination and to give up custody rights permanently upon the birth of the child. Surrogate mothers have been implanted with the egg of a wife unable to bear children fertilised *in vitro* by the sperm of the husband.

Most American states have laws prohibiting the sale of babies (these laws are designed to stamp out black-market peddling of illegitimate, unwanted or abandoned babies for adoption) which may create legal complications for baby-by-contract deals. Motivating factors for becoming surrogate mothers are: (l) Need of money; (2) Desire to be pregnant. Some pregnant women feel more content, complete, special, glowing, feminine and attractive; (3) Feelings of guilt. Women who have had abortions seek to atone for 'killing a baby' by giving one to a family who wants a baby.

To give up the baby is not without emotional strain. Although most women do not expect any feeling of loss, the surrogate mother sometimes experiences a longing for her child. When a surrogate mother decided she wanted to keep the baby and the couple who had arranged to pay for her baby sued for custody; a California judge ruled that the natural mother was entitled to retain the baby. In another suit, the father withdrew his claim to the infant. In some cases, agreements with surrogate mothers stipulated that the natural father was to pay all medical expenses associated with a surrogate's pregnancy and assume legal responsibility for a child born with congenital abnormalities. He was, however, not to be responsible for expenses resulting from psychological problems. The surrogate mother agreed to undergo pre-natal medical care, refrain from smoking, drinking and illegal drugs and not to abort the child unless necessary to protect her health. But such an agreement may be legally unenforceable and many legal problems remain unsolved.

Once a baby is born, the natural father must go to court to gain full custody of the infant and the surrogate mother must sign away her rights.

A childless couple sought a court ruling that the husband, the natural father of the child born by a surrogate mother, was also the legal father but the court refused to make such a decision since, according to existing law, the surrogate mother's husband was the legal father. Then, there is the question whether the father would be obliged to pay child support if the surrogate mother decides to keep the baby, and the liability for the costs if there are complications in pregnancy or childbirth.

The most common problem among surrogate mothers is what to tell her family members; another major worry is whether the adoptive parents will accept the baby if it is born handicapped.

A possible problem is whether the child born by the surrogate mother was actually conceived by artificial insemination. In a recent case, the court decided on the strength of a blood test that a deformed child born by the surrogate mother was not begotten by the alleged father.

Opposition to Surrogate Motherhood

In a report submitted in connection with the government's inquiry into human fertilisation and embryology, the Family Law Committee of Britain's Law Society recommended that 'womb leasing' should be outlawed together with experiments on human foetuses and cloning. It should also be a criminal offense to offer a woman money to bear another's child. Even a contract for the natural insemination by a man of a woman for the purpose of later adoption of the child by a couple including one of the natural parents of the child would almost certainly be illegal. Only married couples or couples living together should be allowed artificial insemination.

The report also pointed out the danger of genetic incest. Artificial insemination with semen of unidentified origin could lead to mating of half-brothers and half-sisters. The committee suggested that all use of artificial insemination and children born as a result of it should be recorded and the identity of the genetic father indicated. Children should be given the right to get details of their natural parents when they reach the age of 18 (the same as adopted children).

The British Medical Association termed surrogate motherhood unethical because of the difficulties, anxieties and uncertainties involved and advised doctors not to cooperate with techniques and procedures leading to surrogate motherhood. But at its 1985 annual meeting, the association reversed its stand and by a vote of 193 to 182 approved a motion stating 'this meeting agrees with the principle of surrogate births in selected cases with careful controls.' A majority of the doctors opposed the view of the ethics committee that 'no human embryos should be created solely for experimental purposes' and the chairman of the association's ruling council called on the government to lay down rules on embryo research.

The first birth by a commercial surrogate mother who was artificially inseminated with the sperm of a man unknown to her on 4 January, 1985, raised the question whether she would be punishable under Britain's 1958 Adoption Act which prohibits payment for a child. The law carries a maximum fine of £100 and/or a six-month jail sentence. An American couple reportedly paid £7,500 through an agency which arranged for the woman to be artificially inseminated with the husband's sperm. His wife was unable to bear children.

Reflecting the widespread animosity against commercial surrogacy, the borough council of Barnet, a north London suburb, stopped the child from being taken out of the hospital and handed over to the American couple. Upon the request of an unknown applicant, the child, dubbed baby Cotton by the media after the surrogate mother's name, was made a ward of the High Court.

On 14 January, 1985, Judge John Latey of the Family Division of the High Court ruled that the baby should be given to her natural father and his wife and allowed to be taken out of the country although she remained a ward of the court. The couple had undertaken to return the child to the jurisdiction of the court if the court should so order — which seemed an unlikely contingency.

The judge noted that the surrogate mother, who has two children of her own, did not want the child. He also ruled that the ban on the media to identify the father should remain permanently in force and declared that the moral issues arising from surrogacy were not for the court to rule on.

The public outcry against surrogate motherhood prompted the British government to introduce legislation banning commercial surrogate mother agencies. Offenders now face penalties of up to three months in jail. Kim Cotton who was paid £20,000 by a British tabloid for her story, strongly defended her conduct in a book, *Baby Cotton: For Love and Money*, by journalist Denise Winn. Answering her many critics, including church leaders who said surrogacy was akin to prostitution, she remarked: 'It maddened me that those pompous people always talked about taking — taking advantage, taking money. I felt I was giving, giving life.' 'Quite apart from the fact that it is difficult to adopt nowadays anyway, surely it is better if one parent at least is represented in the child.'

Since abortion was legalised, the number of babies available for adoption in Britain has drastically declined. Officials handling adoption and fostering estimate that at least 100,000 couples at any one time are looking for a baby and that demand exceeds supply by 80 to one.

Joseph Cardinal Hoeffner, archbishop of Cologne, called the use of a substitute mother morally wrong and a sin against the child who, the Cardinal said, 'had a right to be born by its own mother.' It is difficult to figure out what kind of right (or what kind of child) the Cardinal was speaking about.

The British medical journal, *The Lancet,* suggested that a sterile couple might want to adopt an embryo. A sterile woman from whom no ovum could be obtained could be implanted with an ovum from another woman (for example, from a woman undergoing a sterilisation operation) fertilised by her husband's sperm. The same approach might be taken in the case of women whose offspring were at risk of an inherited disease. (The embryo-transfer process is discussed below in chapter 3.)

A French woman gave birth to a child conceived through artificial insemination with sperm from the husband of her infertile sister. Since the sisters were identical twins, the baby was genetically the same as a child that the woman might have born were she fertile.

Another modern development is the combination of the rejection of marriage and the affirmation of motherhood (see Vol. 1, Ch. 5). Women who do not want to be 'beholden to a man' still consider motherhood as the acme of a woman's existence and an integral part of her self-fulfilment. There are divorcees who, on the basis of their experience, loathe men and sexual intercourse but want a child. Such women may have artificial insemination, often with sperm donated by a friend, and give birth to children.

Couples who reject artificial birth control but do not want to practise abstinence will have to leave it to the natural course of things and accept any number of children. This was the usual situation in most parts of the world until the twentieth century. The enormous infant mortality greatly reduced the number of children in a family who actually grew up. Progress in family planning and birth control methods, growing economic pressures, the weakening of religious convictions and a decreasing willingness to bring the sacrifices required by parenthood have contributed to the drop in the number of children born into today's families.

Desirable Number of Children

There is no ideal number of children per family. Not only economic conditions, but also the capacity of the parents to take care of their children varies greatly, and although it may admit of a certain elasticity, it is limited. The slogan 'quality before quantity' has been frequently used by the proponents of birth control but such an antithesis does not actually exist. While it is true that in poor countries the children of large families are greatly disadvantaged, many eminent men and women have been the younger children in large families. The change in economic conditions necessitating the absence of the father may also have been a factor reducing the family size since it puts a much greater burden on the wife in managing the household.

Qualification for Parenthood

One of the basic considerations in the decision to have children should be the qualifications of the prospective parents to educate their children, but it seems doubtful that such a thought influences procreation. If one reads of a 45-year-old former draftsman who has eleven children by his legal wife and whose mistress has fourteen children, nine by her present lover, one wonders what kind of education these children will receive. The qualification as educator is chiefly a question of personality. Many young couples may be too immature — not physiologically but psychologically — to take on the responsibilities of parenthood. Nobody is allowed to drive a motor vehicle without having given proof of his ability to handle such a machine, but for the incomparably more difficult and important task of education, mankind seems to have taken it for granted that no special qualification is needed. It would be preposterous to institute an official examination for a licence to beget children. In closed societies, the social customs regulating marriage ensure a certain competence but in modern societies, people can get married and start a family without the slightest inkling of the problems they are going to face. Instincts are more or less sufficient to protect the young of animals with a very short infancy from hatching or birth to adulthood, but human childhood is so long and the requirements of human education so divergent that instincts are insufficient to bring up children in the variegated conditions of the human environment.

Education is not only a question of knowledge but, as already noted, it is above all a question of personality, of attitudes and motivation. The educator must be able to treat the children as persons — the basic difference of education from the rearing of animals. Psychological and pedagogical information is readily available but study and even training cannot create educators. The virtues that distinguish an educator — patience, understanding, respect and even reverence for the child and unselfishness, cannot be taught in a crash-course on childrearing. They are much the same virtues as those desirable for all inter-human relations applied to the special situation of human beings who must learn how to live as such. Moreover, there must be a basic harmony of views of husband and wife, otherwise, the upbringing of the children will not only be ineffective but a child may cling to one and reject the other of the parents. In the family, education is not a matter of lecturing children on good behaviour or moral principles but of giving an example. Admonitions, praise and punishment certainly play a role but the most pervasive influence is the behaviour of the parents, their daily life and conduct. The problem, therefore, is whether the parents are living up to the standards they want their children to observe.

An important part of the upbringing of children is to prepare them for living in society. In this respect, the presence or absence of brothers or sisters is of great importance. Today's small families are far from ideal for the children's socialisation. From the point of view of education, families with three or four children are infinitely preferable to the one-child family. The only child is in danger of becoming over-attached to his mother and too remote from his father. Alfred Adler attributed great importance to the sibling order in the development of man's character. The oldest will have to assume responsibility early, the youngest may be spoiled, and a second child may become ambitious and want to overtake everybody. A classical example òf sibling rivalry is the relationship between Heinrich and Thomas Mann. The enormous literary success of the younger brother's *Buddenbrocks* so upset Heinrich Mann that almost everything he thought thereafter, planned and wrote was influenced by the bitter envy of Thomas.

Costs of Raising Children

The material conditions for the foundation of a family and the education of the children naturally depend on the living conditions of society. In Japan, the standard of living has risen considerably compared with pre-war times. This is naturally reflected in the costs of education. An insurance company estimated that total expenses for educating a child up to graduation from college (22 years) would amount to a minimum of ¥15 million and a maximum of ¥37 million (in 1981 prices). These figures do not include contributions to secure the backdoor admission of students to prestigious institutions. In the first year after childbirth, care of an infant requires ¥480,000; the cost of food for the following 21 years will come to ¥5.1 million, that of clothing to ¥1.65 million. Expenses for health, medical care, grooming and sanitation will take ¥800,000, ¥2.06 million will be given as pocket money and ¥1.5 million will be spent on furnishings. Average outlays, not including school fees, will come to a total of ¥18.4 million. If the entire education is absolved in public schools, school fees will require ¥3.28 million; if a student attends public school until graduation from senior high school and then studies at the literature department of a private university, the costs will increase to ¥3.95 million. For a student who attends only private institutions and then studies medicine or dentistry, school fees will amount to ¥20.27 million.

An estimate of the Research Institute of Distribution Issues put the size of Japan's junior consumer market at ¥10 trillion, equivalent to one-fifth of the 1984 national budget. The main sectors profiting from the purchases for or by the over 20 million boys and girls between the ages of 5 and 15 are confectionery, dairy products, stationery, publications, sporting goods, clothing and toys. Parents pay for most of the goods bought in addition to the ordinary household items, and a wife who has a job often uses the money she earns for special purchases for herself and the children. According to a survey made in 1982 by a life insurance company, allowances averaged ¥37,000 a year, and a youngster's average savings amounted to ¥75,000. Boys spent most of their pocket money on comic books, toy assembly kits sold in vending machines and cheap sweets; girls' preferential purchases were stationery, stuffed animal toys and bags.

Preparation for Parenthood

Parenthood, therefore, should be undertaken only after the spouses have honestly appraised their own suitability to raise a child, economically, mentally and emotionally. This advice may be largely academic because a considerable number of conceptions just happen and many parents are unaware of the necessity of being prepared for the arrival of their offspring. There are a number of organisations that provide counselling for prospective parents who are interested in tackling the task of rearing children seriously.

The decision to have children should be made with all due deliberation, but once it has been taken, father and mother must accept all the responsibilities involved. The heart of the matter is to make sure that every child is wanted, not only at the time of conception and birth but forever thereafter. Every woman should seriously question herself whether motherhood is for her. Motherhood is a top-priority job which cannot take a back seat to any other career. It requires preparation, the knowledge of the dos and don'ts of child-rearing, because this is not just 'doing what comes naturally.' Breast-feeding, for example, is not so natural that every mother can do it. A mother must be prepared for sacrifice. Mothers are not lunatics if they don't like the chores and resent the kids, and handicapped children can become such a burden that their parents will kill them. At the time of marriage, many women are unprepared for motherhood. The following conversation of a TV actress with a reporter when she returned to work after childbirth indicates the problem. 'And how about baby care?' the reporter asked. 'That's not my chore.' — 'But don't you sometimes play with your baby?' — 'No. How do you play with a baby who can't even talk?'

Many divorces in marriages under five years occur not because of frictions between husband and wife but because both were unprepared for children. Since children depend entirely on their mother, they make enormous demands on her physical and emotional strength. A mother is at once short-order cook, dishwasher, maid, chauffeur, medical expert and psychologist. A German court has held that the clause in an employment contract entitling a government employee to paid absence from work in case of 'serious illness' in the family covers the case of a small child who is not seriously ill in medical terms but needs constant care and attention.

In the old times, women had a better emotional and practical preparation for motherhood. It was common for a girl in the early teens or even younger to be put in charge for long hours of her younger brothers and sisters or the neighbour's children. Young women knew what to expect and how to handle it.

If a couple is not prepared for parenthood, the impact of the birth of a child on the marriage can be destructive. A difference of opinion regarding the kids may create an undercurrent of negative feelings each partner has about his or her respective responsibilities and role. The confusion, chaos, worry or work resulting from such a situation may poison the atmosphere and a once happily married couple can become so nervous that even trivial irritations or imagined slights can take on exaggerated proportions. Men can run away and get absorbed in their work, but women will usually be left with the children.

Legitimacy

The question who a child's parents are seems fairly simple but since it is of basic importance for determining a child's status and his rights, certain rules have been created by legislation. Most regulations evolved from the concept of legitimacy but in Japanese law, the formal relations derived from the family registration system complicate the matter. For the relation between mother and child, the physiological relation of childbirth may seem sufficient evidence but the Japanese Civil Code lays down: 'Father or mother can recognise a child who is not legitimate' (Art. 779). In case a child has been entered in the family register as the child of a different woman, it is, for the purposes of the family register, the legitimate child of that woman and as long as the family register is not changed, it cannot be recognised as the child of its real mother. For the relation to the father, the basic rule is: 'A child conceived by the wife during marriage is assumed to be the child of the husband' (Art. 772, Par. 1). A child born after 200 days from the establishment of the marriage or within 300 days from the day of the dissolution or annulment of the marriage is presumed to have been conceived during the marriage' (Art. 772, Par. 2). The husband can deny that the child is legitimate (Art. 774). Even if the conception preceded the establishment of the marriage (that is, the acceptance of the notification of the marriage; see Vol.2, Ch.7), the child is legitimate. The law requires a formal act for the establishment of the marriage but in Japan, spouses often live together in a *nai-en* relation prior to the formal notification of the marriage so that the beginning of marital relations and the legal establishment of the marriage do not coincide. There is, however, no proper reason to make a child illegitimate who is conceived by the persons who get married and born during the marriage.

If father and mother are not husband and wife, recognition or a judicial decree is necessary to establish the legal relation to the father. A child born out of wedlock is illegitimate and the mother is obliged to file a notification of the birth together with a birth certificate within two weeks. If this notification is made, the child is entered as an illegitimate child of the mother into her family register and is given her family name (Art. 790, Par. 2). The legal relation with the father is only established if the father recognises the child, and this recognition is retroactive (Art. 784). But he becomes the legal father of an illegitimate child, while the parental rights remain entirely with the mother and the child retains the name of the mother. It can be changed to the father's name if permission of the family court is obtained (Art. 788). If the father reports a child born by a concubine as the child of his wife, the child does not become legitimate.

An illegitimate child becomes legitimate by the marriage of its parents. Legally, such a child acquires the 'status of a legitimate child' but does not become legitimate and is called 'quasi-legitimate.' There are two versions of this status. The first is when the parents of a child whom the father has recognised become married (Art. 789, Par. 1). The quasi-legitimacy starts with the time of the marriage. If a number of children have been born by the same parents and these children have been recognised by the father at different times, they all acquire the status of legitimate children at the time of the marriage. The second case in which a child acquires the status of a legitimate child is when a child is recognised by father and mother during their marriage.

Proof of paternity can be a very difficult process. Blood group sampling, the most common paternity test, has a probability of showing that a man is not the father of 97.5 per cent but it is difficult to establish that a man is the father. Gene frequency tests usually are reliable in indicating the father in 90 per cent of the cases. The most accurate results are provided by chromosome tests which are based on the fact that of the child's 46 chromosomes, 23 are from the father and 23 from the mother. If the father's chromosomes in the child's cells do not match the chromosomes in the alleged father's cells, the man certainly is not the father; if they match, the probability of the man being the father is much greater than in other tests.

In the old Japanese family system, the father could recognise a concubine and a child from the concubine was called *shoshi*, natural child. The old civil law did not recognise the concubine system but recognised the relation of *shoshi* to the father so that, on principle, these children belonged to the family of the father. Under the system of family inheritance, a male *shoshi* preceded a legitimate daughter, making the boy the heir presumptive to the family estate. The system no longer exists under the post-war civil code.

A child born by artificial insemination is considered a legitimate child, but if somebody else's semen has been used without the consent of the husband, he can file a suit to have the child declared illegitimate. A wife who agrees to artificial insemination by a donor not her husband does not commit adultery and her action is no ground for divorce. The donor cannot claim to be the father of the child. The child of an unmarried woman conceived by artificial insemination is illegitimate.

In the Meiji era, a child could not institute legal proceedings for the determination of his father. The relation of the father to an illegitimate child depended entirely on the will of the father. Under present law, a child (or his ascendants or descendants in direct line) can apply to the courts for a sentence or adjudgement declaring his relation to the father (Art. 787). On the other hand, the child or some other interested party can file objections to the recognition by the father (Art. 786). As a matter of fact, such a suit investigates the civil status of the child and his mother, marital relations, *nai-en* relations, sexual relations of a woman with other men and similar questions.

It is extremely difficult to ascertain the mother, let alone the father, of an abandoned child.

In Japan, the number of births of illegitimate children reached a high of 167,011 in 1920 when they accounted for 8.3 per cent of all births (the highest ratio was 9.4 per cent in 1910). In 1981, illegitimate births numbered 13,201, 0.9 per cent of all births. The ready availability of abortion is the main reason for the low incidence.

The distinction between legitimate and illegitimate children has often been criticised. It seems unjust to qualify children on the basis of the presence or absence of legal marital relations between their parents on which the children had no influence whatever. The legal effects related to legitimacy or illegitimacy could be regulated without stigmatising the children.

Different from Japanese law (and most western systems), a child is legitimate according to Islamic law only if it is conceived during the lawful marriage of its parents. In Sunni law, no legal relationship exists between a father and his illegitimate child but there is a legal tie between the child and its mother. Guardianship of the person (such as control of education and marriage) and of the property of minor children belongs to the father or other close male agnate relative, but the bare right of custody of young children whose parents are divorced or separated belongs to the mother or female maternal relatives.

Parental Authority

The imposition of legal restraints on minors is found in many legal systems. In Roman law, all persons under the age of puberty (male 14, female 12) not under *patria potestas* needed *tutores* (guardians). Under his will, the *pater familias* could appoint *tutores* for those who would become independent *(sui iuris)* upon his death. If no appointment was made, certain prescribed relatives became *tutores;* otherwise, an appointment was made by magistrates. Originally, children were considered adults at puberty; in later times, it became usual to have guardians appointed for those between puberty and 25. All women not under *patria potestas* or manus needed *tutores* appointed by magistrates. In the early days of the empire, this was only an irksome technicality which disappeared with Justinian.

The basic provisions in Japanese law regulating the relations between parents and children concern parental authority. Parental authority implies two things, the right of the parents over the child and the restrictions on the freedom and independence of the minor. According to the definition of the Civil Code, 'The person who exercises parental authority possesses the right and owes the duty of care, custody and education of the child' (Art. 820). Parental authority includes the care for the person of the child as well as the management of its assets. Personal care concerns the child's bodily and spiritual development, its upbringing and growth as a good human being. In case of unavoidable circumstances, father or mother can petition the family court to renounce parental power and the right of management, and the court can allow them to resume these rights when the reason ceases (Art. 837). It is possible to divest oneself of the right of management alone but to give up the right (and duty) of care and custody alone will not be permitted. Parental power comprising only the right of management without the right of care and custody is impossible.

Modern law considers parental power as a kind of trust to be exercised by the parents in the interest of the child. If father or mother abuses parental power or in case of serious misconduct, the family court, at the instance of relatives or the public prosecutor, can declare the forfeiture of parental power (Art. 834). In order to prevent the exploitation of a minor's earning power, the Labour Standards Law forbids parents or guardians to conclude a labour contract for a minor (Art. 58, Par. 1). If, however, the contract is disadvantageous for the minor, they (and the labour office) can cancel it for the future (ibid., Par. 2). A minor can demand wages independently and parents or guardians cannot receive wages in place of the minor (Art. 59).

For understanding parental authority, it is necessary to see both, right and duty. That the parents undertake the care and education of their children is a natural right, that is, a right given immediately with the relation of being parent. Parents do not educate their children because they have received a mandate from society or because they have been empowered to do so by the state but because they are the parents of the children. Legal regulations define and specify the relations between parents and children but parents would be entitled to educate their children and bound to do so also if such regulations did not exist. In particular (and unfortunately in too many) cases, parents may be incapable of or unwilling to take over this task and for these cases, society and the state must make provision. But these cases constitute no reason to deprive parents of their right of care and education or to treat education in the family as subordinate and dependent of the state's educational activities. The public institutions of child care and education have never demonstrated that they are superior to family education, and the most satisfactory results outside of family education have been achieved by private institutions.

The care of the children and their education is also the basic duty of the parents. It is first and foremost a moral duty founded, as the reverse of the parents' right, on their position as parents. With the generation of the children, parents must assume responsibility for enabling the children to grow up to valuable human beings. As personal beings, children possess all basic human rights, and parents not only have the duty not to violate these rights but also to help the children to make use of these rights.

Custody

Special regulations related to parental authority are the provisions of the Civil Code concerning the right to determine the residence (Art. 821), the right to discipline (Art. 822), the right to permit the exercise of a trade (Art. 823), and the right to represent the child with regard to property rights (Art. 824–832). The right to fix the child's residence exists not only when the child is unable to make its own choice but also if the child is capable of using its own judgement. But in determining the place where the child has to live, the child's welfare must be taken into account. There is no right to demand that a child be handed over, but it is possible to demand the transfer from a party keeping or restraining a child unlawfully.

In 1973, an 11-year-old boy who wanted to live with his aunt rather than with his parents won a court battle against his parents. The boy was the only child of the proprietor of a beauty shop in Funabashi, Japan. Since the parents did not get on well with each other and they were busy, they asked the man's sister in Tokyo to take care of the boy. The aunt, a graduate of the University of London, raised the boy as if she were his real mother, sent him to kindergarten and later to primary school. The boy first spent spring and summer vacations with his parents but then refused to go to the parental home. The parents, therefore, filed a suit and, in 1971, the Tokyo District Court ordered the aunt to return the boy. The boy, however, went back to his aunt and sought a retrial. As a result, the court ruled that the boy had developed a fear complex against his parents who had paid little attention to him and that it would be cruel to return him to his parents and deprive him of the affection of his aunt.

An international treaty to curb the abduction of children has been ratified by 10 nations (31 July 1986). It provides that a child under 16 years of age abducted by one of its parents to another country must be returned unless it is shown that the child's legal custodian was not actually exercising custody rights, or had consented to or subsequently acquiesced in the child's removal, or that the child's return would expose it to grave risk of physical or psychological harm. The international abduction of children is a modern phenomenon resulting from the increase in international marriages and divorces and the easier conditions of international travel. Recently, a boy who had been brought to the United States by his parents applied for political asylum when his parents decided to return to the Soviet Union. A court ruled that the boy had to accompany his parents but this decision was set aside and the boy was allowed to stay in the United States with his sister (who had already become of age). In a display of stupid fanaticism, the American Civil Liberties Union wanted to force the boy to rejoin his parents in the Soviet Ukraine.

If a child's custodian and, a fortiori, somebody with no custodial rights subjects an infant to undue restraint, somebody qualified to take over the custody of the child can apply to a civil court and ask for the transfer of the child's custody. If it is evident that the undue restraint constitutes an enormous violation of existing legal methods or procedures, the liberation of the infant can be demanded on the basis of the Habeas Corpus Act.

In recent years, the tendency to put small children in private nurseries — so-called baby hotels — has been growing. Parents are reluctant, for various reasons, to raise their children at home. Although there may be cases in which it is unavoidable to entrust children to such homes, this trend is extremely deplorable. A large number of those baby hotels are sub-standard (unsanitary conditions, insufficient safety standards, insufficient number of attendants, misguided child welfare policies). The most serious objection, however, is that the children are deprived of what they need most, the love and intimacy of their parents.

The right to punish is subject not only to moral and educational but also to legal limitations. Courts have held that disciplinary measures exceeding 'social moral views' constitute an abuse of parental power and amount to violence. The government runs institutions for minors whose conduct constitutes a threat to society. Under the Child Welfare Law, minors under 18 can be committed to the National Institute of Juvenile Correction and family courts can order juveniles between the ages of 14 and 23 to be sent to reformatories regulated by the Reformatory Law.

Limitations on Children's Rights

Minors need the consent of their parents or guardians for going into business on their own as well as for accepting employment by a third party.

The right to manage the property of a minor includes the right to 'dispose' of the property. Income produced by a minor's assets can be applied to the child's living and educational expenses. Problematic is the use of income left over when these expenses are met. Starting with Roman law, many legal systems have allowed the holder of parental authority to appropriate this surplus but modern law has generally adopted the rule that it has to be returned to the child. The Japanese Civil Code recognises that income from a child's assets can be used to cover expenses for the child's upbringing and the management of his property. If the interests of the parents and those of the child or children collide, the parents must ask the family court to appoint a special representative for the child. If a third party makes a gift to a child and does not want the parents who exercise parental power to administer this property, he can appoint an administrator, and if he fails to do so, the family court can make the appointment.

The same as a natural child, an adopted child who has not reached majority is under the parental authority of its foster parents. For the duration of the marriage, father and mother exercise parental authority jointly. If, however, one of the parents is unable to exercise parental authority, the other parent takes charge (Art. 818). Since the provisions on parental authority are based on the equality of both parents, the right of the mother is not subject to any restrictions if she exercises it alone. In the old family system, the head of the family alone was in charge of the upbringing, protection and education of all minors and the parental relations were subordinate to his authority. If the mother was divorced or returned to her own family after the death of her husband, she had practically no longer any relations with her children. Under the old civil code, children under parental authority were simultaneously subject to the power of the head of the house to which they belonged which resulted in a double system of subjection. The duty to rear, protect and educate a child was the duty of the father even if both parents were present. If the mother wielded parental authority, she was subject to the control of the family council.

If children did not earn their living independently, they had to obtain the consent of their parents for marriage, divorce by agreement or remarriage up to the age of 30 for males and 25 for females. This was not part of parental authority; these restrictions were a special arrangement to keep children under the domination of their parents. Even under present law, a minor is not able to exercise parental authority which is exercised on his behalf by the parents to whom he is subject (Art. 833).

The law provides no mechanism for reconciling differences of opinion on the exercise of parental authority. In theory, a solution would have to be based on the answer to the question what the child's welfare is and what it requires. The child's life is part of the family life and the parents should have some ideas of what they want to accomplish. On major questions, parents may have their own ideas and it seems rather doubtful that a court would be able to tell parents what they should do. On the contrary, the child may get hurt. It may be possible to stop the illegal or harmful use or abuse of parental power but it is more difficult to promote the welfare of the child. To entrust the formulation of some kind of policy to a family council or a court seems of very doubtful effectiveness.

Financial Obligations of Parents

It is practically impossible to enumerate what parents should do for the sound education of their children. The Japanese Civil Code does not refer to the support of the children in the chapter on parental authority and only states the principle of mutual support among ascendants and descendants in direct line in the chapter on support (Art. 877, Par. 1). Legally, the parents' right and duty to care for, protect and educate the children is different from their financial obligations. Custodial and educational rights and duties are directly connected with parental power while the financial obligations derive from the relations of father and mother to their minor children. A father or mother without parental power (such as in case of divorce) may nevertheless be liable for the support of the children. On the basis of the general principle that descendants and ascendants in direct line are responsible for support, a child's grandparents may have to take care of the child but they are not given any right of custody or education. As between parents who adopted a child and the child's real parents, the adoptive parents are primarily responsible for the support of the child. A father who has recognised an illegitimate child is responsible for its support which may be regulated by agreement between father and mother usually based on the financial resources of the parties.

Step-Parents

The old civil law gave parental authority also to step-parents and to the legal wife over the child of a concubine living in the father's family. In the case of step-parents, the emotional adjustment may sometimes be difficult (a thorough discussion of this subject can be found in '*Step-Parenting: How to Live with Other People's Children,*' by Brenda Maddox.) Naturally, there are great differences depending on the age of the children, the character, maturity and educational talent of the step-parent, and the reason why a step-father or step-mother joined the family (remarriage after death or divorce, marriage of unwed mother to somebody else than the natural father of the child). In orphaned children, the trauma of the separation may coalesce with the distrust and rejection of the newcomer and the negative reactions of the child may make it more difficult for the step-parent to develop an intimate relationship with the child. The situation may become more complicated when step-brothers or step-sisters arrive. On the other hand, the absence of natural ties facilitates the formation of sexually-motivated relations between step-father and step-daughter or step-mother and step-son.

An important factor in the adjustment between step-parent and step-child is the cooperation and understanding between natural parent and step-parent. If they battle out their differences in opinion in front of the children, it will hardly help to have the step-parent accepted as an equal and beloved member of the family.

Parental Authority in Divorces

If the parents divorce, Japanese law regulates parental authority as follows. 1. If the divorce is by agreement, the agreement must also determine the parent who will have parental authority. 2. If the divorce involves a court procedure, the court will determine which of the parents will have parental authority. 3. If the parents divorce before the birth of the child, the parents can determine that the father shall have parental power (Art. 819, Par. 1-3). With regard to a child that the father has acknowledged, the father can exercise parental authority only if the parents agree to name him as the person having parental authority (Art. 819, Par. 4). (Since the child recognised by the father is illegitimate, the mother has parental authority). Parental power exists for the interest and benefit of the children, not for the advantage of the parents. If the sole power of either father or mother seems to injure the interests of the child, relatives can appeal to the court and the person exercising parental authority can be changed (Art. 819, Par. 6). If father or mother abuses parental power or greatly neglects his or her duties, the court, upon the intervention of relatives or the public prosecutor, can strip them of parental authority (Art. 834). In a similar way, the court can step in if the parents squander the child's assets (Art. 835). If both parents exercise parental authority and one is deprived of parental power, the other exercises parental authority alone; if he is also stripped of authority, a guardian is appointed. The general tendency has been to make it easier for the authorities to intervene on behalf of the children against their parents. In England, children can be taken away from their parents on the decision of a magistrate's court.

In order to make use of a clause in the parents' insurance policy which covered injuries caused by an accident in and around the home, a four-year-old Canadian boy sued his parents through his grandmother. The boy had fallen on rusty nails and suffered brain damage while infection set in and the front part of his skull was removed. He will require special attention for the rest of his life.

A difficult problem is how to prepare children for the death of one of the parents or the loss of a member of the family. Naturally, the age of the children will make a great difference in the understanding of the event and its emotional impact. While it is a legitimate concern to spare children grief and sorrow, it is also desirable that children participate in the serious and decisive affairs of the family to the extent of their capacity and learn to cope with adversity, sickness and death. The knowledge that human existence includes both joys and sorrows and the way of handling both is indispensable to the preparation for life.

State and Economic Burden of Family

As mentioned elsewhere (Vol. 2, Ch. 7), in many respects, the existing law does not provide sufficiently for the needs of the family. The law of taxation often puts unjust burdens on the family and fails to take its requirements into account. The adoption of the principle of 'family splitting' would substantially reduce the tax burden on families with children. Education allowances and the inclusion of the years spent on rearing children in the computation of a mother's work years would contribute to the recognition of the social importance of the role of the mother.

Some countries compensate families for the high cost of raising children by child allowances. Under the Japanese child allowance system established in 1972, the government paid ¥5,000 a month to about 2.1 million families for their third child and each of the subsequent children if their annual income was less than ¥4,010,000 in 1984. Under a revision proposed by the Liberal-Democratic Party, parents will receive an allowance of ¥2,500 a month when they have their second child and one of ¥5,000 a month for their third and each of the subsequent children. At present, low-income families are paid an extra ¥2,000 for each child covered by the allowance system. The payments stop when the children . graduate from junior high school. Under the proposed revision, scheduled to be fully implemented in 1988 after a two-year transition period, the payments will cease when the children enter elementary school.

In West Germany, single mothers or fathers who have to meet special expenses for child-care on account of their work can claim a standard deduction of DM 480 a year for each child and deductions up to DM

4,000 for the first child and up to DM 2,000 for each of the other children if the expenses exceeding their own reasonable contribution are itemised.

Statutory maternity benefits are common in industrialised countries but in the United States, 60 per cent of the working women do not receive income replacement during maternity leave. In all countries, however, families without children are better off economically than families with children. The official economy disregards the household economy in as much as the work of the housewife remains unpaid and the production of children has to be financed privately.

Social and educational policies often ignore the functions of the family, create competitive organisations and arrangements encroaching on its activities whereas the creation of institutions supportive of the family is neglected. Actually, many of these developments have been ideologically motivated deviations from the basic tendency of modern law to regard the maintenance of healthy family life as a major national duty. Since Germany's Weimar Constitution, declarations to this effect have been inserted in many constitutions. As mentioned above, the main emphasis of Japan's constitution lies in the equality and individual freedom of both sexes (Art. 24). A number of laws have been enacted to promote the welfare of children. The Child Welfare Law and the Livelihood Protection Law created the legal foundation for helping parents who lack the financial means for rearing their children. In the interest of the upbringing of children, the Child Welfare Law proclaims the functions of their guardians (including their parents) as social duties and provides for ways in which they can be warned and replaced. The tendency is to stress and expand the functions of the state while making light of the contributions of the family.

An aspect which often finds too little attention is the psychological and spiritual gain parents derive from their children. This presupposes that the adult is sensitive to the appeal to humaneness embodied in the child. The child is a human being completely dependent on adults to whom it looks with absolute confidence. The trust of the child forces the adult to become trustworthy. Children trust adults not because they receive material advantages from them but because they feel safe. Tenderness counts more than costly presents. The trusting confidence included in the precariousness and potentiality of the growing life demands a creditable fulfilment of the roles of father and mother which is not content with the external care for the material needs of the child but also looks after his heart and affections. To be father and mother requires the willingness to accept a human being's total trust and to shoulder the responsibility for his future until he can make his own decision. It is a task which not only presupposes maturity but also demands the resolve to shape the future with and for the children.

3

Motherhood

THE MEANING OF SEXUALITY is the transmission of life. The individual may consider the relation of sexuality to procreation irrelevant but in the order of nature, the connection of sexuality with the continuation of the species is undeniable. Only in its relation to life and as an affirmation of life can sexuality be adequately understood. While the individual woman has often been treated or mistreated as property, the incontrovertible fact that human life with all its potential emerges from the womb of the mother has imparted motherhood a dignity and sanctity which has even been exaggerated to the apotheosis of woman and mother.

Religious Homage to Motherhood

Motherhood has often been identified with fertility. In pre-literate religions, the earth mother is venerated as an eternally fruitful source of everything. Different from female fertility deities, the earth mother is not regarded as a specific fountain of vitality requiring sexual intercourse. She is mother pure and simple, nothing is separate from her. The Tibetan name of Mt Everest, *Chomolungma,* for example, means 'Goddess Mother of the World.' All things come from her, return to her, and are her. The totality of the cosmos is her body, she gives birth to everything from her womb and nourishes all things from her breasts. Each separate being is a manifestation of her; all things share in her life through an eternal cycle of birth and rebirth.

In the most archaic form, the earth mother transcends all sexuality. She simply produces everything inexhaustibly from herself. She is life and she is death; she is male and she is female. In other mythical systems, she becomes a more limited figure. She is represented as the feminine earth consort of the masculine sky; she is fertilised by the sky in the beginning and brings forth terrestrial creation.

A different form of fertility worship is the mother goddess. This term applies to a variety of feminine deities and maternal symbols of creativity, birth, fertility, sexual union, nurturing and the cycle of growth. If the emphasis is placed on the sex role, the mother goddess is young and not cosmogenic. Although the male plays a relatively less important role, mother goddesses are usually part of a divine pair, and their mythology narrates the vicissitudes of the goddesses and their (frequently human) consorts. In Babylonia, Egypt, Phrygia and Phoenicia, mother goddesses were worshipped under different names but with about the same attributes (Ishtar in Babylonia, Astarte in Phoenicia, Cybele in Phrygia, Isis in Egypt). Each of these deities personified the same principle: creation of life, rebirth of nature after the death of winter, hope of resurrection of man himself. The cult of these fertility deities spread to Greece and later to Rome and became part of the Hellenistic mythology.

The fertility myths celebrated the revitalisation process. In the Canaan of biblical times, a sacred marriage between the Ba'alim (Lords) and Ba'alat (Ladies) was imitated by sexual intercourse between men representing the Ba'alim and the sacred temple prostitutes *(qedeshot)* representing the Ba'alat. The Ba'alim as gods of weather and sky would send the rains (often identified with semen) to the earth so that it might yield abundant harvests of grains and fruits. Basically, the peasants in some parts of Europe expressed the same belief when they had intercourse on their fields in order to secure a good harvest.

The essential moments in the myths of most mother goddesses are her disappearance and reappearance and the celebration of her divine marriage. Her disappearance has cosmic implications. Her reappearance, choice of a male partner and intercourse with him restore and guarantee fertility after which the male consort is frequently set aside or sent to the underworld.

If maternity is emphasised, the mother goddess is the parent and nourisher of a divine child and, by extension, of all mankind. This form occurs more in iconography than in myth. The male role in procreation has found much less mythical recognition than that of the mother, but the phallus has been widely used for fertility rites.

Different from the goddesses of fertility and reproduction, the mother of the gods *(Mater deum Magna Idaea)* was the goddess of universal motherhood, the giver of life to gods, men and beasts alike. In Greek and Roman literature, she was commonly known as Cybele and under the empire, her cult became one of the most important rites in the Roman world. Her priests, the *galloi,* castrated themselves on entering her service, imitating her lover, the fertility god Attis. From then on, the *galloi* wore female clothing and perfumed their hair with ointments. Some of the mystery religions which arose from Eastern fertility cults with their dying and rising gods were transformed in the Hellenistic age to cults of a saviour god whose dying and rising gives personal immortality...

Hindu mythology links procreation and destruction, birth and death. Devi, the goddess of love, maternity and death, is the consort of Shiwa, the 'Destroyer.' Shiwa is the great god of life, incorporating life and death, sexuality as well as the continence of asceticism. His symbol is the *linga* (phallus) while that of his consort is the *yoni* (the external female genital). Devi, also called Annapurna and Parvati, is identified with Shakti, which means the female principle or organ of generative power, but also with Kali, the personification of creation and destruction. The Indian fertility gods were never spiritualised which led to the identification of erotic and religious experience. Union with the gods was accomplished by sexual union.

The association of life and death is also found in Syrian and Palestine mythology. Astarte, the fertility goddess (called Ashtoreth in the Old Testament), is the goddess of love and war, and so is Anath, the consort of Baal who was celebrated for her ferocity in battle. In Hellenistic times, Anath and Astarte blended in a single figure. Atargatis, the 'Syrian goddess.' The cult of Artemis also included dissonant elements. The huntress of the Olympian mythology was a slayer of animals to whom Greeks and barbarians offered human sacrifices, a reminiscence of the destructive lust of the virgin goddess for the potency of her male partners. She was the virgin midwife and the killing and life-giving mother goddesss.

The mystery of conception and birth has been celebrated by chthonic and phallic cults in the most diverse cultures. Deities originally representing the fertility of the earth became symbols for the veneration of the mystery of human life and the worship of sexual lust as the supreme affirmation of life. Dionysos whose cult culminated in the Bacchanalia, and Demeter whose temple at Eleusis was the centre of the Eleusinian mysteries, typified the belief that the generative power and the transmission of life possessed a dimension transcending merely human potentialities, a persuasion also indicated by the identification of sex symbols with deities (for example, *linga* with Shiwa and *yoni* with Shakti). A similar conviction is expressed in Christianity by the saying that the parents participate in God's creative power. When Eve gave birth to her first child, she proclaimed: 'I have gotten a man through God' (Gen. 4, 1).

A fertility cult related to the sentiments of the prospective mother has been reported from China. A temple on Hengshan, one of China's five sacred mountains, houses a statue of the Bodhisattva Avalokiteshvara (called Kuan-yin in China and Kannon in Japan). According to local superstition, if a woman touches the ear of the child in the arms of the goddess, she is likely to get a girl, if she touches the child's penis, she will probably get a boy. The ear of the infant is intact, but the penis has been almost completely worn away from the touch of tens of thousands of hopeful mothers wanting to escape the shame of giving birth to a girl.

Prayers to local deities for fertility, safe childbirth and the upbringing of children survive in the Japanese countryside. Almost everywhere, statues of Jızô, the god of mercy (in Indian Buddhism, the Bodhisattva Ksitigarbha who saves from the suffering of the nether world) and the patron of travellers, children and pregnant wives, often 'decorated' with a bib, are found at the wayside.

The most idealistic sublimation of motherhood is the Catholic veneration of Mary. It involves the separation of motherhood from sexuality — Mary is 'virgin and mother' — and the greatest exaltation of motherhood because Mary is the 'mother of God.' Mary's relations with her son encompass the heights and depths of motherly affections; she felt the deepest pain of a mother in mourning the loss of her son, but the 'sorrowful mother' is also the 'Queen of Heaven,' united with her son by her bodily assumption into heaven. Raphael's Sistine madonna, a caring and loving human mother, represents the common ideal of the mother for whom the child signifies future and continuation of her own life, but the Mary of the Catholic faith embodies a multitude of symbols far transcending the role of the mother. Mary is the personification of heavenly love and, as 'second Eve,' not only the mediatrix of redemption but also the renovatrix of women and the reversal of 'woman is sin' into 'woman is salvation.'

For the individual woman, the possibility of motherhood depends on her fertility and that of her husband. A woman's fertility starts with puberty and ends with the menopause. These limits, however, are rather elastic and there are great differences in the number of births within these limits. Girls of eleven and women in their late fifties have had children; the highest age according to the Guiness Book of Records was 57 years and 129 days. In Chile, one wife had 37 children of the same husband.

Conception

The process of conception is rather complex. From the immature eggs in the ovaries of the woman, an egg is brought to maturity mainly through two hormones released by the brain, the follicle stimulating hormone (FSH) and the luteinising hormone release factor (LHRF). The immature ovum is encased in a cyst-like capsule called a follicle. It matures in about 14 days, bursts out of the follicle and slips into one of the Fallopian tubes through which it is carried into the uterus. Fertilisation usually takes place while the ovum is in transit.

Sperm production in the male is also controlled by hormones of which FSH seems to be the most important but the process of sperm production is not fully understood.

Sterility

Male and female sterility can result from various causes, purely anatomical obstacles such as blocked Fallopian tubes, hormonal deficiencies, imbalances in the chemistry of the vaginal fluids causing the death of the spermatozoa, and so on. According to American data, about 10 per cent of all married couples are infertile, and a female disorder is responsible in about 60 per cent of the cases. The inability to ovulate causes 30 to 40 per cent of the infertility in women, and this inability may be the effect of the deficiency of the brain hormone LHRF. Fertility drugs directed at correcting hormone problems have become fairly effective and the incidence of multiple births or miscarriages associated with some of them have been reduced, largely as the result of improved drug purity and progress in their administration so as to match the periodic events in the woman's reproductive cycle. A device called a hormone pump has been invented to prevent multiple births in women on fertility drugs.

There are few reliable data on male infertility. Many men are infertile because the internal temperature of the scrotum exceeds about 35°C which makes sperm defective. An apparatus called the testicular hypothermia device developed by a former research engineer cools the scrotum by the evaporation of distilled water.

Anomalies in a women's reproductive system may cause anomalous births. In very rare cases, a woman may have two wombs, bear a child in each and give birth to twins.

Artificial insemination has made it possible for paraplegics to have children. A child was born to a Tokyo couple both of whom are paralysed from the waist down because of spinal injuries, and in New Zealand, a paraplegic couple had identical twins.

Test-Tube Babies

For women with damaged Fallopian tubes, child-bearing has been made possible by the work of the British team of Dr Patrick Steptoe, a gynaecologist, and Dr Robert Edwards, a physiologist. In the test-tube procedure, one or more eggs are taken from the mother, fertilised in a test tube (where the process of cell division starts), and reimplanted into the mother's womb. The first test-tube baby, Louise Joy Brown, was born on 25 July, 1978, and her mother had a second child in June 1982. Numerous pregnancies have been achieved, including those of twins —the first test-tube twins delivered normally were twin girls born in Melbourne in June 1982, test-tube triplets born in June 1983 and test-tube quadruplets born to a 31-year-old Melbourne woman in January 1984. In January 1985, a woman who had been infertile because of pelvic tuberculosis gave birth to test-tube triplets. According to Professor Jan Craft, it was the first case in which in-vitro fertilisation had been successful in a woman who had been suffering from pelvic tuberculosis. The condition can be cured through drug treatment, but the women are usually unable to conceive afterwards.

According to Dr Edwards, there were 590 test-tube babies in the world in May 1984 and 570 pregnancies. Transplants had proved successful in more than 13 per cent of women below 30 years of age, above 12 per cent for women aged 30 to 35, 11.7 per cent for those between 35 and 39 and 7.2 per cent in women over 40.

The first test-tube baby born in Japan was delivered by Caesarian section on 14 October, 1983. *In-vitro* fertilisation programmes are being conducted at a number of universities. There are about 400,000 women in Japan suffering from infertility due to Fallopian tube problems. The majority of fertilised embryos fail to establish themselves in the womb, and an American institute reported that the number of failures is considerable. According to a British clinic, the success rate rose from 10 per cent in 1980 to 18 per cent in 1981. The implantation of the embryo following its replacement in the mother remains the major difficulty. Between twenty-five and forty per cent of the embryos from eggs fertilised outside the mother's womb have been aborted naturally, usually in the first three months of pregnancy.

The scientific discussion concerning *in-vitro* fertilisation centres on the way in which the ripe ovum is obtained. Steptoe and Edwards relied on the woman's natural cycle. This limits the possibility of artificial insemination to one ovum every four weeks. The correct time for removing the ovum must be ascertained by hormone analysis and ultrasonic controls. This procedure has the advantage that the natural generative rhythm is not disturbed and the uterus is prepared for the implantation of the fertilised ovum. The ovum is carefully pealed out of the follicle, fertilised *in-vitro* and implanted in the uterus a few days later. Psychologically, one of the problems is that, if you take sex out of pregnancy, you take emotion out of motherhood, an objection raised particularly against 'wombs for hire.'

Frozen Embryos

Australian gynaecologists at Monash University, Melbourne, under the direction of Drs Carl Wood and Alan Trounson, used fertility drugs to stimulate ovulation so that several eggs could be fertilised at the same time. The method had the drawback that not all eggs were at the same stage of development and that the uterus might not be in optimal condition for the implantation of the fertilised egg or eggs. Embryos can temporarily be put in deep freeze. Of the embryos so treated in Melbourne, some showed defects after defreezing.

A girl believed to be the first baby developed from a frozen embryo was born in Melbourne on 28 March, 1984. The mother had been unable to conceive for seven years and two operations to clear a Fallopian tube blockage failed. Doctors collected several oocytes, fertilised them *in-vitro* and transferred three of the embryos to the woman's uterus but no pregnancy resulted. Six of the remaining embryos developed normally and were frozen in liquid nitrogen at a temperature of -93°C three days after being fertilised. The woman returned for a second attempt two months later and the embryos were thawed. Three of them survived thawing and were implanted in the uterus and pregnany followed. At least six frozen embryo babies, including twins, have been born in

Melbourne and one in Rotterdam. Britain's first test-tube baby from a frozen embryo was born in March 1985 to a mother who had tried to have a baby for eight years. Drs Steptoe and Edwards had removed five eggs from the woman, fertilised them with her husband's sperm, placed three in her womb immediately and froze two. The birth resulted from the two embryos frozen in liquid nitrogen for three months and implanted when the three embryos miscarried.

An unexpected complication arose when a Los Angeles couple died in a plane crash. The woman had come to Melbourne in 1981 after her 10-year-old daughter had died in an accident and she had been told that she could not conceive another child. Some eggs were removed from the woman and fertilised *in-vitro*. One of the eggs was implanted, two others were frozen. The implantation failed after 10 days but until her death in 1984, the woman had not returned to Melbourne for another operation. Dr Wood thinks that the 'orphaned' embryos are unlikely to survive any attempt to implant them in a womb because techniques used at the time they were frozen were defective and the embryos would not survive thawing. Nevertheless, the situation raises the issue whether embryos have legal status. The law has never contemplated the possibility of an embryo existing outside the mother's womb. In the United States, the weight of legal decisions suggests that an embryo is not a person; but is it property? If so, to whom does it belong? Is it subject to donation, disposal or custody? In Australia, Right to Life and Catholic groups demanded that the frozen embryos were given the opportunity to fulfil their potential by being implanted into a substitute mother, but nobody has ever shown that frozen embryos have a right to a womb. Should the embryos be destroyed or raised to maturity and allowed a share in the couple's estate? The Victoria state premier appointed a commission to determine whether the embryos might be implanted in the uterus of another woman. The commission recommended that the two frozen embroys be destroyed but a special amendment approved by the Upper House of the Victoria state Parliament called for an attempt to implant them in a surrogate mother and provided that the embryos be adopted.

The case of the orphaned embryos had become further confused when a Los Angeles lawyer representing the estate said that she had been informed by Dr Wood that the woman's husband was not the donor of the sperm. The husband had a son from a previous marriage who, if the embryos were destroyed, would be the sole heir.

As a by-product of the affair, Victoria's attorney-general announced that, in the future, couples involved in test-tube baby programmes in the state would have to determine what should be done with frozen embryos in the event of their death or separation.

Following the recommendations of a special commission, the state of Victoria passed a comprehensive artificial reproduction law which lays down guidelines for *in-vitro* fertilisation and the use of sperm, eggs and embryos. The true genetic identity of the children conceived by artificial insemination has to be registered. Cloning, cross-species breeding and surrogate motherhood are prohibited. The state minister of health is given authority for deciding the fate of 'orphaned' embryos.

France is the only country with state-run sperm banks. The first centre for the Study and Conservation of Sperm was established in 1972 and 20 such banks are in operation. Under the banks' rules, a donor must be married and have children, and he must have his wife's permission for donating sperm. The banks do not pay for semen. To qualify for insemination, women must be married. Only five women receive semen from any one donor. They are only told the donor's blood type and the colour of skin, hair and eyes. Neither the women nor their children are given the donor's name.

A young French widow who wanted to have a baby by artificial insemination using the sperm her husband had deposited with a sperm bank before cancer treatment that might have made him sterile. The husband died two days after the marriage and the director of the sperm bank argued that the sperm could not be claimed by the widow since the depositor was dead, the sperm had been deposited before the marriage and there was no evidence that the donor intended it to be used after his death. In a court battle, the widow won the right to be artificially inseminated with the sperm of her dead husband but the procedure failed to make her pregnant. The small quantity of sperm and its poor quality — cancer reduced the prospects to about 50 per cent — were apparently responsible for the failure.

In China, the Hunan Province Medical College tried artificial insemination with frozen sperm on five women of whom three became pregnant.

For women with no ovaries, or with ovaries from which eggs could not be obtained or with a genetic defect that would be passed to their offspring, Dr Trounson's team attempted implants of ova donated by healthy women and fertilised outside the womb with sperm from the husbands of the recipients. This method avoids some of the problems of 'substitute' mothers but involves the same question of biological linkage. The same problem poses itself when infertile men become fathers by using donated sperm for *in-vitro* fertilisation. Apart from the legitimacy of the *in-vitro* process itself, there seems to be no objection to the use of other people's sperm or ova. If a couple can adopt a child, why not start at an earlier stage? Doctors at Monash University achieved the first known pregnancy from donated eggs in March 1983 but the woman had a miscarriage after eight weeks. In November 1983, however, a woman in her mid-20s who had been implanted with a donated egg fertilised by her husband's sperm in February gave birth to a normal healthy boy. The woman had been given intensive hormone therapy before and after the transplant to stimulate normal hormone release.

Embryo-Transfer

In the embryo-transfer process, a fertile woman and an infertile woman who wants to have a child are monitored until they ovulate at roughly the same time. Then the donor is artificially inseminated with sperm from the infertile woman's husband. After five days, the embryo is washed out of the donor's uterus and transferred to the recipient's uterus. The first baby from an embryo-transfer pregnancy was born in February 1984 in Long Beach, California.

A successful case of embryo-transfer was reported from Cleveland, Ohio. Doctors at the Mt Sinai Medical Center removed three ova from a 37-year-old woman who had undergone hysterectomy after her uterus ruptured during pregnany, fertilised one of them with the husband's sperm *in-vitro* and placed it into the uterus of a 22-year-old friend who already had two normal pregnancies. Appartently, the embryo developed without complications.

Embryo-transfer enabled couples to have a child that is biologically entirely theirs.

Scientists at Brussels University achieved a pregnancy by implanting an embryo from a donor's egg fertilised by a donor's sperm. Both the woman and her husband were infertile. The embryo was transferred from a test tube when it was 48 hours old and the recipient woman was into her third day of ovulation.

In a new technique developed by Professor Jan Craft of London's Royal Free Hospital, the egg is inserted into the uterus within one hour of normal coitus so that the fertilisation takes place within the woman's own body. But so far, the success rate of this process has been low.

Lately, the problems of the possible transmission of sexual diseases by artificial insemination have attracted growing attention. There have never been deformities among the test-tube babies born so far. One of the twins born in Australia in 1981 was a 'blue baby' suffering from transposition of blood vessels. Naturally, there can be no guarantee against the birth of deformed or handicapped children. Relatively small changes in temperature during the manipulation of sperm, ova or embryos outside the organism can result in defects. A five-year study of Australian and New Zealand hospitals showed that test-tube babies run a high risk of being still-born or dying soon after birth. Based on 909 pregnancies, the mortality rate for the first 28 days was 47 deaths per 1,000 births, four times the normal rate.

In the United States, it was proposed to avoid the drawbacks connected with fertilisation outside the organism by lifting the ovum from its base and moving it past the point of blockage in the Fallopian tubes to a position where it could be fertilised by normal sexual intercourse. But this method has so far not been tried on humans. In the case of infertility on account of blocked Fallopian tubes, the only alternative to *in-vitro* fertilisation is surgery. Thanks to a breakthrough in microsurgery (opening the blocked tubes by fine metal needles heated by a low-voltage electric current), good results have been achieved even for women with severe tubal damage and the success rate has been as high as 70 per cent for operations to reverse sterilisation.

Controversies on In-Vitro Fertilisation

A report of Dr Edwards on 'observations' on 14 embryos which had not been implanted and kept alive for several days caused an uproar and the British Medical Society appealed to doctors to cease cooperation with Dr Edwards. But the appeal was retracted almost immediately when Dr Edwards explained that his 'observations' had not involved 'experiments' with embryos.

Dr Edwards described his work as follows: 'In a few patients three or four eggs are fertilised and two or three are replaced. The remaining embryos will grow for three or four days longer, and it must be ethically acceptable to observe them during this period with the patient's consent. These embryos would be frozen, although we are not doing this work.' Guidelines issued by Britain's Medical Research Council in November 1982 stated that scientifically sound research involving experiments on test-tube babies were ethically acceptable on condition that the embryos used were not transferred to the uterus and the donors of ova and sperm consented to the research in every case. An advisory group to the council specified that sperm from sperm banks should not be used unless collected and preserved expressly for research purposes. Leaving aside the question of who is to decide what 'scientifically sound research' is and the competence of the Council to pass on questions of ethics, the guidelines offend against the sanctity of human life and experiments allowed under the guidelines put human life at the same level as animals. Who is to fix a limit to the period for which experiments can be prolonged if embryos can be grown for experimentation?

The moral problems relating to artificial insemination have become more complicated with the development of techniques for sex selection (see Vol. 1, Ch. 2). In Japan, the sex selection technique separating X-chromosomes (female) sperm from Y-chromosomes (male) sperm through centrifugation was developed by a team of doctors under the leadership of Dr Rihachi Iizuka, professor at Keio University, and Dr Hideo Mori, professor at the University of Tokyo. This group reported in June 1986 that it had been successful in selecting the gender of the babies of six couples who wanted to have girls. Another group headed by Dr Shiro Sugiyama and called the Sex Selection Research Group has been instrumental in the birth of about 40 girls (of 24 women trated at

Dr Sugiyama's clinic, 22 gave birth to girls and two to boys). The cost of artificial insemination is ¥20,000 per attempt; usually, four or five attempts are needed for achieving conception.

Sex selection may be defended as a means of avoiding sex-linked genetic defects (such as haemophilia) but the doctors admitted that they used the technique also in cases in which the parents simply wanted a baby girl. Disapprobation of artificial insemination and sex selection techniques because they constitute a manipulation of the natural order is not convincing. Natural processes as such do not imply moral imperatives and as long as the interference with nature does not mean a perversion incompatible with the dignity of man it is not immoral.

Guidelines on In-Vitro Fertilistion

In a report published in May 1983 announcing guidelines on test-tube babies, the British Medical Association approved the storage of fertilised ova for up to 12 months provided they could be frozen and thawed without damage. Doctors regard the storage of embryos as a means of implanting the embryo in the womb at the same time in the woman's cycle that the egg was removed. The guidelines also advised that observations on embryos should normally be completed within five to ten days and always within a maximum of 14 days after fertilisation, approved most of the techniques pioneered in Australia but not yet practised in Britain, and called attempts to clone embryos or alter their genes unethical if the engineered embryos were to be implanted in a mother.

The report was preceded by recommendations drawn up by a working group of the British Medical Association studying test-tube fertilisation which approved limited research including storage of frozen embryos, keeping 'spare' live embryos outside the womb for 10-14 days, and the use of donated sperm and ova. The report outlaws as unethical any procedure designed to change genetic make-up to induce the formation of multiple progeny, that is cloning, if there was any intent to implant the clone in a woman. The use of donated sperm and ova is deemed acceptable so that a woman can give birth to a child that is neither hers nor her husband's, but surrogate motherhood in which the test-tube baby of one woman is transferred to the uterus of another woman is ruled out.

Britain's Committee of Inquiry Into Human Fertilisation and Embryology, chaired by Dame Mary Warnock of Girton College, Cambridge, proposed that a government body should be set up to regulate embryo research and infertility treatment such as artificial insemination, in-vitro fertilisation and egg, sperm and embryo donation. The report, published in July 1984, endorsed the freezing of embryos until implantation but opposed surrogate motherhood and recommended the banning of agencies that recruit women as surrogate mothers. Experimentation on human embryos should be permitted until the embryo was 14 days old after which it should be destroyed. In the opinion of the committee, 14 days marked the appearance of the first identifiable human-like features of the embryo.

In West Germany, where up to March 1985 136 test-tube babies had been born by 102 mothers, the medical profession has adopted 'Guidelines for the Performance of In-Vitro Fertilisation (IOF) and Embryo-Transfer (ET) as Methods for the Treatment of Sterility' but opposes government regulation which would become an obstacle to research. Dr Liselotte Mettler, professor at the University of Kiel, started to work on artificial fertilisation after meeting Dr Robert Edwards. She maintains that human life begins with fertilisation — that life starts only after 14 days or four weeks is hogwash — nevertheless, she does not oppose all research on human embryos and is inclined to approve the use of fertilised human ova in the first stage of development to cultivate bone marrow cells for treating leukaemia.

A commission of German medical and juridical experts under the chairmanship of Ernst Brenda, former president of the Federal Constitutional Court, examined in-vitro fertilisation and related problems under the aspect of their compatibility with the principle in Germany's Fundamental Law that human dignity is inviolable (Art. 1, Par. (1)). Since human life begins with fertilisation, a manipulation of human embryos offending against human dignity must be rejected. From this point of view, the procedure to fertilise several ova in vitro in order to increase the chances of nidation of one embryo seems questionable. The possibility of nidation should be safeguarded for every embryo since each fertilisation should serve the production of human life. To generate human life in vitro without intending its development to a human being may be constitutionally objectionable. The commission rejected surrogate motherhood, cloning and other experimentation but left the problem of 'spare' embryos, including the treatment of frozen embryos not required for implantation, particularly the extent of their permissible use for scientific research, undecided. There remain numerous unanswered juridical problems, for example, the responsibility of an anonymous donor of sperm, rights and duties arising from the artificial fertilisation of ova of an unmarried woman and the right of children to know their genetic parents.

It seems to me that it is impossible to apply the principle of the inviolability of human dignity to embryos. Human dignity is only meaningful in relation to human personality and the embryo is not a person. But there can be no doubt that the protection of human life should also include unborn life.

The medical team at Sendai's Tohoku University led by Dr Masakuni Suzuki which succeeded in producing Japan's first test-tube baby had adopted the following 'Code of Ethics.' First, the method shall be applied to 'patients' only when other methods to remove obstacles to the natural process of fertilisation fail. Secondly, only legally married couples shall be eligible for the process. Thirdly, the team will refrain from tampering with the genes in the process of fertilisation.

Doctors at Tokushima University's Medical School conducted fertilisation experiments with ova from ovaries excised from cancer and other patients. The press criticised the experiments because the doctors had failed to ask the consent of the women (the doctors said they had obtained the consent of more than half of the 29 patients at the university hospital—additional ova were taken from six patients in other hospitals).

Professor Takahide Mori said that he and his colleagues had taken it for granted that the ova were 'wastes,' not 'beings.' 'Before in-vitro fertilisation became common, life was assumed to start when a fertilised ovum was implanted inside the womb. So our ova were regarded as things.' In their experiments, the doctors succeeded in fertilising 16 out of 78 ova. Of the fertilised ova, five were preserved as specimens, the others destroyed by incineration.

The Monash University in-vitro team is bound by ethical guidelines stipulating that a fertilised human ovum should not be frozen for longer than 10 years. Actually, the longest period an ovum has been preserved before being returned to the mother or discarded has been 18 months. Alan Trounson and Linda Mohr of the Queen Victoria Medical Centre in Melbourne achieved a test-tube pregnany by implanting a defrosted embryo which had been stored in liquid nitrogen for four months. The pregnancy, however, was terminated in the 24th week of gestation because the mother developed a sceptic condition.

Scientists from the British Medical Research Council and Edinburgh University reported that they saw an ovum develop without being fertilised. The ovum reached the eight-cell stage with only 22 female and no male chromosomes. The same team found that only one in four ova they studied contained no chromosomal abnormalities which, a scientist commented, means that test-tube techniques could not be expected to have a better than 25 to 30 per cent success rate.

Australian gynaecologists maintained that there was no biological reason why an embryo fertilised in-vitro could not be implanted in a man's abdomen where it could mature and be delivered by Caesarian section. Apart from the hazards of ectopic pregnancy, it seems more than doubtful that the male body could adjust to the exigencies of pregnancy.

Sperm Banks

In 1980, Robert Graham, an optometrist, founded a sperm bank called 'Repository for Germinal Choice' limited exclusively to Nobel prize winners. The first birth of a girl claimed to be from the sperm of an 'eminent mathematician' was announced in May 1982. The screening of the would-be mother must have been worse than superficial; she turned out to have a criminal record and had lost custody of her two children from a previous marriage after allegations of child abuse. A second baby, a boy called Doron (a Greek word meaning 'gift') was born to an unmarried psychologist from sperm of an unidentified computer scientist and musician. The project itself reveals a distorted approach to reproduction and a seriously flawed image of man. Human intelligence is important but it is not a product that can be packaged and merchandised. There are human qualities that are more important than intelligence, the capacity to love and the willingness to sacrifice, strength of character and a disposition for compassion. The scheme is based on a materialistic misconception of the quality of life and the disregard of factors that make marriage, procreation and education human.

The first privately-owned clinic for test-tube babies, the California Institute for In-Vitro Fertilisation, was opened in October 1982. Its director, Dr William G. Karow, thinks that the procedure is no longer experimental and has become reasonable and practical.

In an extension of the *in-vitro* technique, a team of British doctors extracted sperm from a husband who was infertile on account of a blockage of the *vas deferens,* fertilised eggs from his wife's ovaries in a glass dish and then implanted an ovum in the woman's uterus. The woman became pregnant. In the past, operations removing sperm surgically and implanting it directly in the womb have generally proved unsuccessful.

Moral Problems of In-Vitro Fertilisation

The moral problems involved in the production of test-tube babies query the limits of progress: are we allowed to do everything we can? or, more specifically, is the medically possible morally right? With the development of donor-sperm and donor-ova, today's *in-vitro* fertilisation allows four combinations: homologous sperm and homologous ovum, heterologous sperm and homologous ovum, homologous sperm and heterologous ovum, heterologous sperm and heterologous ovum. If the possibility of a substitute mother is added, three types of mothers can be distinguished: the genetic mother, the child-bearing mother, and the child-rearing mother. These possibilities shatter the old framework of the family, dissociate the origin of human life from parenthood and the child's socialisation from its genetic roots.

In the early stages of the development of the procedure of *in-vitro* fertilisation, the question of the morally licit was sometimes put in the form: 'are doctors allowed to make new men?' Thus put, the question misinterprets the role of the physician in the *in-vitro* fertilisation process because the physician exercises no causal function; he merely makes possible outside of the mother's body what usually occurs inside. A test-tube baby is the 'work' of a father and a mother just as much as any baby conceived in the usual manner. Nevertheless, the morality of the procedure itself has been questioned and the danger of possible misuse exposed. Already in 1949, Pope Pius XII declared fertilisation *in-vitro* as immoral. In an address to the participants of the Second World Congress on Fertility and Sterility on 19 May, 1956, the Pope said: 'Artificial fertilisation exceeds the limits of the right of the spouses acquired by the marriage contract, that is to say, the right to exercise their natural sexual faculties fully in the performance of the marital act. The marriage contract does not give them the right to artificial fertilisation because such a right is in no way expressed in the right to the natural marital act and cannot be derived from the right to the child as the first 'purpose' of marriage. The marriage contract does not confer this right because its object is not the child but the 'acts' able and destined to generate new life. Therefore, it must be said of artificial fertilisation that it offends against natural law and is in conflict with law and custom.'

Church leaders, such as Cardinal Hoeffner, archbishop of Cologne, repeated this condemnation when test-tube babies were born. Some Catholic moralists argued that the lawful purpose (to have a child) does not justify a doubtful and in its consequences dangerous means, the manipulation of a human embryo.

In a 1982 declaration, the Australian bishops, while conceding that the desire to have children is deeply human and that the efforts to find scientific means to satisfy this desire are admirable, condemned test-tube fertilisation and expressed the fear that scientists were trying to carry out experiments that morality could not authorise.

A report by the Joint Committee on Bioethical Issues of Britain's Catholic bishops (1983) rejected any form of experimentation likely to damage the human embryo, any form of freezing or other storage unless there was a definite prospect of transferring each embryo unimpaired to its mother, and any form of selection of the fittest or more desirable among newly-conceived embryos. 'All these practices and procedures,' the report said, 'involve one human being sitting in judgement on the very life of another and treating the other as a mere means to an end.'

The report raises the objection that the child from the *in-vitro* fertilisation is not the fruit of the conjugal union and as the product of manipulation stands in a relation of radical inequality and subordination to the producer. Because of its origin, the child from an *in-vitro* fertilisation does not obtain the same status as a natural child and the attitude of parents will be influenced by the artificiality of the procedure by which the child came into existence. This argument sounds very academic.

The basic objection of the Catholic hierarchy is the dissociation of fertilisation from the conjugal union. The immorality consists in the human interference with the natural order, the technical separation of the processes which are linked together in the 'natural' act of conception.

There are, however, moralists who defend the procedure. Relying on the old maxim *abusus non tollit usum* (abuse does not eliminate use), they argue that the possibility that a means to an end can be misused does not make every use of the means immoral. The possibility of the misuse of drugs does not preclude their use for lawful purposes. The typically juridical construction of marital rights as those acquired by the marriage contract is an arbitrary limitation of marital relations and the use man can make of his body. The removal of the ovum from the mother involves no problem; fertilisation may require masturbation on the part of the husband (which is a secondary problem and not essential to the morality of fertilisation *in-vitro*). The procedure as such does not constitute a misuse of the human ovum or the embryo, and the possibility of failure is also present in 'natural' fertilisation in which ova (damaged or undamaged) may be rejected by the mother's body. The charge that doctors have manipulated embryos irresponsibly and that thousands of embryos have been discarded cannot be substantiated and, even if true, would only prove the possibility of misuse. Although the personal intimacy of marital intercourse is replaced by technical manipulation, *in-vitro* fertilisation is not meant to negate the meaning of marriage but to overcome obstacles to procreation.

A second objection against *in-vitro* fertilisation attacks not the method but its purpose. The medical resources required for the 'production' of a test-tube baby seem out of proportion with its result, the fulfilment of the wish of a mother to have a baby of her own. There are enough babies without parents and to create more babies is a waste of medical facilities.

Together with the approval of organ transplants, the Mecca-based Islamic Fiqh (jurisprudence) Academy approved artificial insemination in 1985.

Israel's two chief rabbis banned artificial insemination unless the recipient is a married woman and the semen her husband's. A notice in Israeli newspapers stated that it is prohibited for any Jew to provide semen to a hospital and for a Jewish woman to agree to treatment involving insemination not from her husband. Under the ruling, Jewish men are not allowed to donate sperm to banks and children born to women as the result of artificial insemination with sperm not from their husbands would be classified as *mamzerim* (illegitimate).

The position taken by this ruling, declared the chairman of obstetrics and gynaecology at the Hadassah University Hospital, is the same as that of Muslims, the Roman Catholic Church, Anglicans and Lutherans. He gave the anonymity of the donor and the possibility of an incestuous conception as the main reasons for the prohibition.

Legal as well as ethical problems arise in heterologous insemination from the clash between the right of the donor of the sperm to anonymity and the right of the offspring to know his or her biological parent.

Swedish Regulations

A comprehensive law on artificial insemination passed by the Swedish Parliament allows *in-vitro* insemination for couples using their own eggs and sperm. Donor sperm can be used only for artificial insemination by injection of sperm into a woman's uterus. All frozen sperm banks in hospitals had to be destroyed when the law went into effect (1 March, 1985). No sperm is to be imported from abroad without permission of the National Social Board which may grant permission for particular ethnic groups. Only married women can be artificially inseminated and the procedure must take place in a hospital. Doctors will choose a suitable donor but may not take into consideration any special wishes of the parents or a donor's talents or qualities. The use of surrogate mothers is prohibited and a one-year limit is put on the storage of frozen embryos.

Hospital records that identify the biological father of an artificially conceived child must be kept secret for at least 70 years but the child has the right to be informed of the name of its biological father when reaching the age of 18. The sperm donor is bound for life to consider himself legally the father of the child.

In a report on his work, Dr Edwards remarked that a by-product of test-tube babies could be the production of 'spare' embryos for research work. While it may be maintained that test-tube fertilisation interferes with 'nature' in order to make up for natural defects, experiments with 'spare' embryos raise a completely different problem. Are these 'spare' embryos human beings? And if they are, when can experiments on human beings be justified? How far can 'spare' embryos be allowed to develop? three weeks? eight weeks? full term? Animal eggs have already been cloned to produce several genetically identical offspring. With new techniques, a single female egg can be split into four separate cells, and each one can be split again. Can this go on?

Embryonic Development and the Beginning of Life

The question whether an embryo is a human being or when it becomes a human being is, of course, the basic issue involved in abortion. The answer requires a closer look at the process of pregnancy.

The cessation of menstruation is the sign by which most women recognise that they are pregnant. Since irregularities in the menstrual cycle are not uncommon, pregnancy tests have been developed which have an accuracy of about 95 per cent. The Chinese claim to have devised a simple 'do-it-yourself' pregnancy testing card costing only a few cents but 98 per cent accurate. With a few drops of urine, the card becomes milky white if the woman is pregnant but turns into a fine powder if she is not.

Recently, Japan's Ministry of Health and Welfare lifted its restrictions on the sale of home-use pregnancy tests. Due to the opposition of obstetricians who claimed that the tests were not always reliable, the ministry had banned advertising the tests and urged pharmaceutical companies and drugstores to exercise restraint in disseminating these products. The ministry had approved the import and sale of about 20 different kinds of tests and they were sold by about 23 per cent of the drug stores. The ministry approved the display of advertisements inside the premises of drugstores for the time being.

The development of a new human being starts when a potent sperm merges with a fertile ovum. This union usually takes place in one of the Fallopian tubes. The ovum has arrived there after its expulsion from its follicle in the ovary. Compared with ordinary cells of the body, the ripe egg is truly large (0.12 mm in diameter); a spermatozoon is 0.06 mm long but the volume of the egg is 85,000 times larger. While some lower vertebrae produce millions of eggs, the human female usually produces only a single ovum at one time. The greater surety of fertilisation and the protected development in the mother's womb allow this limitation.

The fertilisation of the egg in the uterine tube is accomplished in probably less than 24 hours. The spermatozoa deposited in the vagina ascend through the uterus into the Fallopian tube mainly as the result of the muscular movements of these organs rather than through the mobility of the sperm. It takes the sperm about one hour to reach the upper ends of the tubes. In the tube, the ovum loses its outer layer of cells as the result of action of substances in the spermatozoa and from the lining of the tube walls. Loss of the outer layer of the ovum allows a number of spermatozoa to penetrate the egg's surface. Only one spermatozoon, however, normally becomes the fertilising organism, but in the case of identical twins, the same ovum is fertilised by two spermatozoa and there are very rare cases of triplets from the same single egg. Once it has entered the ovum, the nuclear head of the spermatozoon separates from its tail. The tail gradually disappears while the head with its nucleus travels towards the nucleus of the ovum (the female pronucleus). The head enlarges and becomes the male pronucleus. The two gametic pronuclei meet in the centre of the ovum where they unite to form the nucleus of the fertilised egg, the zygote. Their thread-like chromatin material organises into chromosomes.

After the chromosomes merge and divide in the process called mitosis (described in Vol. 1, Ch. 2), the zygote divides into two equal-size daughter cells. The mitotic division gives each daughter cell 44 autosomes, half of which are of maternal and half of paternal origin. Each daughter cell also has either two X-chromosomes, making the new individual a female, or an X- and a Y-chromosome, making it a male. Sex, therefore, is determined by the sex chromosome from the male parent in the sperm fertilising the ovum. Nevertheless, even today, there are numerous prescriptions for influencing the sex of children. Recently, a paediatrician maintained that the mother's intake of minerals such as sodium, calcium and potassium determine an infant's sex. A salty, potassium-rich diet containing foods like potatoes, meat and tomatoes can lead to male offspring while a diet rich in milk products and green vegetables is likely to produce girls.

How long the zygote remains in the Fallopian tube is unknown, but it probably reaches the uterine cavity about 72 hours after fertilisation. It is nourished during its passage by the secretions from the mucous membrane lining the tube. By the time it reaches the uterus, it has become a mulberry-like solid mass called a morula. A morula is composed of 60 or more cells. As the number of cells in the morula increases, the zygote forms a structure called blastocyst, a single, spherical layer of cells that enclose a hollow, central cavity. For a short time, the blastocyst, nurtured by the uterine secretions, floats free in the uterine cavity and is implanted in the uterine lining about the fifth or sixth day after conception. There are scientists who maintain that the blastocyst and the other initial stages of development, although specifically human, remain undetermined as preliminaries of the development to a specific individual.

While the blastocyst lies unattached in the uterine cavity, the cells that will become the embryo form a thickened layer on one side of the bubble while elsewhere, the walls of the bubble consist of a single layer of cells. This layer of extra-embryonic ectoderm is called trophoblast. The trophoblast has a special ability to attach to and invade the uterine wall and plays an important role later in the development of the placenta.

Normally, the blastocyst attaches itself to the upper portion of the uterine lining, but the implantation may also occur in other places. These so-called ectopic pregnancies are one of the major causes of maternal deaths and often terminate in abortion, although not all ectopic pregnancies end with a catastrophic haemorrhage and collapse, and the embryo may sometimes be reabsorbed. One in 300 is an ectopian pregnancy in which the blastocyst attaches itself either in an abnormal location in the uterus itself or an area outside the uterus. Most frequent are ampullar pregnancies (in the ampulla of the Fallopian tubes), ovarian and abdominal pregnancies. Recently, twins were born of whom one had developed normally in the uterus while the other had grown outside on the top of the uterus. The incidence of ectopic pregnancies more than doubled in the United States in the last decade. The reason is obscure but researchers suspect that the pelvic inflammatory disease due to sexually-transmitted disease plays a major role. The number of ectopic pregnancies rose from 17,800 cases in 1970 to 42,400 cases in 1978, and their frequency from 4.5 per 1,000 pregnancies to 9.4. The death rate from these pregnancies, however, declined almost 75 per cent during this period. Ectopic pregnancies among non-white women were more than three times those of whites, and in 1978, ectopic pregnancies were the largest single cause of maternal deaths among non-white women.

After the follicle in the ovary casts off an egg (ovulation), it forms a new structure, the *corpus luteum*. Progesterone and estrogen, secreted by the *corpus luteum*, are essential for the preservation of the pregnancy during its early months. By the 70th day of pregnancy, the placenta is able to replace the *corpus luteum* without endangering the pregnancy. During the first few months of pregnancy, the ovary containing the functioning *corpus luteum* is considerably larger than the other ovary but by the end of pregnancy, the *corpus luteum* has usually regressed and is no longer a prominent feature of the ovary.

By the end of the third week, the first structures have been formed for the uteroplacental circulation which will draw nutrients and oxygen from the maternal blood so as to supply the embryo with all of the sustenance necessary for life and growth and remove its waste products. The body stalk which will become the umbilical cord has already begun to separate the embryo from the outer layer of the trophoblast lying against and buried in the uterine lining, the *endometrium*. The cavity in the blastocyst becomes the fluid-filled chorionic cavity and will ultimately contain the amniotic fluid that surrounds the embryo, the embryo itself and the umbilical cord.

In the basic pattern of human growth, the embryo develops from three primary germ layers, the ectoderm, mesoderm, and endoderm. These layers are not segregated sheets with cells of predetermined, limited capacities and inflexibly fixed fates. Rather, these layers represent advantageously located assembly grounds for carrying out organ-building activities remarkable by the flexibility with which the component parts of the embryo are shaped.

At the end of the first month, a head is discernible which accounts for about half of the total length of the embryo (0.4 — 0.7 cm). At the end of the second month, the embryo has assumed a somewhat human form. Its length is about 3 cm, arms and legs, although short, are discernible and the formation of eyes and ears has started. The growth of the inner organs is showing considerable progress and although it is impossible to distinguish the sex of the embryo, inner and outer sex organs are growing. At the end of the third month, the embryo has reached a length of about 9 cm and may weigh 20 g. The head still accounts for a disproportionally large part of the embryo whose sex is now recognisable. With the fourth month of pregnancy, the growth of the foetus accelerates; at the end of the fourth month, its length is about 16 cm and its weight comes to about 120 g. The skin which had been pellucide takes on a reddish tint. The muscles moving the limbs develop although the pregnant mother does not yet feel much movement, the external sex organs are formed and soft hair appears on the face. Researchers are now inclined to the opinion that the foetus regulates its own development. Many of the changes that occur during pregnancy give the impression that the mother is responding to the tune played on her by the foetus. The foetus and the placenta are the main sources of hormones in pregnancy and manipulate the mother, rather than *vice versa* as previously thought.

There are, as a rule, 266–270 days between ovulation and childbirth, with extremes of 250 and 285 days. A baby girl born prematurely on 1 June, 1983, in Victoria, Texas, was in the 20th week of development and weighed 14 ounces, about 400 g. The earliest recorded premature birth may have been that of a baby girl born in the 14th week of pregnancy on 27 June, 1984, in California who weighed only 330 g. Five months after her birth, her weight had increased to 1.8 kg.

Eight weeks after conception, almost all of the internal organs are in place, and for the remaining 30 weeks, the developing human being is called a foetus. At birth, a child weighs between 2 and 3 kg. Growth is not just an increase in size or bulk. In organisms, cell multiplication is the basic method of growth but cell multiplication must proceed in such a way that it will shape the differences in form and proportions which requires differential rates of growth in different places and at different times so as to conform to a characteristic growth pattern. Organic growth is accomplished in several ways: (1) Most important is the synthesis by which new living matter, protoplasma, is created from available foodstuffs. (2) Another method utilises water uptake; in the early weeks, a human embryo is nearly 98 per cent water while an adult is 70 per cent fluid. (3) A third method of growth is intercellular deposition; cells manufacture and extrude such non-living substances as jelly, fibres and the ground substance of cartilege and bone. Through these activities, a new-born baby is several thousand million times heavier than the zygote from which it came.

Soul

All organic growth is entirely different from the mechanical production processes operating exclusively by external influence. The physical, chemical or electric processes involved in organic growth are directed in a way that adds a completely new dimension to these processes. To explain the direction of growth in accordance with a definite standard programme, the old philosophers postulated a principle they called soul, and for the growth of a human organism, they assumed that a human soul came into being at the moment of conception. It is this theory of the human soul which has made the problem of abortion so difficult. The soul is considered the principle of all life, vegetative, sensitive, and spiritual, and the human soul unites these three functions in the integrity of human life. It is the animating, life-giving principle which ordains and sustains the coherent and teleological development of the organism. Since the soul constitutes one being with the body, both are involved in all human acts and functions, but the physiological processes (for example, activities of the brain) accompanying man's spiritual functions do not enter into the constitution of these actions and it is claimed that man is capable of purely spiritual experiences.

The doctrine of the soul is not an explanation but rather the statement of a problem. As mentioned elsewhere (Vol. 1, Ch. 2), the teleology in the formation and the life of every organism requires some kind of directing, unifying, balancing and enduring capability which is not given with the material elements and their properties. This capability does not come from the outside but is immanent and identical with the living thing — indicated in the description of life as self-movement, self-preservation, self-control and self-regulation. But is the life of the foetus human life because it is directed by the human soul?

Is Foetal Life Human Life?

The intra-uterine life of the foetus is not human life but preparation for human life. Sensitive and spiritual life is impossible in the uterus, and the physiological functions are carried out by a very complex cooperation of the foetus with the mother's body. The outset of the intra-uterine development already poses a difficult problem. The ovum is a living thing, and it can live or be kept alive in a certain way independent of the mother as shown in the in-vitro process. The spermatozoa are also living things, although their existence outside the human organism seems more precarious than that of the ovum. When a spermatozoon fertilises an ovum, they form a new living thing which, however, cannot live separately and independently. It is 'potential human life' but it is difficult to say when this potential starts. If an ovum removed from the mother 'dies' or is destroyed, it is not a question of destroying human life, whether the ovum is fertilised or not.

An unborn child is potentially a human being but it cannot be called an individual or a person without qualification. Philosophically and juridically, these terms imply an independence not present in a foetus. It is only through birth that the child becomes independent in an ontological sense. The German Civil Code states: 'The legal capacity of man starts with the completion of birth' (Art. 1). Prior to its birth, the child's rights cannot be considered apart from its mother because it cannot be treated as an independent subject.

Influence of Mother's Life-Style on the Unborn Child

The life of the embryo or foetus is a symbiosis in which the embryo is the receiver from the mother but everything it receives is used in accordance with its own growth programme. The embryo is not a part of the mother as her limbs or organs are parts of her body. But the interaction between mother and child is just as intimate as if the embryo were a part. The food taken by the mother must suffice to sustain the life of the mother and the growth of the embryo. The effects of drugs, alcohol or cigarettes as well as sickness, over-exertion and other physical or mental conditions of the mother on the foetus have often been discussed. On account of the symbiotic relationship between mother and child, the state of the mother's health exercises an enormous influence on the foetal development. Infant mortality is still high even in some advanced countries and the underweight of the newborn is an important factor. In many cases, the failure of the mother to prepare for motherhood and to observe dietary rules and medical advice during pregnancy contribute to neo-natal defects. Apart from an unregulated sex life, dancing until complete exhaustion, drinking and smoking mark the life-style of many young women. When they become aware of being pregnant, they are faced with the necessity of an abrupt change. To stop smoking can be an enormously difficult undertaking and the severe stress which usually accompanies withdrawal has a highly deleterious effect on the embryo. Abstention from alcohol, which has an even more serious effect on the growing child than tobacco, is often punctured by relapses and sometimes women find it impossible to stop drinking. Drug misuse, not only of hallucinogenic drugs but also of other pills and tablets constitutes another source of potential danger. 'Instant' marriages concluded on account of pregnancy rule out genetic counselling and the prevention of genetically-defective offspring.

According to the American Lung Association, the risk of miscarriage is 170 per cent higher in heavy smokers — defined as 10 or more cigarettes a day. The risk of premature birth is 300 per cent, that of still-birth 55 per cent higher. Pre-natal smoking, especially in the first 28 days, has also been linked to birth defects such as hare lips and cleft palates.

Recently, an American doctor went to court to force a seven-month pregnant woman to stop taking drugs. The woman had a history of drug abuse which had already jeopardised the health of an earlier daughter born prematurely. The case raised difficult questions concerning a woman's rights, the legal rights of a foetus and the right of the government to intervene in the private life of an individual. While there can be no doubt of the moral duty of the mother to avoid everything likely to cause serious harm to the child, it is difficult to construe this into a legal obligation enforceable by court order.

Hormonal Influence

Since all exchanges between mother and foetus take place through the placenta, the hormones secreted by the placenta may affect the foetus. Together with some male hormones, the placenta produces tremendous amounts of female hormones. As a rule, these hormones appear too late to do any harm. The female foetus is fairly immune inasmuch as additional female hormones merely cause a child to be more feminine than usual at an early stage. Boy babies may be born that are truly males but under the impact of the feminising hormones appear superficially to be females and are often raised as such. As a rule, even when they grow older, they have more or less sterile, undescended testes, an imperfect penis, well-developed breasts, an unbroken voice and no beard. In less severely affected cases, the hidden testes begin to secrete their own male hormones during adolescence. The false female characteristics become suppressed, and voice, beard, breasts and sexual interest take on the pattern of the male.

Morning Sickness

A characteristic symptom of the first months of pregnancy is the so-called morning sickness. It is a disturbance of the alimentary system which may involve loss of appetite, nausea and vomiting occurring early in the day, and changes in food preferences, especially a longing for sour foods. The cause of morning sickness is not well known but it is believed to be some toxic secretion from the embryo. Generally, morning sickness lasts until the end of the fourth month of pregnancy but it may also become worse.

Production of Bendectin, a drug specifically made to treat nausea and vomiting and approved for use in 1956 was discontinued in 1983 when the manufacturer lost a law-suit which charged that the drug had caused foetal deformities. But in March 1985, a jury rejected the claims totaling $1 billion of 1,200 women who allegedly had given birth to deformed children after having taken the drug for morning sickness.

The demands on the mother's body increase with the progress of pregnancy and affect all vital functions. A sharp increase in cardiac output (amount of blood expelled per minute) occurs between the 9th and 14th week of gestation, and the load becomes heaviest from the 28th to the 30th week when the heart has 25-30 per cent more work to do than before pregnancy. By the time of delivery, the blood volume has grown by 25 per cent. There are numerous metabolic changes, changes in bladder and kidney functions and other biological phenomena.

Childbirth Deaths

Specific diseases related to pregnancy include acute toxemia, eclampsia and hypertension. Other diseases may affect the foetus, such as acute infectuous diseases with high fever and bacteria in the bloodstream. Pneumonia results in a marked reduction in the supply of oxygen to the foetus; heart disease, kidney disease, diabetes, high blood pressure and other chronic disorders may be associated with premature birth and foetal death. In addition to bodily discomfort, the mother may experience mild emotional disturbances such as increased anxiety, irritability, and fear of labour or for the normality of the foetus. Such restlessness is likely to be more intense during the early months of gestation and tends to be particularly frequent in women who did not anticipate becoming pregnant and who are unduly worried about the baby. Modern medicine, above all pre-natal care, has greatly reduced the number of childbirth deaths. In Japan, child mortality stood at 6.2 deaths per 1,000 births in 1983. Maternal deaths numbered 15.4 per 100,000 births. The major causes were high blood pressure (3.5 deaths), haemorrhage after delivery (3.0 deaths), haemorrhage before delivery (2.0 deaths), and ectopic pregnancies (1.1 deaths).

Paediatricians in Bogota developed a new method of caring for low-birth-weight babies. The tiny infant spends day and night wrapped against its mother's breast instead of in an incubator. The technique called 'packing' performs three functions: It provides the baby with warmth from the mother's body. Temperature control is a major problem with premature or underweight babies. Breast milk is continuously available. Breast feeding of incubator-bound infants is difficult, but breast milk offers excellent protection against infection. The infant benefits from the stimulation of the mother's heartbeat and bodily movements as well as the affection fostered by the closeness between mother and child.

Delivery

An increasing number of doctors have come to the conclusion that the safest place for a baby to be born is at home. One of the doctors holding this opinion said: 'Doctors intervene too much in what is a natural process. They act as if pregnancy were a nine-month disease that needs their help to be resolved.' Dr Robert Mendelsohn of the University of Illinois thought that doctors relied too much on drugs, and anaesthesia, analgesics and inducing birth so that the risk of accidents and infection was greater in hospitals. The Dutch with the highest proportion of home births in Europe have one of the lowest infant mortality rates. In one of the giant German hospitals where babies are delivered as if on an industrial conveyor belt, more than half of all births were artificially induced. There were almost no births on Sundays, few on Saturdays and at night and as few as possible on Wednesday afternoons when doctors went off to relax or to play golf.

A scathing indictment of the treatment of childbirth in hospitals is Michelle Harrison's book *A Woman in Residence*. She objects to the interventionist approach epitomised in the dictum 'child birth is a surgical procedure.' Although each delivery has its own natural pace, doctors, she says, want births to follow the abstract graph of how labour is to progress and turn to artificial means when a woman departs from the curve. Things are speeded up by administering labour-inducing drugs or rupturing the amnion. Women are ordered to push although they do not feel the natural urge to push, and if the doctor's patience wears thin, a Caesarian or forceps-assisted delivery takes place. Episiotomy (an incision that enlarges the vaginal opening) is ordered although it may not be necessary. Harrison charges that there is no humanity in the system; doctors treat patients not as human beings but as objects.

The latest in natural childbirth is underwater delivery. The technique, developed in the Soviet Union and France, is meant to help women relax during labour, reduce the use of drugs and the need for Caesarian sections. The woman remains in a pool filled with water at body temperature until the cervix becomes fully dilated. Sometimes, however, the relaxing effect of the bath precipitates labour and the child is actually born underwater. It is safe because when the baby is underwater, it does not breathe.

On the premise that pregnancy is not an illness and childbirth is not an operation, a growing number of American women are returning to midwife-assisted births. The tendency reflects the desire for more personalised attention and the wish to avoid the sterile, clinical approach to childbirth in which the woman is treated as if she were undergoing major surgery. The popularity of natural childbirth — which eschews anaesthesia and permits the father to participate in the delivery — has contributed to the revival of midwives. For women who have had five or more children, are expecting twins, require a Caesarian section or have a history of miscarriages, a hospital is necessary, also for women with heart, kidney or other health problems.

In the Netherlands, over 35 per cent of pregnant women choose to give birth in their own homes. There are about 1,000 licensed midwives who have undergone a four-year obstetrics training course. They make the decision whether a home birth is safe or whether complications might arise requiring hospitalisation. The midwives who follow the pregnancy from the 10th week are trained to be as flexible as possible. The prospective mother can choose her delivery position and Dutch hospitals, too, offer vertical delivery. According to expert opinion, the 'stranded beetle' position, with the woman lying on her back, her legs raised and strapped at the knees, is of convenience only to those attending and one of the worst for pushing the baby down the birth canal. In order to return the women as quickly as possible to their customary environment, Dutch hospitals arrange 'short-stay' deliveries which have mother and baby back home within five hours of giving birth.

Britain's 1951 Midwives Act prohibits delivery of a baby without professional medical assistance and some men have been fined for violation of this law although the babies were born without complications. One of the convicted men defended his action as the natural right of man as a human animal.

Some hospitals have accepted the point of view that the birth of a child should be a family experience and allow children to be with their parents in the labour and delivery rooms. Parents and their children attend group pre-natal sessions together in which obstetric nurses explain how the baby grows in the mother, how it is born, and what new babies can and cannot do.

A report circulated by the American Foundation for Maternal and Child Health contended that none of the drugs commonly prescribed for use by women in labour and childbirth had been adequately tested to determine their effects on babies. Instead of using drugs, it would be better for women to walk or sit during labour, and to sit up during delivery rather than being kept on their beds. Many experts also recommend birth unfettered by electrodes and monitors. Electronic foetal monitoring should only be used for high-risk, premature babies. The Food and Drug Administration urged a reduction in the recommended concentrations of Bupivacaine, the most widely used obstetric anaesthetic, after a number of women died during labour due to cardiac arrest.

On the other hand, a California hospital was ordered to pay $8.4 million to care for a 5-year-old girl who was left blind, severely retarded and without control of her arms and legs because the obstetrician failed to diagnose and treat a condition called hypoxia — lack of oxygen — during labour and delivery. The obstetrician monitored the pregnancy mostly through the use of a stethoscope which, the court opined. 'in this age of electronic monitors ... is inadequate care.'

Labour pains constitute the acme of pregnancy and the sacrifices of the mother for her child. In the Bible, they are described as a consequence of the fall and the special punishment of woman for her role in the transgression: 'I will multiply thy sorrows in thy conceptions. In sorrow shalt thou bring forth children, but thou shalt desire thy husband, and he shall rule over thee' (Gen. 3, 16). But the travail of childbirth is also the overture to the joys of motherhood: 'A woman about to give birth has sorrow because her hour has come. But when she has brought forth the child, she no longer remembers the anguish for her joy that a man is born into the world' (Jo. 16, 21). What she has done for her child, nobody else can do; it forms the foundation of a relation entirely different from the 'you are mine' of the spouses. 'This now is bone of my bone and flesh of my flesh' is the basis of motherly love and filial affection which, although often disfigured or forgotten, belong to the inexhaustible possibilities of human life. Only a human mother can fear, suffer and die for her child, can experience the happiness of being loved and the disappointment of being rejected. Motherhood means the joy of the mother who gives birth to her child as well as the sorrow of the mother who loses it.

A report compiled by the World Health Organisation and the UK Children's Fund released in January 1986 charged that due to traditional Third World practices during pregnancy and childbirth, half a million women die each year from pregnancy and about five million babies die within one week of birth. Most of these deaths could be avoided by observing the basic rules of cleanliness in childbirth and the availability of skilled help. Because untrained people attend over half of the births in developing countries and dangerous childbirth practices are used, pregnant women have a 200 times higher risk of dying than in developed countries. Infection and serious injury result from cutting the umbilical cord with razor blades, sickles, bamboo sticks and broken bottles and treating the cord stump with cow dung, ash or herbal pastes. Discrimination against daughters, strongest in some southern Asian and Arab countries, leads to a higher death rate for female children as well as malnutrition and sickness. Contrary to the global trend, women in some Asian and Arab countries have lower life expectancies and a higher mortality rate than men.

Childbirth Wonders

Under difficult circumstances, childbirth may bring death to the mother, but there has been a strange case in which childbirth has resuscitated the mother. The incident occurred in 1980 in Philadelphia. The woman, a Chinese immigrant from Hong Kong who spoke no English, was 27 years old and 35 weeks pregnant when she went to the hospital because she was coughing up blood. While the doctor examined her, her heart stopped. The doctor immediately began cardio-pulmonary resuscitation but after 30 minutes without a spontaneous response, he concluded that the woman was dead and decided to perform a Caesarian section. The moment the baby was delivered, the mother's heart began to beat.

The doctors who handled the case waited two years before reporting it so as to make sure that there were no ill effects from the incident. According to their explanation, the stoppage of the woman's heart resulted from a common problem. The swelling uterus pressed against the major vein returning blood from the legs which, combined with the mother's coughing up blood, almost cut off all the blood to the heart. When the baby was delivered, the pressure on the vein was relieved, sending blood to the heart which resumed pumping.

The first recorded successful Caesarian section on a dead woman occurred in 237 BC. The baby grew up to become Publius Cornelius Scipio Africanus Maior (the elder Scipio), the Roman general who defeated Hannibal. The operation derives its name from another famous Roman, Gaius Iulius Caesar, who was supposedly born this way.

Another strange 'post-mortem' delivery happened in 1982 in Buffalo, NY. A 24-year-old unmarried woman died of epilepsy. She was 25 weeks pregnant and the doctors feared that the foetus would be too immature for survival. Despite the 'brain death,' the functions of the heart and lungs were kept going artificially for over a week and the baby delivered by Caesarian section, still very small but viable. In a similar case, doctors in Southampton, England, saved an 11-week premature baby boy born to a 20-year-old mother who had been clinically dead from a stroke for two days. In San Francisco, a woman who was declared legally dead in January 1983 was kept alive for 64 days so as to save her baby. The foetus was only 22.5 weeks old when the mother suffered cardiac and respiratory arrest. Physicians battled infections, diabetes and other complications and kept the woman breathing so that her foetus could mature. The baby was delivered on 29 March when it had reached the age of 31 weeks and its chances for survival were thought excellent. The mother's life-support systems were shut down immediately after birth and her breathing stopped.

In July 1983, a 1.5 kg girl was born to a brain-dead woman who had been kept breathing mechanically for 84 days since she suffered a seizure in April.

In some cases, the courts have intervened to keep a brain-dead mother alive until her baby could be delivered. A 34-year-old California woman, six months pregnant, suffered a stroke caused by a brain tumour and was declared legally dead three days later. Her parents wanted to have their daughter's life support systems disconnected but her fiancé, the father of the child, obtained a court order to keep them on. The brain-dead mother, kept alive for seven-and-a-half weeks, was delivered of a baby girl weighing 1.9 kg by Caesarean section.

In an Atlanta case, a pregnant woman became unconscious — apparently from a drug overdose. When doctors termed her brain-dead, her husband asked that his wife be taken off the life-support equipment but another man, claiming to be the child's father, together with the hospital, petitioned that the woman be kept alive until the baby was born. A Superior Court judge ordered that the woman be kept on life-support systems until birth 'even if this goes against the wish of her husband.' The baby, born 15 weeks premature, died 32 hours after delivery due to the same drug overdose that killed the mother.

No law forces the husband to have regard to the condition of his pregnant wife. As no other event, pregnancy tests the husband's understanding, sensitivity, protection, consolation and help. The bodily and psychic condition of the mother demands special attention and care combining the tenderness of the lover with the solicitude of the protector.

Many men feel they should be with their wives at delivery and some doctors admit that their presence would have a reassuring and comforting effect. But the operating-room mentality which doctors bring into the delivery room has generally led to exclude fathers from being present at the birth of their children.

Post-Natal Care

The relation between mother and child after birth should be a continuation of the intimate consociation during pregnancy. Especially for the first two years of a child's life, the mother is irreplaceable. Naturally, there are many situations in which the mother cannot continue to devote herself primarily to the care of her baby but the possibility of alternative arrangements in case of necessity does not mean that alternative arrangements are desirable. The uninterrupted contact between mother and child starting immediately after birth and phased out only gradually when the child becomes less dependent on the mother constitutes the normal process of rearing a child and is, under ordinary conditions, also the most efficient for its healthy growth in body and mind. The father will often have to help directly with the care of the child but his most important task may be to make it possible for his wife to look after the baby, to support her willingness and to strengthen her confidence in her ability to fulfil the role of mother. In Japan, 92.7 per cent of the infants under one year were taken care of in the family, nurseries cared for 1.5 per cent and other arrangements had been made for 5.8 per cent.

The transition from wife to mother can bring a change and turn a sexual woman into an asexual mother. Some women like the reprieve from sex due to pregnancy and birth and are in no hurry to resume sex with their husbands. The feelings of closeness, warmth and tenderness connected with the care of the baby and particularly with nursing provide sensual and even sexual gratification which can substitute for the sensual and sexual contact with the husband.

As mentioned above, there are mothers who are unable, unwilling or unfit to raise children and sometimes, the mother does not survive the birth of the child. But what is necessary in emergency situations should not be made into a general system and the replacement of the natural mother by institutions is against the best interests of the child and of society.

One of the most discussed aspects of child care is feeding. Except for very extraordinary cases, breast-feeding is considered the most desirable way of supplying nourishment to infants. Mother's milk is a nutritious, easily absorbed food that also provides immunological protection against certain diseases. Sometimes suckling is physically impossible or the health of the mother may not permit it, but it also happens that women find it too bothersome or fear that it may impair their beauty. The growing outside work of women has also contributed to the decline in breast-feeding. A recent survey covering 17 countries in Asia, Africa and Latin America found that more than 87 per cent of the babies in Asia and Africa were breast-fed for the first six months compared with 50 per cent in Latin America. Women in urban and economically developed areas are less likely to breast-feed than mothers in rural districts. Problems arise because many of the substitutes lack the proper nutritional value and poor mothers cannot afford to buy decent food. Moreover, sanitary conditions often make it impossible to ensure proper hygiene. The lack of clean water is a frequent cause of high infant mortality. Unicef's Annual Report for 1982 criticised as irresponsible the promotion and marketing of artificial infant formulas and wanted doctors and hospitals to reassure mothers that breast-feeding is best. In the United States and Europe, breast-feeding is on the increase again thanks to the growing awareness of its importance for the healthy development of babies.

Doctors assert that the quality of a mother's milk can influence the behaviour of the infant. Depending on the ratio of amino acids, babies fall asleep faster or slower (a higher ratio of tryptophan makes the nursing baby fall asleep faster), and the composition of the mother's milk also affects the infant's irritability and alertness.

Breast-feeding tends to increase the period between births because ovulation does not take place. Another important aspect of breast-feeding is the intimacy between mother and child and the feeling of security and belonging fostered by the physical contact.

A problem of basic importance is the economic security of mother and child. In most advanced countries, the welfare systems make special provision for pregnancy, birth and lactation and the protection of motherhood is usually included in labour legislation. But many mothers with children are not covered by the social 'safety net' and only in a few developing countries can mothers count on public assistance.

4

Family and Education

Basis of Education

ONE OF THE DISTINCTIVE FEATURES of mankind is the succession of generations. The sequence of generations in the human race is different from the continuation of generations in other organisms because man not only produces the next generation but also forms it. Children are the successors of their parents not only in the sense of biological successiveness but also because of the spiritual formation by which the parents determine the mould of the next generation. This task ordains the family towards the future, and education constitutes the foremost expression of his ordainment. Education means the shaping of a person, the elaboration of a personal being into a personality. In this process, the oneness of parents and children and the independence of the person are the two poles in the relation between parents and children.

There are greatly divergent views on what education is or should be. J. J. Rousseau asserted that all education is bad. Man is good by nature, and all deviations from man's original goodness are caused by the pernicious influence of the environment. Objectively, education is based on the fact that man is unfinished at birth and that he continues to evolve all his life. For the philosopher, this process poses the question whether this development has a meaning and what this meaning is. Pessimism taught that human existence is meaningless from which some people concluded that it would be better not to be than to be — which, of course, is a *non sequitur*. A completely different interpretation is found in many religions which place the meaning of human existence into the world beyond so that life on earth assumes the function of a preparation for life after death. In such a view, earthly existence has only a preliminary or hypothetical value but, on the other hand, it is given a formidable importance because its meaning is not confined to this world but temporal life decides over eternity. Religion is a matter of faith, and the theological meaning of life cannot serve as a foundation of a philosophy of education based on human nature.

Goal of Education

The goal of education comprises two aspects. Education must prepare the child to live his own life as a person but it must also enable him to function as a member of society and to fulfil the tasks social life will impose on him.

For a long time, the ideology dominating American education was John Dewey's theory of progressive education. Dewey, the most influential representative of pragmatism after the death of William James, contended that the exigencies of modern democratic and industrial society demanded a new educational technique which was popularised under the slogan 'education in a democracy and democracy in education.' Dewey's 'instrumentalism' stressed that cognition is essentially practical and that experience is the only reality. Thought is the instrument for realising man's desires. Action useful for this purpose is truth, and ideas advantageous to the enlargement of experience and action are true ideas. The practical results prove the truth of a proposition or a system. The useful, therefore, manifests the good and the true.

Empiricism

The ideological or philosophical orientation of education has been opposed by pedagogical empiricism. Under the influence of behaviourism, empiricism tried to derive educational principles from polls, surveys and statistics. Empirical data, however, are only 'snapshots' of human society, fragmentary information on conditions which happen to obtain at a certain time and place. Education relying on the normative value of facts fails to provide the orientation required for the coherent growth of man's personality. Under the influence of behaviourism, pedagogy replaced education by the transmission of knowledge and downplayed the conscious and deliberate formation of character, the cultivation of attitudes and the moulding of personality. But pedagogy cannot cease to provide valid norms of conduct and to prepare for the decisions which have to be made in life. Education is essentially linked to the growing-up process which is not only based on a theory of right action but also implants such a theory, not in the form of abstract principles but in the impregnation with a style of living conforming to such a theory.

Behaviourism

Behaviourism has had considerable influence on modern educational theory. According to behaviourism, the objective and accessible facts of behaviour and of activities of man and animals constitute the only proper subject for psychological study. William James, a pupil of Wilhelm Wundt, taught that man should be considered as a living organism with instinctive tendencies to react with his environment. A child's mind is that aspect of his being that enables him to adapt to the world, and the purpose of education is to organise the child's powers of conduct so as to fit him to his social and physical environment. Behaviourism, however, of which J. B. Watson was the leading exponent, rejected terms such as 'mental,' 'consciousness,' 'emotion' and 'instinct' and maintained that human personality should be studied by observing the actual behaviour of men and women. A basic concept used by behaviourism is that of conditioned reaction or conditioned reflex which appear in the simple reactions of animals and small children. All behaviour is a learned process. 'When we are rewarded for doing something, we do it again' (B. F. Skinner) is the basic educational principle. All human activity can be explained ultimately in terms of conditioned reactions and of habits which are formed in consequence.

Commenting on mediocracy in education, B. F. Skinner, today's outstanding exponent of operant behaviourism, remarked: 'It is all a matter of scheduling reinforcements.' The consequences of a subject's action in his environment determine future behaviour. These consequences are either positive or negative reinforcers. Successful action is automatically reinforced. A well-designed instructional programme must provide abundant reinforcement. The major problems in education could be solved if students learned more each day. Efficiency of education could be doubled by letting each student move at his or her own pace which could be achieved by using computers or other teaching machines. In his book 'Beyond Freedom and Dignity,' Skinner advocated a 'technology of behaviour' and proposed that behavioural controls to reinforce altruistic behaviour should be imposed to preserve our culture.

Psychoanalysis

A completely different approach to education resulted from Sigmund Freud's psychoanalysis. As mentioned above, one of Freud's basic tenets was the great significance of sexual factors in the creation of neurotic disturbances, particularly those of hysteria. The sexual instinct is in a process of slow development from earliest infancy. Of particular significance in this process is the Oedipus complex, the tendency of the child to love the parent of the opposite sex and to regard the parent of the same sex as a rival. In the normal adult, the sex instinct is the result of a fusion of a number of minor or 'component' instincts closely connected with certain parts or organs of the body, such as the mouth, anus, and external genitals. Others are less obviously linked but have equally clear aims or satisfactions of their own, for example, scopophilia (desire to look or know), exhibitionism (desire to show off or be admired), sadism (desire to exercise mastery or inflict pain), masochism (desire to submit to or suffer pain).

In the course of the individual's development, these 'component' instincts gradually become integrated and are to some extent put into the service of the reproductive function. But some of that energy becomes displaced and evokes tendencies towards other ends which may be unrealistic and unhelpful, manifesting themselves for example in neurotic symptoms, or useful and socially approved, in which case they are called 'sublimations.' According to psychoanalytic theory, much if not all of human culture is due to the sublimation of primitive instincts to higher ends. A process related to sublimation is symbolism, the expression of a repressed wish in indirect or symbolic form. The ideal ego which man forms of himself contains the ideal qualities that the individual wants for himself. Children attribute god-like qualities to their parents ('my father can do everything') but discover that their parents are not gods. The longing for human demi-gods reappears at puberty when adolescents start to be infatuated with heroes. Formerly, girls had a crash on one of their teachers, boys looked up to the supermen of sports. Now, every star of sufficient fame becomes the centre of a fan club, and the ecstatic frenzy accompanying the performance of rock singers reveals the pseudo-religious undercurrent of these passions. Not incongruously, the worship of those idols has led to the cult of the dead, exemplified by the veneration of Rudolph Valentino a generation ago, and the pilgrimage to the tomb of Elvis Presley in our time.

Psychoanalysis has traced adult neuroses to childhood traumas, but children can outgrow their experiences in infancy without permanent damage. Ill effects from abusive, neglectful or over-protecting parents in the first three years of a child's life can be reversed by attention and care. Children who grow up in orphanages are often withdrawn, but they become open and trusting when adopted and raised in loving homes. On the other hand, the lack of a suitable environment may have a damaging effect. Boys sheltered from children of their own age when others are learning the socially acceptable limits of temper with both parents and peers often become bullies.

Repressive vs. Permissive Education

There are two extremes in education, repressive and permissive education. Repressive education means baculine education intent on 'breaking the will' of the child and relying on the use of force and corporal punishment. But the 'training' of children by mostly aggressive and coercive methods forms psychic and moral cripples whose mental and emotional life has been stunted. Children may be subdued but under the ashes of the burnt-out individuality of the child glimmer the hatred of the educator and the society sanctioning the system. Or children may become social misfits whose defiance and aggressiveness thwarts all attempts at social integration. An educator who wants to subject his pupil to his domination may succeed in enforcing external compliance but he provokes inner resistance and desire for revenge. The children become hot-tempered and imperious bullies and rowdies.

In its most extreme form, permissive education turns into anti-authoritarian education, which is education without education, the negation of education. It results in a chaotic inability of adaptation and discipline. The result is unrestrainable aggressiveness, resistence against educators and rivalry among siblings. In the school, permissive education has led to violence against teachers and schoolmates. The *laissez-faire* education has fostered intolerance, quarrelsomeness and intrigues. Wild growth does not produce individuals who fit into society. Children who have grown up without education often need firm treatment to make them realise the necessity of behaving themselves, but firmness should not give the impression of rejection.

Permissive education is a partial phenomenon of the trend to emancipation which has pervaded the western world since the French revolution. It originated the pathos of liberation which rejects everything traditional and tries to replace it with something autonomous. In Roman law, emancipation was the release from paternal authority to legal independence. But independence was never absolute; it was independence within the framework of the existing legal and social order. Even the emancipation of the mature man does not imply an absolute autonomy but only free and responsible conduct within society. On the one hand, the inalienable dignity of the individual must be protected and his life in freedom and self-determination guaranteed; on the other hand, the common life of society must be respected which is only possible if every individual contributes his share to the common good and receives the share to which he is entitled.

Possibility and Necessity of Education

The conditions of human growth explain the possibility and the necessity of education. Man is born to become man, and human development consists in actualising the possibilities embodied in every human individual. The possibilities transmitted to the child by its parents are limited but they are human possibilities endowing the child for a development of undetermined and *a priori* indeterminable duration. As mentioned above, the physical development of the individual is basically determined by his genetic inheritance although it is influenced by the environment. But man's development also involves the growth of the human psyche. Just as the human organism possesses an *a priori* ordainment for a world in which water, light, air, salt and carbohydrates are found, so in his psychic endowment, man is destined to live in a world in which senses and imagination, mind and heart, intellect and emotions, understanding and resolution can be found. Education does not consist in a mechanical accumulation of experiences; it implies that the individual examines and questions his experiences and therefore may also reject and overcome them. Man is educatable because he has the capacity to determine himself and is not determined by his experience; man needs education because his capacity for self-determination must be developed and formed; man is willing to be educated if he wants to become master of his own destiny.

Socialisation

Education must affect the entire man — body and soul, intellect and heart; it must also further the desirable and correct the defective. Education is a task that must be readjusted to the growth of the child and adapted in contents and form to its stage of development. The child must be recognised and treated as an individual but an individual who must live with and among other human beings. In recent years, the expression socialisation has been in vogue for this process and it has sometimes been equated with education. This is a serious misunderstanding. The proponents of socialisation define it as the acquisition of modes of conduct conducive to life among the members of the species. They see in human conduct a particular case of the conduct of primates and try to find in the formation of animal societies suggestions for understanding human society. The socialisation theorists sometimes assume that man is exclusively a social being and that his value is to be determined by his usefulness to society. But life in society is only part of human life. Training, although it plays an important role in the upbringing of children, is not the key to education. The goal of education is to enable the individual to use his faculties for free and responsible behaviour.

Little children need appropriate care by their parents; without their presence, the socialisation of children is impossible. A premature autonomy becomes an obstacle to the practice and exercise of social skills. Children need instruction, models, practice with feedback, somebody to show them how to do it and correct them when they do it wrong. This includes speech, walking, sitting, the control of the body and the response to others. Children must learn the art of relations so that they know what to do and when and how. This development of social skills cannot be taken for granted and cannot wait until the children start going to school. School does not provide classes for private conversation and can hardly teach good manners if the home has neglected to do so.

Man must be in a position to lead a life 'worthy of man' which, in Aristotle's view, is not 'mere life' but the 'good life.' The good life, however, must be a 'virtuous' life. Today, the word 'virtue' sounds quaint and antiquated. But the failure of an education which tried to manage without virtue is sufficient reason to reexamine the foundations of education.

Goal of Human Existence

According to Aristotle's theory of entelecheia, the complete unfolding of the possibilities proper to man would be the goal of human existence, but such perfection is outside the scope of human experience. There is nothing in man's terrestrial development that could be considered as the goal of human existence. Man's growth curve exhibits no point which would represent the acme of his development. Life can fade away in a gradual slowdown or come to an abrupt end. Of the possibilities given by his genetic inheritance, relatively few mature. An individual can cultivate many and apparently heterogeneous talents but he cannot develop all sides of his mental and physical capabilities. A man may have an exceptional talent for music and also be a mathematical genius or a superlative sportsman but his actual career may be unrelated to his talents and skills. What a man becomes is often not the result of his deliberate choice but of accidental circumstances.

Although it is impossible to fix a goal for man in general or for the individual, education is commonly guided by an idea of man corresponding to the fundamental values of the parents and society. Every society adheres to some basic values, and the common life is moulded by customs and practices which are seldom expressly planned. On principle, society's basic values and the norms followed in the life of the family should correspond to human nature. The determination of what is in agreement with human nature is necessarily subjective which does not mean that it is arbitrary. People usually have a certain idea of what a truly human life should be. The positive contents of such an idea may be rather vague and obscure, but if people fail to achieve that to which they aspire, they are very much conscious of their deficiencies.

The essential element in the idea of man in the Christian occident was man as a person, and the formation of man's personality was regarded as the compendium of what education was supposed to achieve. The formation of a child's personality means education to attitudes and conduct in harmony with human nature and the conditions of human life.

Virtues

The educative role of the family underlines the importance of progress and growth in the emotional integration of its members and its provident functions. The family is no static unit; it must develop with the individuals who compose it and the tasks devolving on it. It is only in the family that the child can acquire the virtues that enable it to master life. Life demands competence; this requires diligence, perseverance and ambition but also obedience and a sense of responsibility. Human life, however, also has softer aspects to which relate cheerfulness, friendliness and sociableness. For social life, virtues such as honesty, forbearance, courtesy, modesty and unselfishness are indispensable.

The same as marriage and the family, education involves the problem of adjusting the relations between the individual and the community. The individual has social duties, but he cannot be sacrificed to society. The pathos of liberation arose from the rationalistic and optimistic tendencies of the period of enlightenment which created the belief in the power of knowledge, science and technology. But man, mankind and society cannot be shaped at will by the means of science and technology. Man is not only a rational, but also an emotional being, and the capacity of reason to function depends on the stability and support of man's emotional disposition. Man's growth must be hatched by careful and sustained guidance. This guidance is not the same as instruction. Its purpose is not the transmission of objective knowledge of facts but the formation of attitudes, convictions and value judgements influencing decisions and actions. This cannot be achieved by inculcating commandments and enforcing norms but ' must be effected by the experience of fundamental human values and basic patterns of conduct in the persons in whom the child or the pupil reposes implicit trust. The persons who can influence the formation of a child's personality are above all father, mother, brother and sister, but also teachers, priests and other educators to whom the child or pupil can establish a relation of full confidence.

Negation of the Family's Educational Functions

Just as education cannot be reduced to techniques and methods, it cannot be taken over by institutions replacing the family. The pedagogical counter-culture considers man as merely a social being unredeemed in society and only redeemable by society. But neither the capacity of educating nor the capability of being educated depends on theories, principles or programmes. The ideologues of equality want to detach the child as early as possible from the family because the family produces differences. The collectivistic attempts on the basis of Marxist fantasy as developed by Herbert Marcuse, for example, in his *Theorem of Educational Dictatorship*, start from the premise that, at birth, the mind of the child is *tabula rasa* and hence unlimitedly formable by the environment. A totally just education, therefore, would produce totally equal citizens. The critical theory of the Frankfurt school (Max Hockheimer, Th. W. Adorno) misinterpreted authority as pure domination (Hitler as the typical representative of authority) and listed the family in its paradigms of dominating and being dominated. Man is the embodiment of civilisation and woman that of nature oppressed by civilisation. The family constitutes a hierarchy of repressions: the man is under the knout of dependent labour, the woman is under the knout of the man, the children are under the knout of the mother. Man's liberation can only be achieved by common emancipatory action for which man's individuality must be absorbed entirely in sociality. From the failure of classical Marxism, the neo-Marxist cultural revolution concluded that only a moral and ideological vacuum left by the destruction of bourgeois culture could create the conditions under which the capitalistic system would be abolished and the moral and cultural heritage of the enlightenment and liberalism transplanted into a socialist society. Only if people act in complete accordance with society can they become social, emancipated beings possessing the 'right consciousness.'

Anti-Authoritarian Education

Out of its chimera of complete egality, the neo-Marxist pedagogy which contradicts the entire experience of reality has created the coercion to egality. In order to realise the goal of complete egality, children must frequent the same kind of school. All workers are to receive the same wages, all men are to live the same kind of life, women have to live the same kind of life as men, children are no longer to be educated in accordance with the natural phases of their development but have to be given as early as possible the right to self-determination and equality. Socialist egalitarianism rejects the recognition of achievement as élitist. But achievement is a legitimate principle of selection in a democratic society and meritocracy is preferable to privilege based on status, wealth or party membership.

The blind rejection of the formation of élites fails to recognise the importance of élites also in democratic societies. Different from feudal times in which a man's social position was generally determined by descent and birth, a truly democratic education does not shut out anybody right from the start. In a democratic society, education should enable the most gifted and the most qualified to come out on top in the competition for influence and leadership, not by patronage and string-pulling, but by ability and performance.

Under the influence of the egalitarian ideology, school education in some of the states of the Federal Republic of Germany has assumed an anti-family bias and attempts to implant in the children not only rejection of the existing social order but also negation of the traditional role of the family and hate of their parents. In order to prevent a 'class-specific' determination by the family, the concept of democracy has to be extended to all spheres of life so as to create new norms. This transformation would have to be effected by the school as a 'therapeutic' institution and the teachers as 'social engineers.' The height of official disdain of the family under the socialist régime in West Germany was the Second Report on the Family (1975) which defined parenthood as a 'production process' by 'amateurs.'

Anti-authoritarian education makes a fetish out of social conflict, particularly the conflict with the parents, and turns it into a beacon for the entire educational process. In Germany, the day centres for schoolchildren are being used for imparting a 'complementary' education aiming at creating 'the preconditions for the emancipation of the child from dependency and tutelage so as to give the child the capacity for political action.'

In her book *Am Anfang war Erziehung* (In the Beginning was Education), Alice Miller, a Swiss psychoanalyst, investigates the formation of Adolf Hitler. She stresses the profound influence of the family on the entire life of the child. Not only the child's self-respect and the feeling of his own value, but also the freedom to develop his innate capabilities depend on the respect and tolerance which parents show their child. Through his entire life, an individual treats himself in the same way in which he has been treated as a small child. Often, the most painful suffering is that which people inflict on themselves. Man cannot escape the persecutor in his own self sometimes disguised as educator.

The role of the family changes with the growth of the children. The period until maturity may be divided into five phases: nurslings, infants, the years of elementary school, juveniles, and adolescents. Children are not unfinished adults but human beings having their own value, while relying on others for protection, support, understanding and care. They possess basic rights but are unable to assert them. Adults can enforce their rights when love fails, but children have none of the means of exerting pressure by which adults can insist on their rights: they have no unions, they cannot strike, they cannot sabotage by observing all rules and cannot refuse work. The real complaints of children are seldom championed by the media.

Children's Rights

On the other hand, the assertion of children's rights has led to some ridiculous postulates. Children are supposed to defend their interests, strive for their own goals, put forward their own claims, and find realistic ways (using methods appropriate to their age) to assert them against resistance. In West Germany, the 1974 draft of a bill on parental rights contained the following passage: 'According to today's juridical understanding, the child is not to be regarded as the object of the extraneous determination on the part of the parents but as the subject of fundamental rights.' The concept of children as subjects of fundamental rights to which the rights of the parents are subordinated is the figment of an emancipation craze which turns the biological as well as the psychological realities of childhood upside down.

State Substitutes for Parents

In the German Democratic Republic, many mothers regard the use of the state-run day-care centres for children of working mothers as a last resort and prefer to forgo the income from a job rather than entrust their children to the state nurseries. Assailing this attitude, an East Berlin publication called it economically harmful and pedagogically wrong. The 'isolation of the nuclear family' could be detrimental to the growth of the child. For the development of a child's personality is threatened not only by the lack of motherly care but also by the exclusiveness of that care. A good day-care centre is better than the family, the article concluded.

The substitution of official regulations to the parents' right of educating their children has been pushed furthest in Sweden. The expression *Children Gulag Sweden* reflects the widely-held opinion that the ideological prejudices and the lack of understanding of Swedish social workers cause numerous serious blunders and that parents as well as children are helpless against the effects of official meddling. Swedes generally seem to accept the position that collective solutions are preferable to individual efforts, and in Sweden's social sector, the collective solutions have created excellent child-care centres, generous vacations for pregnant and nursing mothers and their husbands, and an enormous army of social workers trained in the belief that parents are incompetent to educate their children and that the state should take care of them. The result has been 12,000 children forcibly taken away from their parents and placed in institutions. In a country where both parents are working in 90 per cent of all families, a certain amount of child neglect may be unavoidable but compared with the other Nordic countries in which the number of institutionalised children is much lower (Denmark 700, Finland 500, Norway 200), the actual conditions seems to make the expression *Children Gulag* quite appropriate.

Childhood Autonomy

In the nineteenth century, the child was treated as an immature adult. Clothing and conduct of children and adolescents were fashioned after those of adults. The psychological and biological standing of children conformed to their destination to transmit tradition in thought, attitude and conduct as a continuation of their parents. Since the beginning of the twentieth century, the opinion has been gaining ground that youth constitutes a special, independent, self-conscious and self-reliant part of society not necessarily related to the preceding adult generation. J. J. Rousseau had already proclaimed that childhood was not just preparation for adulthood but an autonomous part of human life (he himself, however, sent his children to an orphanage). The youth movement which met on the Hoher Meissner in 1913 and formed the *Freideutsche Jugend* proclaimed the necessity and legitimacy of a self-styled form of living proper to the world of youth.

One of the most difficult problems of today's education is the trend that in many respects, young people mature earlier than before but that the educational system does not correspond to this advance. Adolescents are said to be more adult, more sceptical and less innocent than in the past; they are more wordly-wise but they are locked in an educational system built on very different premises. Children outgrow childhood early and are drawn into the adult world without being prepared for it. This problem is complicated because the acceleration of the growth process is very uneven. Apart from physical growth, the younger generation has much more intensive contacts with society and social phenomena than used to be the case. Today's youth is familiar with many things of which adults are ignorant, and this advantage reaches from the knowledge of computers and other electronic gear to the ways of obtaining drugs. But the social sophistication does not necessarily mean mental and spiritual maturity, just as a vast array of practical knowledge is not the same as maturity of judgement and ability of thinking. It is clear that these adolescents cannot be treated like children but it is also evident that they need education. The problem is, what kind of education?

The United Nations' Charter of the Rights of Children announced on 20 November, 1959, demanded special legal protection of children. By legislation and in other ways, children should be given opportunities and facilities for their healthy spiritual, moral, psychic and social development. Legislation should be determined by the child's best interests.

Impact of Environment on Children

The actual situation of children bears little resemblance to the ideals set forth in official documents in industrialised as well as in developing countries, but in different ways. In the rich countries of the West, most children are well-fed, well-clothed and have too many toys but they may be spiritually neglected. The word 'not by bread alone doth man live' applies also to children. The environment is hostile to children. People who desire the maximum of individual comfort are not very willing to have children. Other couples only want children if they can afford it, which means if they can maintain a standard of living far above the ordinary household. In the developing countries, 800 million people are undernourished of whom 300 million are children. Infant mortality is higher than 150 per 1,000 births and in the hunger areas of Africa, one out of five children dies before it reaches the age of five.

There are parents who resort to drugs in order to control the behaviour of their children. If children lack concentration, indulge in day-dreams, get sulky or fretful, some parents have a doctor prescribe medication. In the city of Hamburg, between 30 and 38 per cent of the children receiving medical treatment because of difficulties at school or problems of concentration were given psycho-pharmacological drugs. But in most cases, children's difficulties in learning or recalcitrant behaviour are not the result of bodily disorders or sickness which can be cured by medicines. More often than not, these symptoms are distress signals, reactions to conditions in family, school or society with which the children or adolescents cannot cope. The attempts to improve scholastic achievements by drugs have no lasting effect and the replacement of the cane by pharmaceuticals in order to maintain discipline can have disastrous long-term consequences.

Although Japanese society is still dominated by feudalism and conformism, post-war education brought an over-emphasis on individualism. The social atmosphere changed from the despotism of a totalitarian régime to the unrestricted freedom of an affluent society. Religion, patriotism, tradition and even etiquette have lost their grip, and the disorganised family has been unable to use its own freedom and to teach children how to use theirs. The unrestrained self-expression of the individual became the foundation of education or the lack of it, and the post-war generation has now taken over as educators. Typical of today's society is the breakdown of social discipline. Among adults, the most common manifestation is the rudeness in the rush-hour traffic, but most disturbing is the failure of young mothers to teach their children the elementary rules of decent behaviour. Children are allowed to run around freely in stores and railway stations and to play ball or ride bicycles in crowded streets.

When children grow up, they want to have their own room. Naturally, not all families can afford to give everyone of their children a special room but even in Japan, where housing is behind the standards in advanced western countries, high school students usually get a room of their own even at the expense of the comfort of the parents. The preparation for the entrance examination to university is considered so important that no sacrifice is too great. When children have their own room, they do not want their parents to enter it but they do not clean it themselves. In a family in which each of three children has his own room, the mother collects the three keys on a fixed day in the week and cleans the rooms while the children are away at school.

Small Children in Japan

There are some noteworthy differences in the education of small children in Japan and in the West. The basic trend of western education stresses independence. The baby should sleep alone, preferably in his own room. In playgrounds, mothers expect their children to play by themselves while the mother is sitting on a bench reading a book. When a child is naughty, it is immediately chastised, also in public, and it is made to feel guilty. The Japanese baby sleeps in a *futon* or crib next to its mother, and as soon as it shows the need to be closer to its mother, it is taken out of its bed and sleeps with her. In the playground, mothers actively amuse their children who always form the centre of attention. Mothers are very reluctant to scold or discipline their children and usually let them do what they want. Discipline and respect for others begins with school. In the West, children are expected to help with the household chores suitable to their age, Japanese children watch TV while the mother sets the table or does the dishes. Even if children do not help at home, they get all the pocket money they want. Since Japanese society is ruled by shame and not by guilt, Japanese children are happy because they know no shame.

In families living in Japan in which the mother is not Japanese, language may become a problem. The mother's Japanese and the children's English (or whatever their mother's native language may be) sometimes are insufficient to communicate on a deep or abstract level. The impossibility to communicate fluently in the language the other family members are using may make father or mother an outsider in the family.

On account of the different attitudes to the education of children in Japan and abroad, education may cause some problems in mixed families. A Japanese parent may be overly patient while the foreign parent may be annoyed by the extent to which the Japanese parent puts up with unruly and disorderly children. One of the most important decisions facing couples in cross-cultural marriages is whether to send their children to an international school or to the ordinary Japanese school. This will largely depend on the plans of the family for the future, particularly whether the parents intend to stay permanently in Japan (which may often be the case if the father is Japanese) or move abroad.

Moving and Adolescents

A related problem is the change in the attitude and behaviour of adolescents when the family moves. Children form friendships with their peers, and these friendships are particularly strong among adolescents. They not only involve deep emotional ties but also form the basis of a group to which the teenager belongs and with which he can identify. Depending on the character of the group, it exercises a profound influence on its members — for good or for bad. As pointed out above, influence always implies the readiness on the part of those who are influenced to yield to the impact. The plasticity of adolescence explains why the influence of the peer group can outweigh the formative action of home and school and hold the adolescent firmly in its grip.

When the family moves, these bonds are severed which may be a wrenching experience for the adolescent. Not only is he or she torn away from old friends but he (she) may find it difficult to make new ones. Although there is a great similarity in the way teenagers think, speak, dress and act, each group has its own character and spirit and a newcomer may find the boys and girls in his new school or neighbourhood not to his liking and they, in turn, may not accept the newcomer. These difficulties are compounded when the family moves to a foreign country. Language, life-style, values and the way of thinking make it hard for adults to fit into the new social environment, it may be doubly hard for adolescents — although it may happen that an individual 'hits it off' and finds congenial friends.

Children and Modern Living Conditions

Modern housing conditions deny children an environment in which they can grow up in bodily and mental health. The parental home is often small, walls in the large apartment blocs are thin, the crying of young children, the noise from radio, television and musical instruments rattles nerves. The cramped living conditions hardly allow privacy. The traditional Japanese house was not built to provide private rooms for individual members of the family. Now every child wants to have his or her own room and some children want to replace the Japanese sliding doors (fusuma) with doors that can be locked. Children have no place to play. The streets are dangerous and playgrounds are not always conveniently located.

In the old days, children could be sent outside to play with reasonable safety. Now, many mothers are afraid of letting their children go out alone. If the family lives in a high-rise building, mothers of small children may have to carry their babies down many stairs and up again, or if older, the children have to climb the stairs themselves if they want to play outdoors. The children of families living in high-rise apartments play less outdoors than the children of families living in one-family houses although large apartment buildings often have playgrounds or open spaces. In the large cities, children have little opportunity to encounter nature, and they may even find it difficult to find playmates of their own age which, in view of the prevalence of nuclear families, would be very important.

Family as Educational Mould

The crisis in education indicates that children are not prepared to adapt to life in society. The many facets of social life should be experienced in the family. The family is a community of creation, a community of education, a community of interest, a community of responsibility and position of dependency and submission to its parents must feel that they are worthy of respect and affection and that the way of life obtaining in the family agrees with its own interests. The family transmits traditions a community of remuneration. Parents can and should demand of their children cooperation with the work of the household. It used to be an unquestioned custom that children would help not only with the household chores but also in the parental business or the work on the farm. The old education emphasised the child's 'duties' of obedience, affection, respect and deference. To speak of the 'duty' to love and cherish creates a psychological block in the modern mind but there can be no doubt that the parent–child relationship has reciprocal moral implications.

Although education does not consist in enforcing commands, the formation of right habits must constitute an integral part of the children's upbringing. The educator must see what kind of influences are having an impact on his charge and if it is imcompatible with the values and norms he considers appropriate, try to make him or her see what is wrong.

Adolescents are easily attracted by fads, and some fads may have disastrous effects. In recent years, food fads have played havoc with the health not only of adolescents but also of adults, and these tragedies underscore the necessity of implanting good eating habits into the young generation.

Man only learns to live together with other men and to observe social forms and customs if he learns to form himself. A child does not learn by understanding principles and rules but by imitation. The first three years are said to be decisive for the way a child grows into this world. Just as the child learns to speak by repeating what it hears, so it learns behaviour by imitating those with whom it comes into contact. But the child does not imitate those whom it dislikes and against whom it feels antipathy. The precondition for education is the feeling of security resulting from love and recognition. It is not important that children grow up to become what their parents want them to be but that they experience a family in which they are loved, find attention and can expect understanding and help. The child must feel that the educator is not motivated by envy and the lust for power, but by love and responsibility. It must know that it can count on sympathy and support in all its needs and difficulties, and that it can always cry away its sorrow in the loving embrace of its father or mother. Trust is the irreplaceable basis of education, and a child's trust in its parents must be cultivated from the beginning of its life. The attention given to a child in the first period of its existence builds its sense of security and creates a bond with those who care for it. If a baby experiences inconsistent caring, pain and frustration, a basic mistrust will develop.

Mere knowledge does not make an educator because it does not form his character or enhance his personality. Intellectual preeminence is no guarantee of educational competence. A child who experiences its not by theoretical reflections but by the community of life of people who trust and love one another. What the family is to transmit is the interpretation of human experiences.

Assertion of Parental Authority

In the course of their development, children from time to time become disobedient and recalcitrant and try to go their own ways. In such situations, the parents' authority is put to the test. The aim of education is not to further the interest of the parents but those of the children. The children need somebody who cares not only for their material needs but who is also responsible for their mental, emotional and spiritual development, who gives them support and direction and, if necessary, admonishes and punishes them. An educator must take the child's thoughts and feelings, its expectations and dreams seriously, understand its problems and show their solutions. Based on the experience of age, the educator can try to direct youth from ideological fallacies to goals that are possible. It is the fate of youth to rebel against the ossified, outdated and one-sided views of the old generation and it is the task of age to convince youth that there are precepts, laws, forms and structures without which the individual as well as society will perish.

In every community, authority is based on the purpose of the community and is responsible for the attainment of this purpose. In the family, therefore, the authority of the parents is meant to ensure the fulfilment of the purpose of the family, the life in common. The growth of the children and their development as human beings forms an integral part of the common life. This goal constitutes the foundation as well as the limitation of parental authority. Parents have the right and duty of educating their children because they are parents, and in the fulfilment of this duty, they are first of all responsible to their own conscience. Parental authority is not based on a social mandate. Such a mandate would give the parents some kind of sovereignty to which the child would be subordinate. John Locke was of the opinion that the will of the parent was to take the place of the will of the child until the child was able to form its own will. Such a construction involves the voluntaristic misinterpretation of authority characteristic of the modern age and, furthermore, disregards the fact that authority cannot be arbitrary but is bound by the meaning and purpose of the family.

Education requires a balance between authority and freedom. A child does not comprehend authority as a principle of an objective system, and the recognition of the parents' authority depends on their credibility as models of acceptable behaviour. This credibility is built up by the personality of the educator. Children remain indifferent to moral values if their parents lack moral convictions. In their later development, children may reject moral norms because they revolt against the hypocrisy of their parents. Parents cannot educate if they are selfish, contentious and immature.

Father and mother can demand obedience of their children not because they are father and mother but because as father and mother they have the task of recognising the requirements of family life and the right to make the decisions necessary for meeting these requirements. Parents are not commanders or leaders who give orders by virtue of their personalities or because of a superior mission. The assertion *hoc volo, sic iubeo, sit pro ratione voluntas* ('I will it, I so order, let my will stand for a reason' — Juvenal) has nothing to do with authority. Obedience does not mean to do something because it is unreasonable. He who wields authority has not only the task of making decisions, but also the responsibility of making his decisions understood.

To renounce authority is not the way to reconcile it with freedom. The tendency to avoid the impression of authority and to place oneself on the same plane as the child is against the meaning of authority and education. Parents and teachers who want to function as 'big brothers' and have the children call them by their first names so as to be as 'equal' and as 'near as possible' misunderstand the necessity of a model and the requirement of direction which creates certainty and confidence. Parents pretending to be partners of their children try to escape the role as models which constitutes an essential part of their task as educators. They find the burden which their position imposes on father and mother too heavy.

Although education involves give-and-take and should not be understood one-sidedly as the influence of the adult on the child, it would be basically wrong to propel the child too early into the adult world and its sorrows. The child does not belong in the centre. A 'companion family' giving equal responsibility to parents and children destroys the world of the child. The child lives in the 'now.' In the life of the child, neither joy nor sorrow lasts forever, and neither past nor future has the same importance as in the life of the adult. Children do not know the grief and heartache of the grown-ups and they lose their gaity and cheerfulness if they are forced to shoulder the burdens of adultness.

Father and mother have the task of protecting the child as long as it cannot protect itself. This task includes the need for parents to convey to the child the confidence that they are taking care of its well-being and show by their way of living that they bear the responsibility for its physical and spiritual development. The time and effort spent by the parents on impressing on the child that their actions are inspired by love and concern are not superfluous. But it is also necessary that parents can say 'No.' For this, it is important to feel when a 'no' is required and even more necessary to know how to say 'no' to one's children. If every 'no' is accompanied by ill-tempered indignation or hysterical rage, it no longer is a matter of refusing a single request or denying an expectation, but rather the impairment of the basic trust and the poisoning of the faith of the children in their parents. The 'no' to a two-year-old baby must necessarily be different from the 'no' to a sixteen-year-old adolescent, and the adaptation of the 'no' not only to the age but also to the temperament and mood of the child is the key to the prevention of tension and clashes.

When children grow older, it becomes increasingly necessary to make them understand the decisions of the parents. It is not enough to tell them what to do or not to do; they must also be told why they should or should not do it. Man needs motivation for his conduct and the insight into the rationale of an order or prohibition is an essential prerequisite for its inner acceptance in addition to outward compliance. Naturally, father or mother cannot give a philosophical lecture every time a decision is made, but the child must feel that it is loved and respected.

Parents are human and make mistakes. It is a sign of the maturity of an educator that he acknowledges his mistakes — if the children are old enough to understand it, also before the children. At the same time, the educator must have faith in himself, no matter what others may think.

Children undoubtedly curtail the personal freedom of their parents and their social activities outside the home. There may be an ambivalence of parental feelings, love on the one hand and, on the other, resentment.

A comparative study commissioned by the Prime Minister's Office in 1982 found that, compared with parents in the United States, Britain, France and West Germany, Japanese parents spend less time with their children, take a less active part in sports, games and other recreational activities, help their children less with their homework, and admonish their children less to behave in public, to be considerate of the aged and disabled, not to litter streets and not to jump queues.

Parents' Concern for Children's Future

Better food and generally better living conditions and better medical care have contributed to a generally healthier physical development of today's children, but their mental, spiritual and emotional development has been exposed to greatly divergent influences. Children receive an enormously discordant variety of impressions, mainly on account of the media, but most of these experiences remain superficial so that they have no lasting effect. This implies two things, first, that most influences are not absorbed so that few particular events have any formative value, and, secondly, that the dilution of impressions greatly hinders the effectiveness of the influences in home and school on which the children's basic education depends. Father will be a poor second to Superman or whoever the current hero may be in impressing on the child the way to behave, and the obliteration of the difference between reality and fiction may have disastrous results for a child's behaviour, its expectations and orientation.

RP-I

The anxiety of Japanese parents to set their offspring on the right track has pushed the beginning of the educational rat-race down to pre-kindergarten level. Infant education has been propelled by two quite different trends. One sprang from the idea of detecting and nurturing talent. This is the aim of the Early Development Association founded by Masaru Ibuka, chairman of Sony Corporation. The other trend stems from the desire to have one's child 'succeed' in the sense of landing a job with a prestigious company. This means being admitted to the right kindergarten. Parents preoccupied with the child's later career make the preparation for passing examinations the only consideration in the child's upbringing.

Japan's early education courses have not yet reached the sophistication of the baby curricula in the United States. While the ambitions of Japanese mothers are geared to the country's élite pattern, American mothers follow much more individualised paths in their attempts to prepare their children for joining the ranks of the meritocracy. Parenting courses teach parents how to raise superbabies, and believing in the creed that the years until three are the period in which infants are most receptive, parents push their development in all spheres from physical exercise in baby gyms to computer-aided mathematics. The mother may work as the child's private tutor but she may also enrol her baby in classes or courses and take it to lessons. The thought that their offspring could be left behind has caused deep anxiety in many parents but what better babying will do to the children has many educators and paediatricians wondering. The increased parental attention may stimulate the infant's growth but the emphasis on intellectual stimulation may prejudice emotional stability. The pressure for high achievement may even create physical ills and psychic traumas.

The intrusion of the rat race into the nursery induced by the pressure for achievement appears also in the attempts in the Soviet Union to discover promising athletes at the earliest possible time. Soviet scientists have been conducting genetic tests on infants to identify potential gold medalists in Olympic competition dominated by young athletes. The sports research programme at Moscow's State Physical Culture Institute includes studies on 'genetic markers' — blood groups and skin types — so as to direct youngsters into sports for which they are physically best suited and avoid sports that would not be good for them. These studies represent a step beyond sports morphology, the selection of young athletes on the basis of biological maturity rather than age, and try to identify children who could benefit from early training at élite schools.

The ultimate aim of education must be to make the child independent of the educator. The educator, therefore, must make himself superfluous. The adolescent must learn to form his own judgement and to follow his own conscience. He must know the principles of moral life and know how to observe those principles. Family education does not teach abstract principles but it must transmit a consistent pattern of action in which the right values are chosen and the binding norms affirmed. If the parents do not provide the example that enables the children to know the right pattern of action, merely verbal remonstrances will be ineffectual.

The educator should not yield to the temptation to mould the child in his own image. When the children grow up, he has to take the feedback into account, listen to what the children have to say. Let the children talk: they will share their feelings if you let them. Find out what they are thinking and what is bothering them.

Education cannot anticipate the problems of real life and solve them beforehand. Education should prepare for life: *non scholae, sed vitae discimus*. But the problems of life become real only later and cannot be foreseen. The educator cannot provide ready-made solutions and recipes, because he does not know beforehand in what environment and in what kind of society the pupil will have to prove himself. All an educator can do is to serve as model for the way in which problems should be handled.

Roles of Father and Mother

Traditionally, the father is seen as the person wielding authority in the family whereas the intimacy of the relation with the mother is connected with protection and shelter. The close relationship between mother and child in the early years of infancy is essential for the psychic stability of the young generation. The nearness of an always present caring mother in the beginning of life creates a reliable refuge where the child feels secure and confident in its own existence. The experience of a just, protecting father who sorts things out when something goes wrong is particularly important for the education of adolescents when it comes to teaching them responsible and conscientious conduct. The image and spirit of the father should teach the road to independence and self-reliance. The influence of the father should also afford protection against being spoiled by mother or grandmother.

Erich Fromm makes a strict distinction between the paternal and maternal style of education. The love of a mother is unconditional. The small child is best cared for by the mother. Children owe their psychic health to the mother while the father's contribution is more dubious. He may prepare children for life in society but he is more demanding than the mother, he judges and punishes. Fromm thinks that the image of God has been shaped by the image of the father. He is merciful and loves the prodigal son if he repents but He is awesome in His wrath.

For a father who takes his responsibility seriously, the absence from home and the failure to be deeply involved in running the household and in the education of the children may become a cause of concern. While he may be important and even irreplaceable at the office, he is a stranger at home where everything seems to run smoothly without him. Of course, he will still be responsible for the basic decisions affecting the family and the children, whether to move or to which school to send the children. It greatly depends on the relation between husband and wife whether the husband feels that he belongs. It is not a question of the father reserving some decisions or activities to himself — preparing breakfast or putting the children to bed when he is at home — but of making himself a companiable member of the family when he is home.

Parenting is not a popularity contest. Loving one's children does not mean to please them. Momentary happiness and absence of distress are not synonymous with balanced adjustment. Decisions that may cause annoyance in the short run may be necessary for long-range goals. Material favours are not the same as love. Money and presents are no substitute for intimacy and warmth.

Japanese fathers tend to be willingly or otherwise immersed in their work. They are away from home from early morning to late at night, six days a week, too exhausted to do very much on the seventh. According to a 1982 survey of the Prime Minister's Office, mothers were in charge of home discipline of the children in 71 per cent of Japanese families, fathers in 6 per cent, and both parents took equal charge of home discipline in 22 per cent. Japanese children are to a great extent deprived of a father's attention and guidance. The father becomes a stranger to his family who does not perform a father's normal role. When he comes home, he tends either to spoil or to scare his children. A father who is too little at home is in danger of becoming a bugbear with the role of scaring or intimidating the children.

Parents should avoid dividing roles into a scolding mother and a soothing father. Scolding can become a habit. In Japan, this is particularly a pitfall in urging children to study. Because the father is not at home, the task of supervising the children's homework falls on the mother who easily becomes a *kyōiku mama* constantly nagging the children. Only too often the mother becomes emotional when she scolds a child. There are unruly children who refuse to obey, lie down on the floor of a store or on the street, cry and bang the floor or pavement with their heads or feet. Mothers of such hysterical children often become hysterical themselves, shouting and wailing and unable to cope.

If an educator gets excited and even loses his temper when admonishing or punishing, the child perceives the episode as an emotional outburst rather than the enforcement of an objective norm. This naturally creates resentment and even hatred because it is felt as an injustice and the impression of injustice has a devastating effect on education.

On the other hand, parents should not shirk their responsibility and shift the burden of keeping children in check on others. A schoolboy from primary school got on the bus with his mother and once inside, he met one of his friends. So he started to shuttle between his mother and his friend. 'You should not run around like that,' the mother chided him, 'the driver will scold you.' The driver heard it, took his microphone and announced: 'The bus driver does not scold you for things like that. Scolding unruly children is a mother's responsibility.'

For the maturing of the children and accustoming them to self-reliance, weening them away from the mother is indispensable. Often, a child is very close to the mother and rather indifferent to the father. This may lead to over-protection by the mother which, in turn, results in the mother being controlled by the child. The child may take advantage of the mother to secure special favours for itself and keep up this relationship as long as possible. The contrary may happen if the family is numerous or the mother working outside the home and has too little time to care sufficiently for each of her children. The emotional ties between mother and children will be weak and prevent children from seeking help and advice when they need it. Relations with their parents may influence the way children develop relations with the outside world. If they trust their parents, they will be open about their relations with teachers, friends, classmates and acquaintances while children who have no confidence in their parents will try to hide their lives from them. Children may have more intimate and trusting relations with their friends than with their parents and look to them for advice and help.

Generational Differences in Parents

The Second World War has deeply affected family traditions. The mentality of the post-war generation differs completely from that of their parents. The image of man and the value judgements of the people who grew up in the post-war era reflect the change to a less inhibited individualism. Young parents seem unaware of the virtues required for a harmonious family life: mutual respect and considerateness, patience and the readiness to help, understanding and the spirit of sacrifice. Even among spouses, selflessness has become rare. Relations between parents and children remain superficial. Parental care does not exceed material succour and neglects mind, heart and soul. Parents care too little about the inner life of their children, not their learning, but their spiritual and moral growth.

To bring children joy seems to be a natural task of educators. The educators themselves should see not only the negative aspects of reality, the evil, injustice and baseness in the world. There is also much that is good, beautiful and enjoyable and children should be taught to discover the positive without naïveté but with an open and unbiased mind.

The education of an only child has its special difficulties. The claims on the mother are much heavier because she usually is the only companion of the child. Socialisation is harder. An only child lacks the wealth of human relations and feelings which brothers and sisters can give whose presence constitutes a natural introduction to and training for life in society.

If a second child arrives, the older child should be prepared. Small children will feel frightened, upset and left out if the mother who has been so close to them is suddenly bundled off to a hospital.

Communication

Education requires communication. Although education does not consist in instruction, lectures or sermons, verbal exchanges constitute a large part of the common life of the family. Listening to the children is indispensable for gaining and keeping their confidence. Communication is necessary for preventing a child from becoming shy and withdrawn. The desirable goal is the medium between brashness and shyness. Shyness means lack of self-confidence and self-esteem. The sense of self-worth is the key to identity and the conviction of having a role to play. Children are not born with shyness although Prof. Jerome Kagan of Harvard University thinks that it is genetically predetermined in some cases. It is often rooted in early childhood experiences but may also arise from difficulties in school, unfavourable comparison with siblings, relatives or peers, loss of usual social support by frequent family moves out of a neighbourhood or change of school, from an upset in social relations through to divorce or death. It may come from poor parental models or a lack of experience in social settings which may happen when children grow up in isolated areas or in a restrictive household. As in other situations, shyness cannot be overcome by ridicule, coercion, logical persuasion or shock treatment. Children must find their own way but parents can help if they are able to answer the questions or uncover the problems in the child's attitude. It is no use to give superficial answers to questions that camouflage rather than reveal the difficulties. Such situations require the ability to interpret indirect questions and give an answer to the personal problems behind them.

Corporal Punishment

A much-discussed issue is the use of corporal punishment in education. Corporal punishment is emphatically not the same as child abuse. Punishment means the infliction of pain or the denial of some enjoyment in retaliation for a wilful infraction of a rule or disobedience to a lawful command. In corporal punishment, the infliction of physical pain takes the form of beating, often with a rod or some other instrument, but shackling or binding of hands or feet, forcing somebody to keep standing for a considerable period of time or assume an unusual and painful position, confinement to a room and the denial of food or drink also constitute physical punishment. Any infliction of pain which leaves a welt or draws blood, results in more or less permanent crippling, deformation or weakening, the application of heat, fire or electricity (except in therapeutically-sanctioned treatment of an illness) are not punishment but torture.

There are two schools of thought concerning corporal punishment of children, one that asserts that corporal punishment is never justified, another that considers punishment not only useful but sometimes necessary. The first point of view is represented by a law that went into effect in Sweden on 1 July, 1979. It outlaws spanking and makes it illegal to treat children in a 'humiliating way.' The law is not directed against child abuse but is meant to control the way in which people discipline children. The law, the brainchild of a group called Barasraett (Children's Rights), intends to change people's attitudes towards physical punishment. The proponents of the law contend that corporal punishment elicits fear rather than love in children, that the reaction of children when hit by parents is one of revenge and not of respect, that punishment does not lead to self-examination but to obstinacy. The law does not spell out what 'humiliating treatment' is but it seems to include things such as depriving a child of a meal, forbidding contacts with friends or reading the child's mail. Sweden is well advanced in the replacement of the family by institutional child-care largely based on the tenets of progressive education.

In the Swedish town of Gallivari, an 11-year-old boy who had been spanked by his father for disobeying his order and taking a bicycle ride with his younger brother went straight to the police and reported his father for violating the 1979 Anti-Spanking Law. A jury found the father guilty and fined him $12.

Seven Swedish parents appealed to the European Commission on Human Rights against this law. They claimed that the law was incompatible with the European Convention on Human Rights, especially the paragraphs protecting the integrity of the family and the freedom of religion, and that it was impossible to raise children without respect for authority which cannot be upheld without punishment.

Corporal Punishment in Schools

In February 1982, the European Court of Human Rights ruled that corporal punishment in schools violated human rights, and fined Britain for two cases brought by two Scottish mothers who claimed that corporal punishment in Scottish schools offended their 'philosophical convictions.'

In one of the cases, a boy to be punished refused, with the agreement of his parents, to submit to the whipping and was expelled from school. In the other case, no actual punishment was involved but the mother of a boy claimed that he was gripped by permanent anguish over corporal punishment. The court stated 'In the exercise of its functions in the field of education and teaching, the state must respect the rights of parents to assure that this education and this teaching conform to their religious and philosophical convictions.'

The court did not outlaw caning as such and the court's ruling is not legally binding in Britain, but the decision may accelerate the disappearance of corporal punishment from British schools. For government schools, 49 of Britain's 125 educational authorities had banned or were planning to ban corporal punishment at the beginning of 1982. In 1983, 81 per cent of secondary schools in England and Wales used the cane. In November 1984, the government announced legislation to give parents the right to forbid their children from being beaten in school and a law passed in February 1985 gave parents the right to decide whether their children should be punished or not. Liberal MP's and teachers raised apprehensions that children liable to corporal punishment would have to be marked or made to wear a special uniform and that a system of 'class justice' would emerge.

The London Diocese Board of Education (Church of England) had stated that corporal punishment was ineffective, damaging psychologically, and incompatible with Christian ideals and aims. The authorities of the Roman Catholic Church in England considered corporal punishment a question for individual schools and recommended that schools be mindful of local pressures. Some educators have asserted that the act of beating has sexual connotations and that the child's sexual development may be distorted because beating may lead to a desire for sexual flagellation in later life. Sir Laurence Olivier is quoted as having said: 'The first time a schoolmaster ordered me to take my trousers down, I knew it was not from any doubt that he could punish me efficiently enough with them up.'

The 1982 convention of the National Union of Teachers, Britain's largest, reversed the long-standing policy of letting teachers decide for themselves on the use of physical force to discipline pupils and voted against caning and other corporal punishment in school.

The Times reported that 65 per cent of those responding to a British opinion poll carried out at the beginning of 1985 favoured caning as punishment for misbehaviour at school while 33 per cent were opposed to corporal punishment. The approval rate was 6 per centage points higher than in 1949.

In 1983, the island of St Vincent passed a Corporal Punishment of Juveniles Act which requires caning to be administered in private and on the buttocks. The recipient must be certified medically fit to receive the punishment and a doctor must be present while the caning is inflicted. The cane must be a light birch, tamarind or similar twig.

Japan's Ministry of Education reported that 115 teachers were admonished in fiscal 1984 for meting out physical punishment. The figure was much higher than in former years (the lowest was 69 in FY 1981) which does not necessarily mean that teachers have become more violent but may indicate that the authorities have become more concerned about abuses.

A report entitled 'School Life and Children's Human Rights', released by the Japan Federation of Bar Associations, stated that corporal punishment is inflicted on students who violate school regulations. In its survey of 1,000 public junior and senior high schools, the federation found that in 56 of 597 junior high schools and eight of 388 senior high schools corporal punishment was common. Teachers, including women teachers, slapped or hit students with their fists when they failed to do their homework, chatted during class or neglected cleaning their classroom. In a junior high school in Chiba Prefecture, students got one slap for every five points their marks were below the average in exams and they were slapped again if they failed to say thank you after being slapped.

In a particularly unfortunate case, corporal punishment for a trifling infraction of school rules caused the death of a second-year high-school student. On a school trip to the Tsukuba Exposition in May 1985, the boy used a hair dryer with an attached brush at the hotel where the class was staying — which was against school regulations. Kazunori Amamori, the teacher in charge of the class, beat and kicked the student relentlessly for some minutes. The student, a quiet and gentle boy who loved sports and music, took the punishment sitting up straight without resistence, collapsed and died of shock. The school, which had been opened only in 1976 and grown into an oversized institution of about 1,300 students, had problems in maintaining discipline and the school authorities had connived at corporal punishment for the violation of school rules. Amamori, who had been transferred to the school just a month before the fatal trip, testified at the trial that he was personally opposed to corporal punishment but had been upbraided by his fellow teachers for being too soft in enforcing discipline.

Right or Wrong of Corporal Punishment

The view that corporal punishment is all right is held by many parents and educators. One of them is Dr Matthew Israel who directs a school for severely emotionally disturbed children. Dr Israel is a pupil of Prof B. F. Skinner. As mentioned above, Dr Skinner maintains that all behaviour is a learned process: 'When we are rewarded for doing something, we do it again.' Dr Israel adds that punishing inappropriate behaviour is also necessary and that the combination of reward and punishment is more effective than reward alone. Dr Israel has had great success in restoring disturbed children to normal lives by using a reward and punishment method that includes spanking. Corporal punishment, he says, is less harmful than not to correct the deficiency.

This school of thought advocates what is called tough-love. Love must be combined with discipline. Parents should lay down the law to their children with love — 'Shape up or ship out.' They think that this is the only way to solve the problems that permissiveness, the general hedonism and particularly the drug culture have created. Tough-love takes courage but the alternative of continuing to support irresponsible behaviour is worse.

Psychologists subscribing to operant conditioning maintain that behaviour is more strongly sustained when it is rewarded on an intermittent schedule than invariably after each active response. Teaching by punishment for error serves merely as a negative reinforcer; it teaches avoidance of undesirable behaviour so long as the punishment continues but puts no positive behaviour in its stead.

The 'battered child syndrome' was mainly concerned with the physical abuse of children but the psychic health of children may also be impaired by emotional abuse. While emotional abuse at home is not infrequent, it may also occur in school. In a particular case, children reported that their teacher screamed at them until they cried, used homework as punishment, called them 'dummy' and 'stupid,' allowed some children to belittle and harass others, and imposed unrealistic academic goals for age and grade levels.

Emotional abuse easily slides into physical abuse. The same teacher pinched, slapped, shook and pulled ears of students, tied string to a child's chair and pulled it out from under him. The children reacted by crying and developing headaches, stomach aches, nightmares, school avoidance, withdrawn behaviour and depression.

Parent's Right to Education

Parents have a natural right and duty to maintain, rear and educate their children. This means that the parents have the right to educate their children because they are parents and their duty to raise and educate their children is likewise based on the same 'natural' relation. The right of the parents is connected with and conditioned on their duties but it is an autonomous right, although not absolute and not illimitable. The natural rights and duties of the parents can be interpreted and concretised by social customs and circumscribed by positive law but they cannot be taken away from them unless this is necessary for the well-being of the children — which raises the question of who determines what the well-being of the children is and what it requires. The parents always retain responsibility for the human being they created and put into the world, and the essence of this responsibility is that a personal human being must be enabled to develop its personality.

Today, the right of the parents is threatened in a variety of ways. The nature of the parental right is contested. The draft of a law of the German Federal Republic stated: 'Society transfers the education of the children to the family and extra-familial institutions.' This sentence is in open conflict with the principle laid down in the country's Fundamental Law which says in Article 6, Paragraph (2): 'Care and education of the children are the natural right of the parents and primarily their duty. The community of the state supervises their exercise.'

The state is not the author of the parents' right to education and the state itself has no educational mandate. The function of the state to supervise education does not legitimise dirigistic interference. It only justifies substitutional activities if parental education fails or corrective intervention if the well-being of the child is endangered. As a matter of principle, the state can prescribe neither method nor content of education. The change in terminology in German law from 'parental power' to 'parental care' is indicative of the trend to limit the right of the parents as much as possible. There have been attempts to fix legal standards of the well-being of the children and make them binding on the parents as goals of their education. Because parental rights are disparaged as 'outside (heterogeneous) determination,' parents are to be obliged by law to discuss measures they intend to take with their children and obtain their consent to the extent that the children are capable of judging their affairs. Under certain conditions, the court shall be empowered to make decisions concerning the training and profession of the children even though their well-being is not in jeopardy. An important consideration in the tendency to displace the family and have the state or the community take over the upbringing of the children is the inequality of opportunity inherent in family education which is repugnant to an egalitarian philosophy.

In a 1982 decision, the German Constitutional Court declared unconstitutional a provision in the new Marriage Law which ruled out joint parental authority of divorced parents even if this arrangement was in the best interest of the child. If both parents were able and willing to take care of their children despite their separation, the court ruled, there were no reasons to exclude them against their will from the right to education guaranteed in the Fundamental Law. The situation is different in the case of a child without a legal father. If the natural parents refuse to get married, the natural father can be excluded and parental authority entrusted to the mother alone.

The basic mistrust of the family and the unlimited confidence in state action is in conflict with the needs of the child which require the warmth and security of close personal relations and the loving care of devoted parents. Neither pedagogues nor bureaucrats are qualified to define moral or pedagogical ideals that should be binding on parents. The over-emphasis on parental duties and children's rights eliminates the responsibility of the children for their parents and the family.

This does not mean that the parents' right and duty to educate their children are not subject to state intervention. But such intervention is only justified if required for the well-being of the children. As a rule, the right of the parents can only be superseded if the parents neglect their duties and if such neglect is culpable. But there are cases in which state action is called for although the behaviour of the parents does not involve any subjective wrong-doing. Parents may suffer from psychic disorders, they may be dependent on drugs, or may oppose medical treatment of their children (for example, blood transfusions) on religious grounds. It may happen that the parents cannot agree on important decisions affecting a child. In German law, the view of the father was to prevail (Civil Code, Art. 1634) but the Constitutional Court decided that this arrangement violated the constitutional equal rights provision (Fundamental Law, Art. 3, Par. 2), and the new Family Law provides that the parents must try to reach an agreement (Civil Code, Art. 1627). Japan's legal provisions on parental rights have been discussed above (Ch. 2). Instead of assuming direct responsibility for education, the state should recognise the importance of the family for this task, emphasise the parents' duties as educators and assist them in fulfilling their duties.

Compulsory Education

While there is no question that the welfare of the child should be the decisive consideration, the problem is who should decide what constitutes the well-being or the 'best interest' of the child and what the child's welfare requires. Children elect no representatives; they constitute a 'silent minority' which can stage no protests. The state has no right to substitute an official or even a constitutional value system to the value system of the parents — although it can protect constitutional values and prevent their violation. On the other hand, the extension of state activities has created many opportunities for influencing education. The most far-reaching influence results from compulsory school education. The schools' original function was to provide 'instruction,' but the activities of today's schools go far beyond such a limited objective.

Japan's School Education

The system of compulsory education started when Frederick the Great of Prussia decreed compulsory school attendance in 1763. The French Revolution proclaimed a 'universal right to education' in 1791 and ordered that education should be 'secular, free and compulsory.' Voicing ideas already expressed by Plato, J. G. Fichte asserted that all children should be educated by the state. Public educational systems were established early in the nineteenth century in Germany and France, somewhat later in Britain and the United States. Universal school education is impossible unless it is financed and at least partially undertaken by the state.

In Japan, the transition from yesterday's to today's education was occasioned by the Meiji Restoration (1868). The ideas behind the Meiji Restoration were stated in the 'Oath of Five Articles' *(Gokajô no Seimon)* pronounced by Emperor Meiji on 14 March, 1868. Particularly significant was the sentence, 'Knowledge shall be sought from among the nations of the world,' which pointed to the basic programme of the Meiji era to elevate Japan's culture and education to the level of the advanced nations and assimilate their achievements as quickly as possible. State regulation started with the 'School Regulations' *(Gakusei)* of 1872 but compulsory education actually began with the 'Elementary School Ordinance' *(Shôgakurei)* promulgated by the then minister of education, Arinori Mori, in 1886. The eight years from the age of 6 to 14 were described as the school age of children but school attendance was made compulsory only for the three or four years of ordinary elementary school. Compulsory education was extended to six years in 1907, to eight years in 1941 and to nine years (divided into six years of elementary school and three years of junior high school) in the post-war educational reform of 1947.

Right from the beginning, Japan's state-regulated education was centralistic and had a strong ideological orientation. The main vehicle of indoctrination was moral training *(shûshin)*, a course which was to teach the essentials of morality but served, particularly in the interwar period, for imbuing the children with the Emperor system, the uniqueness of Japan and the nationalistic *Weltanschauung* incorporated in the pamphlet entitled *Kokutai no Hongi* (Essence of the National Structure, a widely used slogan of the pre-war period) published by the Ministry of Education in 1937. The post-war educational reform intended to decentralise education and make it egalitarian. The first objective was completely rolled back by subsequent revisions of the laws passed under the Occupation (Basic Law of Education *(Kyôiku Kijun-hô)* and School Education Law *(Gakkô Kyôiku-hô)*, both passed in 1947).

Legally, compulsory education comprises elementary (from the age of 6 to 12) and junior high school (from 12 to 15); actually, however, most youths advance to senior high school (from 15 to 18). In 1984, an estimated 1,883,000 students graduated from junior high school and 1,767,000, 93.9 per cent, went on to senior high school or technical college. The rate was 92.4 per cent for boys and 95.0 per cent for girls.

Today's schools with their large classes and rigid curricula do not educate children but teach subjects. Japan's post-war school education has been warped by two contradictory factors, excessive softness in the demands in instruction and irrational demands in the entrance examinations. Due to a distorted notion of equality, standards for evaluating achievements, particularly at the elementary level, are set to accommodate the slowest learners and it almost never happens that a pupil has to repeat a year in the courses of compulsory education (elementary and junior high school). The stupid egalitarianism propounded by the Japan Teachers Union demands that all pupils be treated the same. Some teachers give all pupils the same marks. Respect for the children's personality is interpreted to mean that children should never be admonished, let alone punished. The teacher should not be a person of authority but a 'big brother', standing at the same level as the pupils. As an external manifestation of this philosophy, the teacher's platform has been removed from most classrooms. This educational policy has succeeded in eliminating all discipline from the schools.

At the same time, there is immense pressure to prepare for entrance examinations (which now start with the entrance examination to kindergarten). These examinations are mainly memory tests; the student has to commit to memory an enormous amount of unrelated facts or methods so that the examinations are essentially quizzes rather than tests of ability. Once a student has passed the entrance examination to the university, he can relax and enjoy life; he will be able to graduate almost automatically. Naturally, not all undergraduates take this view; those intending to take the state examination for the civil service or the medical examination, for example, have to study hard, and those studying natural sciences or engineering know that their future depends on their qualifications.

The system leads to learning by rote a mass of incoherent facts, formulas and methods of calculation. Gifted students get bored and often neglect to develop their capabilities. On the whole, children regard learning and study as a burden and vexation. There are few remedial courses and at the lower levels, students cannot select subjects according to personal preferences and special talents. As a result, the performance of students is far from satisfactory. Teachers often speak of the seven-five-three system (the children's festival in November is held for the seven, five and three-year-olds): 70 per cent of the children follow instruction at the elementary level, fifty per cent in junior and thirty per cent in senior high school.

Japanese high school students spend some of the most precious years of their lives cramming for university entrance examinations. Years that should nurture their creative talents are filled instead with memorising textbooks and preparing for a gigantic quiz which has no relevance to understanding and is only concerned with memory. Today's school education in Japan miserably fails to stimulate intellectual curiosity, to launch students on a quest for knowledge and to introduce them to the great spiritual problems of man.

Europe's traditional secondary education intended to prepare for an academic career and constituted a propaedeutic or preparatory 'general' study in the form of a canon of subjects (languages, mathematics, history) which provided the basis for the scientific study encompassed in the general study called philosophy. The propaedeutic study was considered to impart a 'formal' education in the sense that it gave the student the mental maturity enabling him to engage in scientific pursuits. The dazzling array of humanistic, social and natural sciences which evolved from the old philosophy has made it impossible to interpret the 'general' study any longer as a 'universal' education, and in view of the enormous differentiation and specialisation of modern science, the old canon of subjects which transmitted the formal education has lost much of its propaedeutic value. It seems evident that a one-track secondary education is unable to prepare students for the immensely complex conditions of modern civilisation. To increase the number of electives is no solution to the problem of chartering a course of study enabling the student to cope with the demands of today's society and shifts the burden on the student who is utterly unequal to this task.

Reforms of the Japanese educational system have often been discussed in recent years and the need to improve the admission system has been stressed in all proposals. In the absence of a reliable and uniform system of grading scholastic achievements, some kind of entrance examination will remain unavoidable for senior high school (if it is retained in its present form) and college.

A survey carried out by the Japan Teachers Union revealed a significant increase in school drop-outs. High school students find school life empty and meaningless; they don't care about school and only continue going to school because there is nowhere else to go. Many students go to school because it is the place where they can find friends, and they stop going when they lose their friends.

Because children are forced into a uniform school system which denies individuality and inhibits achievement, they sometimes manifest an almost instinctive rejection of the system from which they fear a denial of their personality. It is difficult to fit problem children into a strict school system because they need individual education, they need teachers who remain composed even when faced with absurd behaviour, they need teachers who think of education from the point of view of the pupil, and they need teachers who do not neglect or pass over anyone of their charges but show serious concern for all. Children expect the teacher to understand and they clam up when they feel that they are being overlooked.

It may happen that the aversion of children to school is not general but that, for some reason or other, they do not want to go to a particular school and are eager to study when given the opportunity to enrol in a different school.

In the last year of elementary school, signs of rejection of education and educators may appear. The resistance against parents and teachers grows stronger in junior high school. Boys, in particular, band together in gangs and behavioural problems appear, including alcohol, smoking, drugs, sex and sometimes theft, notably shoplifting. Vandalism, especially defacing and destroying school property, and violence against teachers and schoolmates has become widespread.

In senior high school, the students who want to enter university limit their studies to the subjects required for the entrance examination of a particular university while those who are not interested in going on to a university stop studying altogether. To the violence committed on junior high school campuses come the disturbances caused by car and motor-cycle gangs and serious cases of assault against teachers and parents. Politically-oriented groups are relatively small but there is more political activity among university students. A few radical groups still engage in ideological warfare but the large majority of the students pay little attention to politics. They spend much of their time in part-time jobs, partly because they must earn their own living expenses, partly for augmenting their pocket money.

Many teachers, particularly those at public schools, suffer from health problems. A report of the Senior High School Education Research Association stated that three in every five high school teachers had considered leaving the profession at least once because they could not understand the views and behaviour of their students. Others were discouraged because their efforts were useless — the students were just too dull and uninterested. Some were upset by the disregard of school regulations and the sexual behaviour of students.

The nominal uniformity of the Japanese school system conceals profound differences between individual schools. Many factors influence the quality of the school and the quality of its students. Basic differences exist between public and private schools, schools in the metropolitan areas and schools in the provinces, schools going back to pre-war times and schools established after the war. Schools enjoying a traditional reputation attract the best students or students whose parents can spend plenty of money on private tutoring or cram schools.

Senior high schools are popularly rated according to the number of their graduates who succeed in passing the entrance examination to Tokyo University. In a place like Tokyo, the location of the school already implies differences in the social environment from which the students come. In the public schools located in Tokyo's so-called *shitamachi,* children preponderantly come from families of shopkeepers, artisans, employees of small companies or other workers. But today, parents are willing to spend a great deal of money on education and send their children to good private schools. Generally speaking, however, a large part of the students enrolled in 'famous' private schools come from well-to-do families. Their parents may have a university education and their fathers may be company executives or employees of large corporations, government officials, businessmen, doctors or lawyers.

Although the system seems to involve a certain amount of élitism, Japan's post-war affluence has been accompanied by a considerable degree of social mobility. The worst example of élitism is the preponderance of the graduates of Tokyo University in the higher echelons of Japan's bureaucracy but theoretically, at least, and in most cases practically, admission to the university is open to everybody regardless of the social status or the wealth of the family. The nature of the entrance examination favours intellectually-inclined students which may be connected with a certain one-sidedness of character.

Costs of School Education

In the discussions prompted by the growing school violence, the proposal was made to abolish compulsory education, at least at secondary level. Compulsory education is a product of the nineteenth century when child labour was widespread and many parents would not send their children to school unless forced to do so. Today's situation is completely different. Most parents want their children to go to school and many parents could afford to pay for it. There is no reason why the state should maintain an expensive and often inefficient school system. The relatively few parents unable to pay for education could be helped by child allowances which would be much cheaper than a state-run school system.

But even with free compulsory education, the costs of education born by the parents have been rising significantly in post-war Japan. According to the Japanese Ministry of Education, average costs of a 12-year education in public schools exceeded ¥1 million in 1981. In 1982, the average yearly costs born by the parents for a pupil attending a public elementary school came to ¥160,098; they were ¥194,676 for a public junior high school student and ¥252,631 for a public senior high school student. These expenditures included only stationery, textbooks and other materials, travelling expenses and lunch. For children enrolled in private schools, costs were much higher. Average tuition amounted to ¥481,000 for private high schools, and in some private high schools, total yearly costs exceeded ¥1 million.

A recent survey of the Tokyo Metropolitan Government found that the average monthly outlays for education of Tokyo households amounted to ¥63,000, roughly 20 per cent of the monthly family income. A large part of these outlays resulted from the expenses for supplementary education, such as cram-schools (juku) which children attend in preparation for the entrance examinations to senior high school or university. The Fair Trade Commission reported that there were more than 100,000 juku throughout Japan at the beginning of 1986 and estimated their total yearly revenues at ¥870 billion.

In a survey covering 783 students and 114 juku, the commission found that 24.5 per cent of the elementary school pupils and 50.2 per cent of the junior high school students went to juku. The average fee amounted to ¥12,200 a month for the former and to ¥12,600 for the latter. In an extreme case, the Tokyo survey found that a 50-year-old company employee spent ¥248,000 a month for the education of his three children. How the wife managed the family household with the rest of the income was not told in the survey.

According to an estimate of the Ministry of Education, 16.5 per cent of Japan's elementary school pupils and 44.5 per cent of the junior high school students attended *juku* in 1985. Together they numbered 4.5 million, or 26.3 per cent of the boys and girls in the age classes subject to compulsory education. In the third year of junior high, when the students prepared for the entrance examination to senior high school, the ratio of those enrolled in *juku* reached 47.3 per cent. Mathematics and English were the subjects most frequently studied at the *juku*. Families spent a monthly average of ¥7,800 per child at the elementary school level and ¥10,200 for a junior high school student. The reputation of a *juku* depends on its success in preparing its charges for the exams, and in contrast to public schools, they use a no-nonsense approach to instruction.

Some junior high schools have allowed unruly students not interested in learning to come to school once a week and spend the rest of the time doing a job (for example, in restaurants or motor-cycle repair shops). Besides being highly irregular, the problem of this procedure is that these students get a certificate of graduation without having fulfilled the academic requirements.

Large enterprises not only operate their own research facilities but also provide advanced training for their employees. Many of the courses instituted by manufacturing firms for their engineers provide a better education than graduate schools. Different from the problematic school system, training institutions seem more efficient. They inculcate definite procedures and teach a step-by-step approach to every operation. By stressing observance of a fixed sequence in the execution of each task, the training ensures a great deal of regularity. The method facilitates team work and enables each operator to take the place of his colleague without detriment to the process. The results of this training are apparent in such simple things as the wrapping of goods in department stores but also in the work of typists, bank tellers and nurses.

Constitutional Basis of State Education

The constitutional role of the state in education is very vague, to put it mildly. There is no provision in the Japanese Constitution concerning the right of the state over education. Article 26, Paragraph 1 states that all people have the right to receive an equal education correspondent to their ability, as provided by law. Paragraph 2 makes it obligatory for all people 'to have all boys and girls under their protection receive ordinary education as provided by law.' This obviously implies that the state can regulate education but the only thing which can certainly be settled by legislation is the extent of compulsory education. The clause, 'Such compulsory education shall be free', has been interpreted to give the state authority to set up a school system since the state cannot finance educational enterprises 'not under the control of public authority' (Art. 89; actually, public funds are used for financing private schools from kindergarten to university).

In a number of decisions, the Japanese judiciary has put the seal of approval on the Ministry of Education's assertion of state supremacy in education. On the pretext of instituting an administrative survey, the ministry ordered a nationwide achievement test for second- and third-year students of junior high school. The attempts of the Japan Teachers Union to stop the tests by strikes led to a series of lawsuits in which the lower courts were split on the question of the legality of the tests. In 1975, the Sapporo High Court ruled that the enforcement of the tests was beyond the authority of the Minister of Education but with unseemly haste, the Supreme Court overturned the verdict in 1976 and decided that the state had the right to intervene in education, that the tests had been lawful and that the state, as part of its administrative activities, could establish educational policies and determine, 'to the necessary and appropriate extent,' the contents of education.

In the latest (March 1986) decision in a series of lawsuits brought by Professor (now emeritus) Saburo Ienaga in a fight involving the censorship of textbooks by the Ministry of Education, Judge Kiyoshi Suzuki of the Tokyo High Court repeated most of the arguments by which the judiciary has propped up the attempts of the Education Ministry to regain its pre-war authority over the entire educational system. In order to show that the freedom of teachers can be regulated, Judge Suzuki reasoned that, on the basis of the Constitution, the state is given a mandate by the people and thereby possesses the function of establishing and enforcing wide and appropriate educational policies. The Diet, directly or by empowering administrative organs, can enforce necessary and reasonable controls on the contents and methods of education and determine, 'to the necessary and appropriate extent,' the contents of education. In order to ensure equality of opportunity in education, the state must ensure the same nationwide standards and a uniform content of education.

Just as in earlier decisions, the ruling of Judge Suzuki said nothing about the right of the parents to choose the education they want for their children, he was silent about the legal limitations on the competence of the Ministry of Education (which has direct administrative responsibility only for the national universities) and disregarded the view that, contrary to the assertion of a nationwide uniform educational system, 'public schools' can be erected by the state, or by local public bodies or by private school corporations (Fundamental Law of Education, Art. 6, Par. 1; School Education Law, Art. 2, Par. 1) and that the equality of educational opportunities does not require uniformity of the contents and methods of education.

Judge Suzuki also repeated the ridiculous argument that the censorship of textbooks is not censorship (which is prohibited by Art. 21, Par. 2 of the Constitution) because the books could be published as ordinary books although they could not be used as schoolbooks.

Although private schools can be established, primary education is almost completely in the hands of the state. In 1984, only 169 out of 25,064 elementary schools (0.7 per cent) were private institutions so that the state has an actual monopoly on education at the primary level. Japan may have become a pluralistic society but its educational system is uniform, bureaucratic and, up to secondary level, egalitarian.

At the same time, education has become more and more professionalised. The union leaders are dominated by the job thinking of 'workers in educational institutions.' Teaching is professional labour based on an employment contract stipulating a certain kind of work paid on a certain wage scale. Many teachers, however, are poor educators.

The state's interest in education is hard to define. While the state has neither an exclusive nor the primary right to education, it has the right to safeguard the interests of the community and the substitutional right to educate children if they have no parents or if parents are unable or unwilling to provide an education. Even social and political education is primarily part of the education to be given by the parents.

The degree of literacy is often regarded as an indicator of cultural development but the modern state-promoted literacy is not for the lofty purpose of culture but on account of the requirements of industry and defense. Even conceding that the maintenance of a certain standard of education is in the national interest, a uniform educational system or a uniform curriculum is by no means a national necessity. On principle, parents should be able to have their children attend schools that correspond to their convictions and the school system should not make it impossible to educate each child as an individual. No parliamentary majority guarantees the protection of the rights of parents of a minority, and there are no rules that force a pluralistic state to provide for alternative educational opportunities.

Problems in School Education

Financial considerations impose limitations on the educational system the state can afford but there seems to be more centralisation, uniformity, monotony and routine than necessary and certainly more than desirable. A school should not be turned into an education factory and education cannot be accomplished by conveyor-belt methods.

The basic question is: who controls the schools? Japan's monolithic, rigid and unadaptable system has not been structured for the needs of the young generation but for the convenience of the administrative agencies. Compulsory education under state supervision is the invention of Prussian absolutism. The state bureaucracy has replaced freedom and choice of teacher and school by administrative regulation and centralised standardisation of curricula and teaching methods. It seems unlikely that the bureaucracy should know better than parents and teachers what children need and what is necessary for education. Bureaucratic arrogance makes the adaptation of the school to local conditions and the wishes of the parents impossible.

There are two basic faults in the present system. First, it gives parents no choice to put their children into a school that corresponds to their views on education, and, secondly, it forces children to put up with teachers and a school environment with which they may be completely out of tune. School curricula and textbooks are structured from the point of view of teaching a certain subject within a certain period of time instead of how a certain subject can be taught to children of a certain age. Generally, the children's interest in a subject has little to do with the subject but much to do with the teacher who teaches it, but in most cases, the children cannot change teachers even if they have a deep-seated aversion to a teacher. Neither parents nor children have any choice or influence with regard to the educational environment in the form of school facilities or classmates and they have to accept the educator who happens to be put in charge of a class.

Parents hope that the school will develop the skills and talents of their children but today's educational policies do little to fulfil this hope. In the name of democracy, education is often dominated by a stupid egalitarianism which makes study boring to bright children and fails to equip less talented children with sufficient knowledge to get started in life. Broadly speaking, school education can serve four purposes: formation of personality, acquisition of culture, preparation for a profession, and graduation (obtaining of a diploma). The present system places the greatest emphasis on graduation, but a diploma says nothing about character and culture and very little about professional ability.

In Japan, the entrance examination system has turned the entire teaching and learning process upside down. School education is not for life but for passing examinations. For the students, the most important rule is 'it doesn't matter what I study, if I only get good marks.' The president of the World Teachers Federation, Wilhelm Ebert, characterised this tendency as follows: 'Do not be interested in truth and knowledge, but in rewards, marks, scores, recognition, money. This is the secret curriculum of our schools which turns out children into moral morons.'

School keeps children away from home for a considerable part of the day. The situation is particularly bad in Japan. In addition to the regular classes, all schools have a large variety of extra-curricular activities (usually in the form of 'clubs'), and for some of these activities, participation is compulsory. On account of the rigorous entrance examinations, parents enrol their children in a *juku* where they learn what they should have learned in school. Children may take part in 'sham' examinations and have all kinds of other private lessons so that they have very little time left to play. When they are at home, they are too exhausted to do much besides watching television.

One of the developments that have contributed to replace the functions of the family by the school is the extension of school activities to fields unrelated to instruction. School lunches, school health care, school career counselling and employment services may be convenient but they are outgrowths of the welfare state mentality which have made education more costly and often intrude on the rights of the parents.

Professor Reginald W. Revans, examining the English school system, concluded that the schools and not the over-maligned parents did most to create anti-social attitudes. Children who are not allowed to ask intelligent questions about silly organisational messes soon come to resent authority.

In the United States, the Gardner Report on the American school system compiled by a commission under the chairmanship of David T. Gardner and entitled 'A Nation at Risk' called for a longer school year, more homework and better teachers at higher pay. It proposed tightened requirements in the 'new basics': science, mathematics, English, social studies and computer science in high school so as to respond to the situation created by the communications revolution and the advances in information technology.

In Communist countries and in countries where party politics dominate educational policy, the school is turned into an instrument of social revolution. Jürgen Habermas considers emancipation by the revolutionary activity of militant classes the supreme goal of learning. The school no longer functions as an institution supplementary to the family but as an alternative to the family. The family is at most tolerated as a supplement to the school. In this view, deficiencies in socialisation can only be compensated by the school. By depriving the family of its educative functions, it is deprived of an essential part of its mission.

The limitation of the rôle of the family in the realm of education does not result from an equally valid mission of the state in this field but is a consequence of the unification connected with collective education. If the state institutes a system of compulsory education, the modalities of the school organisation and the school activities will necessarily infringe on the parents' right to education.

Personality and Public Education

In the supposition of compulsory school education, the school has the duty of contributing to the development of the children's personality and their preparation for the future, their private lives as well as their occupational and public activities. Although the main task of the school is instruction and the transmission of knowledge, it must also prepare for the use of this knowledge and relate knowledge to the totality of man's personality. School education cannot address itself exclusively to the intellect.

Parents and children must be in a position to guard their view of life against the state and public education. The right to develop one's personality freely is only protected if the public school system recognises differences in the pupils' talents and capabilities. The school is unable to change elementary differences such as 'basic disadvantages.' The denial or rather the disregard of differences in abilities, character and inclination has led to serious shortcomings. All men possess a right to education but the assertion that all men possess the right to the same education is utopian. Such a demand stems from socialist egalitarianism which replaces Justinian's canon of justice *suum cuique* (to everyone his due) by *idem cuique* (to everyone the same). Equal opportunity in education does not mean that everyone follows the same road but is able to follow his own road. This requires a choice in educational options. It is erroneous to regard the selection and furtherance of talented people as granting a privilege. Not differentiation, but the downgrading of everyone to the same level constitutes discrimination. Handicapped children and children with learning difficulties require special help but, on the other hand, it is an injustice to keep talented children to the same pace as the slowest learner in a unitary school system. Sound pedagogical principles demand differentiation based on ability and willingness to study.

The school cannot replace the family. The educational function of the family does not mean that parents should act as teachers, although parents should keep themselves posted on the scholastic standing of their offspring, not only when they bring home their school reports. The influence of the home is of greater importance for the career and the later life of the children than the school. But this supposes that the educational impact of the family and its human aid, particularly the personal relations to the parents, have been preserved intact.

Some parents are completely oblivious of their own responsibilities. If the children misbehave at home, they blame the school and the teachers for not having taught their children to be obedient, courteous and well-behaved.

Co-Education

Co-education has been one of the basic expressions of egalitarianism in education. The equal treatment of boys and girls started in kindergarten with the complete absence of any sex-specific influence. Throughout their entire school life, the curricula are strictly the same for both sexes and in the Federal Republic of Germany, the chances for occupational training have been made the same. The results of these methods in hitherto segregated schools have been startling.

In kindergarten, the boys intensified their rivalries until the strongest emerged while the girls were meekly content to play second fiddle to the boys. In school, the polarisation of the sexes was striking; girls played exclusively with girls and boys associated with boys, and both groups stuck to characteristically sexually-preferred activities. Throughout the school years, the ascendancy of girls over boys became stronger. Girls showed more diligence, more regularity, more obedient listening, more perseverance and therefore achieved better exam results and better marks. Generally speaking, girls become less neurotic, they are better drivers, have fewer accidents, are socially more adaptable than boys, more peaceful, more tender, more affectionate, more reliable and more competent. But there are very few geniuses among the girls. In tests designed to find out the most promising students for academic degrees, not a single girl qualified. No girls are among either the over-achievers or the complete failures.

The development curve for boys and girls is different. Girls grow quicker in younger years, they mature earlier sexually and their interests relate to persons rather than things. Egalitarian education cannot eradicate natural differences but only create obstacles to a differentiated development.

Very remarkable has been the improvement of the achievements of girls in sports and the lowering of the age at which girls set records, notably in gymnastics and swimming. This development has been particularly pronounced in the Soviet Union.

Egalitarianism in University Education

Egalitarianism in education has had devastating effects in university education. A university used to be an élitist institution. Not all universities were good, and universities were judged by the quality of the élites they produced. A serious university is inherently hierarchical and even authoritarian. Those who are qualified to be students go there to benefit from supervision by people who know more than students do, especially about what is good for students. The attempt to make universities all things to all people ignores the fact that not all good things are good for all people. Today's universities are, as George F. Will put it, 'academic cafeterias serving junk food for the mind.' Because students are unprepared for academic studies, most students start with nothing, acquire only a little and finish with not much more.

Boarding Schools

Japan has very few boarding schools. Before the war, some of the state high schools (different from today's high schools) were boarding schools.

They played an important rôle in training the country's pre-war leadership and lasting friendships were formed through the experience of a community life in which intense competition went hand in hand with ardent comradeship and fierce loyalty. There are famous boarding schools all over the world, the best known being Britain's public schools, and some of the institutions run by religious orders have been very successful. The reasons for sending a boy or girl to a boarding school vary greatly. Sometimes, family problems, not necessarily those of the child, may be involved, but often the desire to give the child a better education than he or she could have received at home impels parents to choose a boarding school. But it may also be for the sake of prestige, social ambition and, in a few cases, family tradition.

It is, of course, impossible to say that boarding school education is good or bad or that the decision of parents to send their child to a boarding school is good or bad. The proverbial strictness of boarding schools has been relaxed in recent years, co-educational boarding schools have increased, and curricula are generally those required for recognition by the educational authorities. The great advantages of boarding schools are the coherence and integration of their education, the unity of purpose of their staff, the evenness of their atmosphere, the regularity of everyday life, and generally conducive conditions not only to study but also to self-discipline, character formation and sociability. But for some adolescents, both boys and girls, the discipline of boarding schools may be oppressive, life emotionally boring or disturbing, and the restriction to one place, one community and a monotonous rhythm of life unbearable. These possibilities must be taken into account if the decision to send a child to a boarding school is made.

The rôle of boarding schools in the development of homosexual tendencies has often been mentioned. Cases of sexual abuse or seduction of students by teachers or supervisors certainly occur, but homosexuality among students is sometimes rather more a matter of common masturbation or sex play.

Children and Media

An important problem in today's education is the rôle of the media, particularly television and radio. The media do not replace the family or the school but they strongly affect not only the children but also educators and educational processes and conditions. They constitute an independent educational force to which parents or teachers may limit access but which they cannot control; on the other hand, the media cannot shut out the influence of the educational cartel of family and school.

A survey of the newspaper, *Mainichi Shinbun,* found that, in 1981, the average Japanese above the age of 15 (which makes the survey unrepresentative for the youth group) spent 257 minutes a day involved in one element or another of the mass media. This time was divided as follows: reading books and magazines 41 minutes, reading newspapers 35 minutes, listening to radio 44 minutes, and watching television 137 minutes. The average American child — age 9 to 12 — will spend about 1,000 hours in the classroom over a year but will spend 1,340 hours in front of a television set. By the time the average child is 18, he or she will have spent 22,000 hours watching television and only 11,000 hours in the classroom. Parents significantly underestimate the amount of time their children spend watching television and are often not well aware of the programmes they select.

In a West German study carried out in 1984, over 4,000 minors and young adults between the ages of 12 and 29 were interviewed about their use of the media. On average, these young people devoted four-and-a-half hours a day to television and radio and 45 minutes to reading books, magazines and newspapers. The most popular element of the media was radio to which the interviewees listend an average of 117 minutes; television was next with 101 minutes while cassettes and records were a distant third with 28 minutes. Books got 20 minutes and newspapers 13.

There were significant differences between the various age groups. The time for listening to radio increased with age from 71 to 138 minutes a day while cassettes and records lost their attractiveness: they got 31 minutes of the time of those aged 12 to 15 but only 17 minutes of the 25 to 29 age group. Time spent watching television decreased from 118 minutes for the low teens (12 to 15) to about 88 minutes for those aged 16 to 24. But the average went up again for those over 25. A similar curve appeared in the time devoted to reading books: 25 minutes for the 12 to 15 group, 17 minutes for the group from 16 to 24, and 20 minutes for those from 25 to 29. The time given to reading a newspaper(s) increased from 6 to 18 minutes.

Overall, books are not read by one out of five among the young generation, one out of six spurns magazines and one out of eight can do without newspapers. Education influences the interest in the printed word. Only every fourth graduate of elementary school reads books regularly but 80 per cent of university graduates do. The credibility of the various media is likewise different for different ages and different levels of education. On average, 63 per cent of young people consider television most creditable, while only 19 per cent think newspapers and 17 per cent radio most reliable. But 45 per cent of university graduates hold newspapers most trustworthy and 36 per cent television.

The Nielson rating may not reflect the tastes of the young generation. Only 30 per cent watched youth programmes more or less regularly, TV movies and news were most popular with 55 per cent followed by pop and rock music, the hit parade and other popular music with 46 per cent. Almost 70 per cent disliked programmes concerned with culture and the economy, and 58 per cent were allergic to comedy, political commentary and advice on living.

Music serves for entertainment and recreation, but also as a sound backdrop for study and work. Pop is the favourite idiom whereas there are few lovers of classical music, opera, musicals and folk music.

The media are used as 'domesticated' collaborators in the school where electronic equipment is often available in a greater variety than in the home. Outside the school, the media are 'untamed' purveyors of entertainment and information, largely used by children and adolescents at their own discretion and for less specific purposes than at school.

The influence of the media on children must be seen in the context of the child's ability to handle media offerings. In kindergarten and in the first two years of school, immediate apprehension predominates. Children prefer one-track, successive narratives. For reading, picture books and comics are the favourites which is linked to the preference for animated cartoons and commercials. In their seventh year, children learn concrete-logical operations. They can understand the sequence of events and their background but their interest remains with the concrete. They become capable of following short films and a series of oral statements. Between the ages of eleven and twelve, children develop their capability for formal operations. Actions are understood even if they are not strictly linked to concrete objects. Contents and form can be grasped beyond the concrete meaning as having figurative or symbolic significance. When they advance to junior high school, children understand more complex representations and the editorials of newspapers.

In today's world, children start watching television at a very early age; they then take up comics and books. The TV curve shows a slight decline after nine, and movies or newspapers hardly attract much attention. With the beginning of school, books start to attract more interest, and in the course of school life, books may serve to escape from the pressure of home and school. Listening to audiophonic media such as radio, records and cassettes begins to become a habit when adolescents reach twelve and takes up more of the time of fifteen-year-olds than books. But the infatuation with audio is of short duration and television regains a stronger position in later years. Of importance, however, is the dance-and-disco culture which attracts many adolescents.

The habits related to the use of the media show a wide range of variation for the different age groups. Reading and the use of books and other print media depends greatly on the conditions of the parental home on the one hand and, on the other, on scholastic achievements. Television now forms the basis of the communication experiences in the home since almost all households are equipped with radio and television sets.

Speaking (in the sense of formulating one's thoughts), reading and writing are often the exclusive province of the school. The school has the unenviable task of organising the intellectual digestion of the uncritical intake from the media. Experiences from the media are seldom discussed in the home which has become silent and less concerned with education. There is no dialogue with the screen and there is no discussion with parents or others on the programmes. Because TV stops conversation, to switch on TV during meals, particularly when the whole family is together, is hardly conducive to fostering the family spirit.

The basic shortcoming of television is the passivity which it brings into the development of the children and the limitations on other activities which result from spending many hours in front of the tube. While TV may stimulate the imagination — an effect which has been disputed — it impedes the creative use of free time and, in the long run, inhibits creative imagination and initiative, intellectual alertness, resolute exertion and spiritual maturity. TV tends to make children dull, passive and unsociable. It encourages the tendency of spoiled children to react defensively, to retreat into themselves when they are confronted with something that they consider an excessive demand. One of the things children must learn is to cope with unpleasant situations and to bear failure with equanimity. This they cannot acquire by watching TV but only in play and fellowship with other children.

The emotional impact of TV is stronger and more durable than the cognitive influence. Facts and figures shown on TV are soon forgotten but affections may be stimulated. The educational and therapeutical potential of TV has not been exploited. No systematic attempt has been made to use TV for indoctrinating children by showing models of polite, friendly and helpful conduct, for encouraging compassion, for conquering fear and bringing consolation.

If children become spoiled with television, they become self-indulgent and impatient, less sensitive to the pain and suffering of others, and more fearful of the world around them. The effects are the same as those of any other kind of immoderate indulgence. Every restriction of or interference with their enjoyment produces grumbling, recalcitrance, abuse and quarrels. It is, however, not only on those occasions that the influence of TV on speech and manners appears. Television not only depicts violence and crime, but conversation is often uncouth, vulgar, insolent and threatening. Children get used to this kind of language and behaviour and consider it the normal way of speaking and acting in everyday life.

A report of the US Department of Health and Human Services supported findings of studies conducted during the 1970s which linked television violence with aggressive behaviour and concluded that children who watched a lot of violence on television may come to accept violence as normal behaviour. Research findings have destroyed the illusion that television is merely innocuous entertainment. Violence on TV is a much greater threat to the civilised behaviour of young people than sex. The use of physical force, intimidation and even killing is depicted in an everyday context and appears as part of the ordinary world. Children get the impression that verbal and physical abuse are socially acceptable forms of behaviour. Even small children get used to uttering phrases like 'Kill him!' Conflict with parents, fighting and delinquency are all positively correlated with the total amount of television viewing and not just viewing violent programmes. The only remedy would be the total prohibition of violence on TV and video cassettes. Films shown only in cinemas pose less of a threat to children because they are less accessible than television.

Television induces viewers to overestimate the incidence of violence in real life and makes them more fearful and apprehensive. The experience of violence has no cathartic effect; the viewer is given no opportunity of purging himself of his aggressive inclinations.

The distinction between fiction and real life is obscured by TV as well as movies — even adults often behave as if the real world could be shaped in the image of the fantasies on the screen. Media imagery becomes a substitute for reality. There are children who, to the question, 'What do people die of?' answer: 'Usually of murder.'

Among the unrealistic messages conveyed by TV are the impressions regarding the use of drugs, alcohol and tobacco and the portrayal of sexuality. Adolescence, in particular, is associated with a continuous involvement in sex, the rapid development of sexual relationships and a constant state of sexual crisis. Television promotes ethnic and racial stereotypes and may reinforce social prejudices.

Most countries have tried to protect minors from the undesirable influence of films shown in cinemas, usually by rating the films to which minors can be admitted. But no restrictions can be enforced on the viewing of TV or video cassettes in the home.

In West Germany, the Penal Code prohibits publications depicting violence against people in a cruel or otherwise inhuman way — and thereby express a glorification or exculpation of such violence or incite to racial hatred (Art. 131) — and expressly forbids the sale of such publications to persons below the age of 18 (Par. 1, No. 3) or the diffusion of their contents by broadcasting (Par. 2). In addition to the restrictions making pornographic publications inaccessible to youth (Penal Code, Art. 184), three special laws have been enacted for the protection of youth: the Youth Welfare Law, the Law for the Protection of Youth in Public, and the Law Concerning the Diffusion of Publications Endangering Youth. Until now, West Germany has had only public television (no independent network) and the standards are appreciably stricter than in some other countries.

The new Youth Protection Law which went into effect on 1 April, 1985, subjects video cassettes to the same restrictions as films. Video cassettes to be made accessible to minors under 18 years of age have to be vetted by a voluntary self-control panel of the industry and the age class for which they have been approved must be indicated. Video cassettes not approved for minors or not submitted to the panel cannot be sold by mail order or in shops; they can only be leased in special shops not accessible to juveniles. The prohibition of Art. 131 of the Penal Code has been tightened and the production of films or video cassettes representing violence 'in a manner violating human dignity' has been made punishable. New rules have been laid down for the placement of automatic vending machines and video games which cannot be placed in the lobbies of cinemas or in shopping malls. Alcoholic beverages cannot be sold to juveniles under 16 years unless they are accompanied by their parents.

Although the intention of the law to protect the sound development of the young generation is laudable, the prohibition of the representation of violence 'in a manner violating human dignity' is too loose and opens the door to artistic and political censorship.

Parents and Control of TV Consumption

As in everything else, parents have to set an example in television consumption and exercise wise self-control. They have to educate their children to self-restraint and explain to them why such self-mastery in enjoyment is necessary. They should select the programmes together with their children, arrange a schedule and look to it that it is adhered to. The worst thing to do is to switch off the TV in the middle of a programme in a fit of anger or disgust. Children usually feel that such an abrupt action is unfair and unjust. While public censorship of the media is inadmissable in a free society, self-censorship is desirable to protect not only the children but also the level of family entertainment. Actually, however, people willing to forgo dubious programmes seem to be in a minority — this, at least, appears to be what the percentage of people subscribing to X-rated movies on cable TV indicates.

Video Games

Video games, the latest development in automated entertainment, are attracting thousands of teenagers who even squander their lunch money on purchasing new programmes. Different from television, video games are no mere exposure to a spectacle that rolls on without regard to the viewer's reaction; the viewer tries with entranced attention to win. A teenage addict who wrote a book on video games claims that they produce amazing reflexes, help kids to become familiar with computers in general and promote analytical thinking. But in video games, the opponent is not a person as in chess or card games but a microchip so that these games constitute a further step in the depersonalisation of entertainment.

Automated entertainment has become an important industry. In

Japan, a home entertainment system called 'Family Computer' (a console used with a TV set) was the undisputed best-seller in the 1985 Christmas season (the console sells for ¥14,800, cartridges start at ¥4,500). Since putting the game on the market in 1983, the manufacturer had sold 5.8 million consoles by the end of 1985.

In West Germany, 284,444 automated entertainment machines were in operation in the beginning of 1984 of which 69,619 were video games. In 1983, total income of manufacturers, dealers and operators of entertainment equipment, including such items as music boxes and pool tables, amounted to DM 3.7 billion, down from DM 4.2 billion in 1982. The operators of video games have adopted a voluntary control system to keep games not suitable for juveniles from being installed in places accessible to young people.

A West German study based on interviews with 120 young (up to 17 years) players of video games disputes the danger generally associated with those games: inclination to violent solutions of conflicts and reinforcement of destructive tendencies by imitation. The study which does not claim to be representative denied the validity of the image of isolated players entirely absorbed in their individual pastime. Common play with friends and the aspects of skill and entertainment predominate in the consciousness of the players. The games are only one of a number of leisure activities in which sports receive the strongest emphasis and the togetherness with friends contributes greatly to the feeling of relaxation. The ideals and wishes of the young video players showed no difference from those of other groups of the same age: rejection of aggressive life-styles and dreams of an existence with the need for accomplishment, without fear for the future and without the pressure of competition. The study concluded that video games do not lead to 'socioethical disorientation' (which the 'Law Concerning the Diffusion of Publications Endangering Youth' lays down as a criterion for prohibiting access of minors to such publications).

Video games may present intellectual challenges but they also have an addicting and narcotising effect. In England and the United States, cases of epileptic seizures have been reported from playing the Pac-Man video game. Dr H. James Holroyd who specialises in 'technology abuse,' arrived at the conclusion that video games are not innately dangerous but that the impressionable child can become so absorbed in the game that he or she may dodge reality and human contacts and become alienated from his or her environment. Opponents of the games charge that they glorify violence, destruction, space wars, killing and racing. Some games require the player to drive a speeding car into a road full of pedestrians. Some Asian countries, notably Singapore, Malaysia, Indonesia, the Philippines and Thailand, have banned or restricted the operation of video games.

In some Western European countries, video games contribute to social problems. The boyish habitués of Amsterdam's video-machine parlours are prey to cruising older homosexuals who finance the youths' games in the hope of favours in return.

On Thursday nights, when the stores stay open late in the city, gangs of youths often swoop down on shoppers, mugging and robbing to support their game addiction. Several of the young thugs have calmly confessed to murder. In Stockholm, young game addicts scatter after closing time to terrorise people in the subways and streets. These games can become very expensive; with the console version of *mah-jongg* and draw poker, some plungers risk $10,000 a month.

Besides the psychological risks of video games, players have experienced eye strain, wrist pain, high blood pressure and, in some cases, paralysis of the hand resulting from pressure on the outside part of the wrist where the nerve leading into the hand is closest to the surface.

Most girls are turned off by violence but the industry was not interested in developing non-violent games. 'Boys are the market,' the industry was reported to think and most games were said to have been designed 'by boys for boys.'

One of the most controversial forms of printed material reaching the Japanese public are comic books. Actually, 'comics' is not a good translation of the Japanese word *manga* (Hokusai, one of the masters of woodblock prints, coined the word for a collection of sketches) and most of these publications are not comic at all. There is no limit to the subjects covered in *manga* form but eroticism and violence are by far the most common themes. Publishers aim *manga* at definite classes of readers, divided principally by sex and age (adult men, adult women, boys, girls). The reading public, however, disregards these classifications. Sales of *manga* are estimated at over 1 billion copies a year, and the industry provides work for about 3,000 illustrators.

5

Sex Education

Secrecy or Openness?

SOME TIME AGO, Miss Ilona Anna Papajcsik, a Hungarian-born university graduate, was convicted on charges of gross indecency. Miss Papajcsik, at that time 25, worked as a playground supervisor for the local education authority in Swansea, Wales. When some of the children under her care, two boys and two girls aged eight to twelve, quizzed her on sex and sexual inhibitions, she stripped in front of the children to answer their questions and the boys also exposed themselves. Said Miss Papajcsik: 'I believe it was right. I don't feel my conduct was indecent. I did not want to fob them off with lies and half-truths. They wanted to know about sex and as I have been teaching them that the body is not something to be ashamed of, I felt I could not refuse.'

This incident illustrates the basic problem of sex education, taboo or openness, and if openness, how far and how early. Humans are not equipped with an instinctive mechanism for control or regulation of sexual impulses which means that sex is not instinctively managed towards biological ends and that sexual satisfaction can become an end in itself. Sex education should prepare human beings to deal with life situations and social relationships directly or indirectly arising out of the sex instinct and to keep sexual activity, and particularly sexual satisfaction, within the limits of morality, health and social requirements.

Children's Sex Consciousness

Children's interest in sex may start at an early age. When three-year-olds play 'doctor,' it may be a euphemism for sex play. In pre-school years, children become interested in the physical similarities and differences between themselves and others. This interest in body and sex is natural and occurs in all children. But this does not mean that children should be given practical training in sexuality in kindergarten or in the home. Young people want to know the truth about sex and are entitled to learn the truth, but the whole truth about sex may be even beyond a life-long experience.

If children do not get absorbed in sex play and do not continue to do so for a long time, there is no cause for concern. If parents think that the curiosity is overdone, they can stop it because at that age, children are usually responsive to the parents' approval or disapproval. But children need supervision because they may place objects within their bodies or the bodies of others or may masturbate in public. The attitude expressed in the remark, 'A mother should rejoice more when her baby first clutches his genitals than when he first smiles' (Helmut Kentler), reveals a complete reversal of human values.

An Australian educator observed that parents risk making fools of themselves if they wait until their children are teenagers before explaining about sex and drugs. By the time the average Australian child reaches his teens, he knows more about these subjects than his parents are ever likely to know. This opinion may not be entirely accurate. Despite the curiosity about sex, the early and often premature sexualisation and the frightening increase in teenage pregnancies and abortions, there often is an abysmal ignorance of the functions of the human body and the organisation of sexuality.

Children get their sex information in bits and pieces and most children are self-educated. A study of two Australian educators involving interviews with 838 children between the ages of 5 and 15 in Sweden, Australia, England and North America (United States and Canada) found that Swedish children were most knowledgeable with the Australians and English far behind and the North Americans least informed. Although they know least about sex, American children have sex earlier than children in other countries. In Sweden, official sex education is compulsory for all children and starts at the age of eight; in other countries, sex education is generally given in secondary school.

According to a survey of Japan's Prime Minister's Office covering young people between the ages of 15 and 24, 70 per cent of the adolescents were sex conscious before leaving elementary school (12 years of age); for 60 per cent, active interest in the opposite sex started during junior high school (12–15–years–old). About 70 per cent of the junior high school students had girl or boy friends with whom they spent their free time. They liked club activities in which they could meet with members of the opposite sex but few had sexual intercourse. Talks about sex of 60 per cent were with their friends, mostly of the same sex, 1 per cent with parents, 0.6 per cent with teachers and none with doctors. Their main sources of information were magazines, above all weeklies, and talks with friends.

First Sexual Experience

A Japanese survey covering 857 young people (of whom 846 or 98.8 per cent were unmarried) inquired about the first sexual experience. Of the respondents, 24.4 per cent had intercourse 2 to 3 months after becoming acquainted and 20.6 per cent after 4 to 6 months. Altogether, 72.4 per cent had intercourse within 6 months, including some who started one week after their first meeting. In the opinion of 58.2 per cent, intercourse poses no problems. Curiosity was the motive for having intercourse in 18.6 per cent of the cases and force or violence was used in 11.0 per cent. Nine out of ten considered pre-marital intercourse acceptable if the partners loved each other. Six out of ten girls were surprised when told that they were pregnant; 39.3 per cent kept their pregnancy secret from their parents. Contraceptives had been used by 63.1 per cent but 44.5 per cent had never received instruction on sex. Many were unconcerned about a possible pregnancy because they could easily have an abortion. Doctors point out that the uterus of teenage girls is small and easily damaged in abortions. In some cases, abortion leads to infertility. Of the teenage girls giving birth, many leave school and take up prostitution.

Teenage girls taken into police custody because of sex-related delinquency numbered 9,813 in 1984 (1983: 9,676). Most numerous were 16-year-old girls (2,678), followed by those aged 17 (2,387). 357 were under the age of 13. About 30 per cent of the girls, 3,043, were unemployed, 2,558 were junior and 2,496 senior high school students. Of the 5,935 girls who had become delinquent of their own free will, 1,836 had done so out of curiosity, 1,834 said they had done so for love and 1,339 for money. 3,546 girls had been seduced.

A survey undertaken by the Tokyo Metropolitan Government in 1982 and covering 1,200 senior high school students (age 15-18) found that 10 per cent of the boys and 9 per cent of the girls had had sexual intercourse. Other forms of heterosexual contact were kissing (boys 28 per cent, girls 26 per cent) and petting (boys 18 per cent, girls 14 per cent). Male students usually go through masturbation (about 80 per cent masturbate), kissing and petting to intercourse. Masturbation is practised by about 20 per cent of the girls; their sex experience usually starts with kissing.

Because boys and girls are no longer afraid, more and more and younger and younger adolescents engage in intercourse. Fear of the unknown or fear of being caught does no more deter young people when they decide to experience sex for themselves. Of the girls engaging in sex, a third become pregnant within three months and a half within six months after their first experience. In Japan, 28,020 girls between the ages of 15 and 19 had abortions in 1984 which means 6.5 abortions per 1,000 girls of this age group (in 1975, the rate was 3.1). This figure, however, only covers reported abortions and estimates put the actual number of teenage abortions at 80,000.

Cases of pregnancy among junior and senior high school students that were referred to obstetricians and gynaecologists in the Kanto region trebled between 1968 and 1981. About 30 per cent of the girls severed relations with their lovers a few months after becoming pregnant, over 10 per cent ended their association within a year and 22 per cent married the father of the child.

Of the students at a high school in Kobe, 66 per cent were in favour of dating and 48 per cent had steady dates. 58 per cent talked about sex with their friends, 10 per cent had been kissing and caressing and 2 per cent had had intercourse. 27 per cent were against pre-marital sex but 38 per cent were willing to lose their 'virginity' to their dates if they were truly in love.

In Miami Beach, police arrested a 12-year-old boy and a 10-year-old girl who willingly had sex with each other. The boy was charged with sexual battery and the girl accused of lewd and lascivious conduct. After the arrests, the authorities expressed dismay over the way the case had been mishandled.

Teenage Pregnancies

A study by the Alan Guttmacher Institute of teenage pregnancy in the United States found that, in 1981, 14 out of 100 women between the ages of 18 and 19 and six out of 100 girls between the ages of 15 and 17 had become pregnant. This was about double the rates in England and Wales. Six out of 100 teenagers have had at least one abortion by the time they reach the age of 18, about twice as many as in Sweden and France. Recent estimates surmised that out of a total of 29 million American adolescents between the ages of 14 and 19, 7 million boys and 5 million girls have had sexual intercourse. The average age of the first sexual experience is 16. Two-thirds of the girls who became pregnant had used some form of birth control. The United States registers one million pregnancies of teenagers and 3 million new cases of venereal disease each year. Of the teenagers who became pregnant, 220,000 gave birth out of wedlock. 360,000 married to cover up the pregnancy, and 400,000 had abortions. In 1983, the last year for which national statistics are available, 261,260 babies were born to women between the ages of 15 and 19. In a California high school, 150 of the school's 692 girls became pregnant in the 1984–85 school year.

Girls as young as nine or ten years have had babies. Young people who are the most promiscuous and who have sex at early ages like 11, 12 and 13, are the ones who are least informed. In the period from 1960 to 1974, 48 per cent of the American women between the ages of 15 and 44 delayed sexual intercourse until marriage, but only 21 per cent of the women who married in the years from 1975 to 1979 were virgins when they married.

In West Germany, 22 per cent of the boys and 12 per cent of the girls had their first sexual experience between 13 and 15. In East Germany, some youngsters exchange bodily caresses before they are 12, but for 60 per cent, the first caresses such as kissing, petting or embracing occur between the ages of 14 and 16, and by the age of 18, 70 per cent of the boys and 71 per cent of the girls have had their first intercourse. In a recent survey covering over 5,000 youths, 84 per cent said that they had had sex by the time they were 18. Almost all young people tolerate pre-marital sex but most boys would prefer to marry a virgin. Of the teenagers who had had sexual experience, 5 per cent slept together the first night after becoming acquainted, 13 per cent had had intercourse after having known each other for one month, 29 per cent after three months, 22 per cent after six months, 15 per cent after one year and 12 per cent after a longer period of time.

The first ever sex survey carried out in Malaysia found that children were changing but adults were not. Pornographic publications were banned in Malaysia and in films, kisses are censored, but 29 per cent of the respondents (equally divided between men and women from 20 to 34 years old) had had pre-marital sex at least once, but 69 per cent disapproved of pre-marital intercourse, 82 per cent had never discussed sex with parents, 61 per cent had gathered their knowledge on sex from books and magazines and 18 per cent from friends. Although 50 per cent professed Islam, only 11 per cent had had religious instruction related to sex.

These facts and figures show that today's society is hardly conducive to sexual restraint. No teenager ever asked: 'May I have sex?' Today's social surroundings and conditions abet irresponsible sexual behaviour. Sexual stimulation in the form of films and pornography is not counterbalanced by sexual information and education. Only too often, general education leaves young people without a sense of purpose. They are not very future-oriented, lack a sense of responsibility, want to have fun now and worry later. Frustration and a sense of alienation may result from seeing the trappings of an affluent society while being left out from the blessings of that society.

Many educators have operated on the assumption that knowledge is harmful. If you tell young people about sex, they will try it out. But the experience all over the world shows the opposite. Young people who are educated and well-informed tend to be responsible in their behaviour.

Encouragement of Childhood Sexuality?

Sex education has become difficult for a variety of reasons that also make it more necessary. Restrictions on human conduct such as moral norms or religious precepts have lost much of their effectiveness and the freedom of urban society facilitates behaviour incompatible with traditional standards. Furthermore, in the world of sexology, prestige usually came from attacking taboos and repression, not from assessing the psychological damage of the ideas unleashed. Under the label of science, the most irresponsible assertions were circulated. A child, it was said, should be allowed, and possibly encouraged, to conduct a full sex-life without interference from parents and the law. Children are sexual beings who need to develop skills early in life. The child has a basic right to know about sex and to be sexual. The latency period is a myth invented by a prudish society. Infant boys get erections and the vaginas of young girls lubricate. 'It is almost certain that human beings, like the other primates, require a period of early sexual-rehearsal play.'

The most pernicious assertion is that adult-child sex is not harmful, that paedophiles should be allowed to copulate with children, and that it causes a lot of problems not to practise incest. The trend of this thinking is that there should be no restrictions whatever on sexual conduct.

Childhood sexuality is like playing with a loaded gun. People who think that small children are capable of making free decisions about sex with adults are evil idiots. Pre-pubescent children are not taboo because this is a sex-negative society but because they can be physically hurt and may be psychologically injured as well by sexual intimacy with adults. Premature sexual behaviour of children almost always leads to psychological difficulties because a child is acting out a rôle for which he or she is not cognitively and emotionally ready. Most people who were seduced early in life go through the motions of living and may seem all right but psychologically they are damaged.

At the Sixth World Congress of Sexology held in May 1983, Dr Mary S. Calderone reported that sonograph pictures of male foetuses in the womb show regular erections of the penis — one erection every five hours, about the same rate as sleeping adults. She concluded that sexuality is present in children even before birth and that parents should accept childhood sexuality as a part of being human and rather than denying it, they should teach children the proper time and circumstances for expressing it. Parents should inculcate responsibility, educating children to engage in sex in private, without exploiting others nor being exploited.

Sexuality is a rather vague term, and intra-uterine erections can hardly be interpreted as 'private sex life.' As far as human conduct is concerned, sexual phenomena resulting from purely internal, physiological causes (such as nocturnal emissions) are completely different from the activation of man's sexual potential by external stimulation. That the sexual response system is natural does not mean that man should satisfy every sexual impulse. Responsibility implies self-control, and sex education must combine the affirmation of sex as a basic human endowment with the acceptance of norms regulating man's conscious behaviour. Self-discipline is not the same as suppression, and to make young people understand and observe the golden mean of self-restraint between the extremes of licence and denial is the difficult task of sex education.

The attitude of children to sex may be influenced by their experience of sex relations in the family and their social environment. Children may receive favourable reassurance from the strength of the parents' community of life or a frightening shock from the parents' squabbles, fights and divorce which might even dissuade them from assuming the responsibilities of marriage.

Sex Instruction

Opinions on sex education have often been influenced by the general philosophical and pedagogical tenets of the educators. Some of the viewpoints echo the nature versus nurture controversy. In his book *Behaviourism*, John B. Watson asserted that appropriate education could make healthy children into doctors, lawyers, artists or businessmen but also into beggars or thieves. The optimism of permissive education regarded the transition from adolescence to adulthood as a problem that would solve itself in a proper social environment. If the bonds of the family were not too strict and the young people were allowed to gain sufficient sexual experience before and outside marriage, the development from sexual awakening to sexual maturity would proceed without conflicts.

The late Margaret Mead wrote her *Coming of Age in Samoa* as a vindication of a *laissez-faire* sex education and, as she indicated in the subtitle of her work *(A Psychological Study of Primitive Youth for Western Civilization)*, a model for advanced societies. Miss Mead contended that Samoan youths possessed a positive and simple attitude towards sex, that rape was unknown, that marriage did not impose exaggerated demands of faithfulness and that jealousy was relatively rare. Miss Mead was influenced by the hypothesis of her teacher, Franz Boas, that biological determinism was wrong and cultural determinism right. She wanted to show that thanks to Samoa's cultural environment, adolescent girls passed through the teenage years with little stress, free from anxiety and sexual restraint.

Later researchers took exception to Miss Mead's description of Samoa and her account of its sexual mores. In his book *Margaret Mead and Samoa: The Making and Unmaking of an Anthropological Myth,* Derek Freeman, an anthropologist at the Australian National University, challenges Miss Mead's representation of Samoan mores as well as her basic thesis. Samoa's society emphasises differences of rank; brothers watch sharply over the virginity of their sisters; children and adolescents are subject to draconian punishment by their parents. At present, Samoa's rate of rapes and venereal disease is much higher than in the United States and Britain, and so are the rates of suicides and murders. These social disorders are nothing new, Professor Freeman asserts, but existed already when Miss Mead, in 1925, spent nine months on Tutuila (East Samoa) where she lived with an American family. The real intention of her work was to demonstrate 'the downfall of our belief in a single standard' which would result from our knowledge of divergent cultural patterns.

Contents of Sex Instruction

Sex instruction usually covers the biological facts regarding reproduction in plants, animals and humans, anatomy and physiology of sex organs, general sex hygiene, pre-natal and post-natal care of infants, treatment and prevention of venereal disease and birth control. This enumeration shows the importance of adapting sex instruction to the age of those being instructed.

There are three completely different levels of sex eduction. The first regards pre-school children up to puberty. They should learn about their own body and bodily functions, the differences between boys and girls and also get an answer to the question 'Where do babies come from?' This instruction should be given by parents or people with close personal relations. The second level comprises puberty and concerns the physiology of sex, the sex act and birth control. Parents as well as the school should provide this information. The third level consists in the preparation for marriage. Young people contemplating marriage should know something about marital relations, sex techniques and family problems. Special courses given by doctors, health officials and social workers would probably be an appropriate form for such instructions.

Moral Guidance

The goal of sex education should be to inculcate responsibility in the attitude towards sex and in sexual behaviour. All moral education aims at encouraging man to behave responsibly 'in thought, word and deed.' Sex education must teach respect for the meaning of sex in oneself and in others; it must also inculcate reverence for sex and the conviction that sex is not a commodity but something inseparable from man's total self. Such an attitude demands respect for one's own body and mind and the body and mind of others. Sex education, therefore, must go beyond knowledge and understanding and also include motivation and orientation. An understanding of the biological, hygienic, psychological and social implications of sex must be complemented by an explanation of the individual and social significance of sex and its inherent values.

Mere biological enlightenment may defeat the purpose of sex education, not necessarily in the sense that mere sex information will make sexual intemperance possible while guarding against pregnancy but on account of the insecurity and lack of confidence created by knowledge not integrated with everyday life. The adolescent, intent on emancipating himself from his dependence on parents and loosening his ties with his family, is searching for the meaning of his existence and looking for his own form of the values that the family provided: security, tenderness, affection, love and partnership.

Japanese girls complained that sex instruction at school was long on moral exhortation but short on solid information. Without knowing what he or she must control, adolescents cannot be expected to understand the necessity of moral constraints.

Sex education, therefore, cannot be limited to the mere transmission of knowledge without value judgements. Sex information will influence action and it is worse than useless if it does not provide norms of conduct. Mere definitions of the sex act, pre-marital sex, masturbation or homosexuality are of little value in themselves; a discussion of these matters also requires an evaluation, an indication of the way in which they should be approached and handled. Information without norms leaves young people bewildered and insecure. They must learn how to use their freedom, how to form their conscience, how to deal with what the 'old religion' called 'temptations.' An adequate understanding of sexuality also includes orientation on its use and its place in the framework of a human being and humanity.

Children and adolescents need guidance on their road to the maturity of body, soul and spirit. Such guidance should be better than what young people can pick up haphazardly from rather dubious sources. The important questions are how this can be done and who should do it.

Some time ago, The Vatican released a statement deploring sex education for children below the age ten as 'a frightful denudation' of the 'mystery of sex.' Children should learn about sex on the knees of their mothers rather than from 'crudely precise and detailed' illustrations of sex organs. A comprehensive exposition of the teaching of the Church on sex and sex education published in December 1983 under the title 'Educational Guidance in Human Love' stresses the primary responsibility of parents for the sex education of their children which should be undertaken within a moral system as the basis for content and method. Educators cannot remain silent on this subject and sex education in the family should be backed by Church, school and government.

Methods of Instruction

In response to The Little Red Schoolbook, Denmark's controversial manual dealing with sex, drugs and revolutionary politics, Danish and English parents and educators produced a Christian answer to permissive propaganda which stated that today's world resembles the situation in the Roman Empire when Christianity made its breakthrough. Teaching children the philosophy of false freedom and including in a children's book chapters on sex before marriage, adultery, homosexuality and sexual adventures outside marriage can only lead to destruction, degradation, disgust and disillusionment. Such sexual information does nothing to prevent venereal disease; the only certain protection against venereal disease is faithfulness to sex in marriage.

Many attempts to break the taboos in sex education have shown an appalling lack of common sense. An educational book for children was illustrated with photos of masturbation, several positions of intercourse, homosexuality and childbirth. 'Growing Up,' an educational sex film, included a sequence showing a couple having intercourse. BBC produced a film entitled 'Where Do Babies Come From?' for use in sex education programmes for junior classes, that is, children aged eight and nine. The film showed naked male and female bodies and the birth of a baby but did not depict sexual intercourse although the act was explained. Male and female genital organs were represented as well as a cutaway illustration of the foetus in the womb of the mother.

BBC says the children's reaction to the film was absorbing interest without becoming self-conscious or embarrassed, much less prurient. But the programme may arouse the children's curiosity to the point where they may well experiment. Curiosity is there and it will be satisfied anyway, but badly, so that 'objective' information may have some value. The London *Daily Mail* asked 36 children age 8 - 9 where they thought babies came from. Twenty-four knew: your mummy's tummy. Most of the rest credited the Almighty.

Sex education in family and school often stops at an explanation of the sex organs and moral exhortations. Some educators add concrete information on birth control. Japanese gynaecologists criticise sex education at school as too timid and following the advice 'to let sleeping dogs lie.' The Ministry of Education's opinion was that in view of divergent customs and individual differences, uniform instruction on birth control could have bad effects.

A revision of the guidelines for senior high school textbooks in 1973 providing that health and physical education manuals should include an explanation of the functions of the sex organs drew sharp criticism from parents.

Who Should Teach What?

Just as difficult as the problem of contents and methods of sex education is the question of who should provide it. It undoubtedly is part of the parents' role in rearing children but parents often hesitate to broach this subject. Mothers talk to their daughters about menstruation but they limit their instruction to the fact that it happens about once a month, combined with the warning not to be caught unprepared and get their panties dirty. Anyhow, one talk on sex does not last a lifetime — it is not like an inoculation. If parents take up the subject, the children may think that their parents suspect them of doing something they shouldn't do. And children are reluctant to ask because they fear the parents might get the wrong message. Moreover, parents often are unsure about their own sexuality. For many adults, sex is sacred and sinful, exciting and nasty, something people speak about only when they tell dirty jokes.

Unless parents are at ease with their own sexuality, they feel uncomfortable in the role of sex instructors.

Reluctance of Parents

One of the difficulties of sex education in the family arises from the aversion of most parents to talk about sex. Parents find it awkward to mention a subject that is taboo in everyday conversation and adolescents have no chance of asking questions. A mother may feel embarrassed if she talks to her daughter about contraceptives when the girl starts dating. She does not want to give the impression that she expects her to have intercourse. And the girl may be offended if the mother actually gives her advice because her mother thinks she might do 'such a thing.' A father who wants to warn his son against premature intimacies or encounters with prostitutes will wait in vain for an occasion to have a heart-to-heart talk with his boy. Sex instruction in the family should not be given as a special lecture or sermon but interwoven with the general communication between parents and children.

Leftist pedagogues dispute the parents' qualification to provide sex education. They contend that in today's society, the family's sexual experience is limited and that the lack of scientific reflexion makes parents unfit to give sex instruction. But even if the parents were not equal to the task, it would not mean that their function would devolve automatically on the state or the school. It would require that parents should be enabled to carry out this part of their educative duties more efficiently.

Sex Instruction in West Germany

The problem of the conflict between the parental right to education and compulsory school education has been thrashed out thoroughly in West Germany where the school policy of several states inspired by leftist doctrinaires has tried to uproot traditional views on parental authority and moral norms. On the basis of the recommendations concerning sex education in school adopted by the permanent conference of the ministers of education in 1968, sex education starts in elementary school (for 6-12-year-olds) in all states of the Federal Republic.

During the first six school years, the children are to be instructed on the basic facts of human reproduction (conception, pregnancy, birth), the physical and psychic changes during puberty as well as menstruation and emissions.

Until the end of the ninth or tenth school year, instruction, while avoiding encyclopaedic treatment, shall cover conception, pregnancy and birth in man, sexual problems of adolescents (for example, mutual behaviour of the two sexes, premature sexual activity, masturbation), social and legal foundation of sex and family (such as engagement, marriage, family rights and duties of parents, rights of legitimate and illegitimate children), problems of social ethics related to human sexuality (such as birth control, promiscuity, prostitution, homosexuality), and penal provisions for the protection of youth and sex crimes (such as rape, abortion, procurement, spread of venereal disease, crimes of passion).

Role of School in Sex Education

In a decision on sex education, the Federal Constitutional Court declared in 1978 that the school's general mandate for instruction and education was not subordinate but coordinate to the right of the parents. From this, the court deduced the necessity of a compromise. In the sex education of the school, an adjustment with the parents has to be achieved in which both parties, in accordance with their respective rights, can make demands and express criticism but must also be ready for conciliation. The decision stated that the school must desist from attempts at indoctrination of the pupils aiming at advocating or repudiating a certain kind of sexual conduct. The school must respect the natural feeling of shame of the children and generally have regard for the religious and moral convictions of the parents affecting the sphere of sexuality.

Citing Art. 2, Par. 2 of the Fundamental Law, the court asserted that these provisions protected not only the sphere of sexuality but also the right of every individual to determine for himself his attitude to sexuality. He can choose himself whether, to what extent and for which purposes he will accept the influence of third parties on his attitudes. This also applies to children and adolescents who are not merely objects of parental and public education but must be treated as persons which has to become more explicit with their growing age.

The court pointed out that young people can suffer psychic damage and their development impaired by pedagogically wrong educational measures.

Although the decision set limits to sex education at school, it is erroneous on several important points. The statement that the school's general mandate for education is not subordinate to the right of the parents but of the same rank disregards the qualitative difference between the 'natural' right of the parents (Fundamental Law Art. 6, Par. 2) and school education instituted by the state. The school has no right and no business to make 'demands' upon the parents. Although cooperation between parents and school is indispensable and parents should listen with respect to the opinions of teachers on their offspring, parental education is not subject to intervention by state or school. As long as parents do not violate the law, their way of treating their children is, for better or for worse, immune from interference. A 'compromise' between parents and school is a legally unfounded and practically impossible postulate. The question of the standard on which such a compromise should be based is actually unanswerable.

The basic problem of sex education in the school is that instruction is supposed to be neutral. Schools are assumed to impart knowledge involving biological, social, juridical, cultural and ethical data — without committing teachers and pupils to a definite point of view. Sexual instruction should refrain from ethical value judgements and treat all moral norms as relative standards corresponding to certain social conditions. If this course is followed, the adolescent is thrown back to the authority of his own experience because he learns on the basis of the authority of the school and the authority of science that there are no binding guidelines. This kind of sex education is unable to provide the integration of the sphere of sex with the totality of human personality and an all-embracing image of man. There is an unbridgeable chasm between sex instruction on the basis that man is just a special species of primate 'doing what comes naturally' and sex education on the premise that man is a personal being responsible for his acts.

In actual educational practice, 'indoctrination' is a problematic issue in public schools (private schools are chosen by the parents because they provide the indoctrination favoured by them) and similar questions arise when teachers are politically oriented. Curricula and guidelines of sexual pedagogics intend the implementation of educational goals indicating and determining socially desirable conduct. These goals are not merely guarded defensively but pursued offensively. Although sex instruction may be labelled ideologically neutral, purely biological information without values and norms is practically impossible. Many concepts already include an evaluation and teachers consciously or unconsciously rely on their own systems of norms.

Respect for Children's Personality

The court demanded respect for the natural feeling of shame of the children. The concept of a natural feeling of shame is controversial. J. J. Rousseau considered shame the product of education: 'Although shame is natural to man, children do not have it by nature. It arrives only with the knowledge of evil, and how should children who do not and should not have this knowledge know its effect, the feeling of shame?'

What sex education should respect is conscience, the conscience of the children and the conscience of the parents. The formation of conscience is one of the basic tasks of all education, and especially of sex education, and parents have the right to demand that their religious and moral convictions according to which they have formed the conscience of their children be not attacked and undermined by the school. This brings back the problem of adjustment of home and school. How can an adjustment be reached in spheres in which values and norms are the essential elements? The impossibility of an adjustment makes the legitimacy of the school system doubtful. Parents have at least the right to demand that the school should not oppose their own values. Pedagogics discrediting the norms and values of parents as 'antiquated,' 'bourgeois,' and 'backward,' is obviously on a collision course with the parents' right to education. The educational models of many pedagogues consider the family merely as part of the wide social environment into which the child is to be integrated as soon as possible. Such models establish society as the dominant and determinant factor for human development and substitute a system of social standards to the norms held by the family.

Respect for the child's personality which must be a leading consideration in education recognises that even minors are not totally malleable. This respect is not merely accidental but a basic requirement of the educational process and the main reason why the educator must take the feedback into account. It also indicates why sex education can only be effective within the framework of total education. The gradual enlargement of the children's autonomy is a vital part of education, and sex education constitutes an essential aspect under which parents have to measure the expansion of freedom to be granted children when they grow older. The supervision of friendships and restraints on the children's conduct are meaningless if they have no confidence in their parents. Children must know that they can always appeal to their parents and have them consider special situations. Over-protection can lead to defiance and revolt against sexual restraints.

State of Sex Education

The actual state of sex education in the schools of various countries shows that its problems have not been solved. Because of a sharp increase in unwanted pregnancies and venereal disease, Denmark extended compulsory sex education for children aged nine to eleven. When parents complained, the European Human Rights Commission decided that this measure did not constitute an infringement of human rights. Mrs Antanina G. Khripkova, who as vice-president of the Academy of Pedagogical Sciences visited Sweden, was frightened by the sex education in Swedish schools which she found too explicit. She had been an advocate of early sex education but her trip to Sweden changed her mind. She doubted the necessity of explaining to young children what sexual incompatibility or frigidity means and objected to the co-educational sex classes conducted as if there were not two sexes in the audience. She still thought that schools had a tremendous rôle to play in shaping the sexual mentality of teenagers. But parents cannot be replaced as the prime sex educators. A teenager doesn't have to attend long and boring lectures in order to master the basics of sex. The best teacher for a boy is his father and for a girl her mother. Unfortunately, only too often, parents themselves lack the knowledge and the will to do this job.

Generally speaking, sex education seems rather cautious in Communist countries. In the Soviet Union, sex instruction met with strong resistance from party circles and government hesitation. Only the schools in the Baltic republics provided sex education, and it was only in 1981 that a pilot course became part of the curriculum of Moscow schools. The instruction is given in two courses, basic biology of sex relations and childbirth to fourteen-year-olds and the moral and psychological aspects of partnership and marriage to 15- to 16-year-olds. This course also includes warnings on the harmful effects of early sexual intercourse. In 1983, it was decided to make sex education a subject in all Soviet schools, and in order to combat the growing divorce rate, courses preparing for marriage were introduced. Experimental courses to which young people were invited offered a series of lectures on sexual techniques, contraception and emotional aspects of marriage as well as routine matters of running a household.

According to Mrs Khripkova, many young people enter into marriage completely unprepared and it is most often the wife who suffers from it. Many men simply do not know how to handle their wives in bed and one of the consequences is a high rate of frigidity.

Soviet sex education is less concerned with specific problems of sex as it is and more with sex as it should be, emphasising the formation of ethical notions and a correct moral outlook. The approach to sex in the courses is conservative. Sex education is linked to the whole system of moral education. Teenagers are urged to refrain from sex until their early 20s and their marriage. The consequences of an early sex life, they are warned, are a weakening of sexual desire, dissatisfaction, bad feelings, physical weakness and a complete breakdown of the endocrinal system. Young people become incapable of real love. Masturbation, young Russians are told, creates pressure on nerve centres which quite often leads to their untimely exhaustion.

In the German Democratic Republic, the government opposed early sex life not for moral reasons but because it was considered a threat to the willingness of youth to participate in the social policies of the party and strive for outstanding professional achievements. In recent years, however, the official attitude has changed. Surveys showed that affectionate relations had little influence on the accomplishments of adolescents. Of the young people covered by an inquiry, 42 per cent declared that love increased their joy of life; 59 per cent of the young workmen and 75 per cent of the students felt a stronger impulse to work.

The authorities in the People's Republic of China generally treated sex education with caution, but in 1980, a publication entitled 'Sex Knowledge' offered a frank discussion of sex. In an interview with an American reporter, Zheng Junshih, principal of the Nr. 1 Middle School in the city of Fuzhou stated: 'Sex education is not a matter of teaching teenagers about sex. It is a question of teaching ideals and morality.' Sex education is conducted separately for boys and girls. To the question whether the instruction covered the use of contraceptives, the principal replied: 'No, they are still young.'

Abuses

Sex instruction at the college level has led to abuses that have nothing to do with either science or education. A professor at the California State College at Long Beach ceased to give course credits for sexual activity in his 'Psychology of Sex' class after a faculty review committee objected. His course included 'homework' involving homosexual, extra-marital and group sex. Other homework options were dressing in drag for a day, or taking 'field trips' to homosexual bars or bath-houses and nudist camps. The professor's explanation of the homework options: 'The idea is not to go out and do some kinky things just to see what they are like, but to see a change in your behaviour and feelings. ...It can be a very powerful growth and learning experience.' The implicit assumption seems to be that anything goes as long as it is a new experience. No sane person will supplement the training of fire fighters by sending them out to commit arson. The professor admitted to being 'romantically involved' with students in his class and of attending parties given by his students marked by nudity and sexual activity.

The episode illustrates the complete rejection of standards and the negation of any hierarchy of values by some of today's educators. While learning can have a powerful influence on behaviour and school education cannot be restricted to instruction, the classroom should not be abused for changing the character and life-style of the students to conform to a teacher's ideosyncrasies.

Very difficult problems are posed by the sex education of the handicapped. Blind children and the blind in general are threatened by the danger that others may take advantage of their disability and the deaf may face similar risks. Particularly difficult is the situation of paraplegics. Their legs and the lower part of their bodies are completely without feeling due to spinal disease or injury, in many cases as a result of car accidents. The victims can never experience orgasm. Few males can have intercourse or father children. Women paraplegics cannot have normal sexual feeling but can bear children.

Being forever deprived of sex is deeply frustrating, especially for young people. Sex education must help the individual to understand that there are many ways of being sexual. Kissing, caressing and petting are possible. A film shown at the first international congress on 'Handicap and Sexuality' held in Paris in 1980 depicted a young wife and her paraplegic husband soaping each other in the tub. The rehabilitation programme for paraplegics at Utrecht University urges them to discover the erotic portions of their upper bodies so that their mate can express affection in different ways.

Protection

A negative but important aspect of sex education is the protection of children and adolescents against corruption. Criminal law generally prohibits and punishes sexual abuse of children and although legislation for protecting children against pornography and sexually explicit movies and video cassettes is difficult to enforce, it is part of the state's responsibility for maintaining public order.

The West German Penal Code contains detailed provisions for the protection of children and minors against immorality. It punishes sexual abuse of minors under the age of 18 who have been entrusted to the care of the abuser for education or training (this also applies to natural or adopted children) or who are employed by him (Art. 174). More severe punishment is inflicted for the sexual abuse of children under 14 years of age (Art. 176). Punishable behaviour includes not only acts committed on minors or children but also to have them perform sexual acts on the abuser, have them perform sexual acts by themselves in front of the abuser or third parties, to perform sexual acts in front of children or stimulate children sexually by showing them pornographic pictures, having them watch sexually explicit performances or listen to pornographic tapes or talk.

German law also prohibits the admission of minors to 'brutalising' performances such as wrestling in other than the Greco-Roman or the Olympic styles, wrestling of women or in mud. Employers of minors under 21 years are prohibited from inflicting corporal punishment or otherwise mistreating them or using minors for occupations endangering morality. In particular, women under 21 years cannot be employed for dancing in the nude or serving as bar hostesses. Persons who have been convicted of serious immoral crimes are prohibited from employing minors.

6

Youth Problems

Battered Child Syndrome

ONE OF THE SADDEST CHAPTERS in the story of the family is child abuse on the one hand and, on the other, the maltreatment of old parents and other old members of the family household. The extent of what is called the 'battered child syndrome' is unknown. In the United States, about 6,000 cases of child abuse are reported to the police each year but there may be as many as ten times this figure because many cases, especially in middle- and upper-class families, remain unreported. Kidnappings of children are estimated at 6,000, and 80 per cent of the children disappearing from home run away because of physical or psychic maltreatment. Every fifth girl is sexually abused before she reaches the age of 18. In the Federal Republic of Germany, cases of child abuse and child neglect referred to the police amount to about 30,000 a year, but the actual number of cases of maltreatment of children may be nearer to half a million. About 600 children are tortured to death each year. Injuries range from bruises to fractured skulls and broken limbs, and damaged organs from punches to the stomach are not infrequent.

A deteriorating social environment has been blamed for the growing problems of child abuse and child murders in Britain. Government statistics showed 86 children under the age of 16 were killed in 1984, including 54 under the age of five. The National Society for the Prevention of Cruelty to Children reached the conclusion that these figures represented a serious underestimate and that between 150 and 200 child deaths a year may involve violence. In 1984, at least 1,500 children under the age of 15, 87 per cent of them girls, were sexually abused by adults. Some of the victims were as young as two or three. One in ten adults may have been sexually abused in childhood.

Marital discord and unemployment were considered the prime underlying causes of child abuse. About 2,000 children a week see their parents separate, 1.7 million live in families that are on or below the poverty line and 400 are made wards of the state each week because of ill treatment or neglect. Drug addiction among children has tripled since 1981 and 83,000 families were homeless in 1985, 73 per cent with children.

Among the cases that made the headlines in Britain was the death of 3-year-old Leoni Keating who disappeared from a campsite where she had been left alone by her mother, a battered wife estranged from her husband. She was raped, thrown into a ditch and left to drown. Tyra Henry, 21 months old, was bitten 57 times and battered by her father who left her at a London hospital (where she died) and then went to celebrate his twentieth birthday. Three-year-old Heidi Koseda was locked in a filthy, cold room and left to starve to death by her step-father who decided to stop giving her food after she took some sweets from a cupboard.

Tina's mother had a habit of holding out lighted cigarettes for the girl to touch 'to teach her not to grab for lighted things,' the mother said. The little girl woke up with nightmares screaming 'Don't, Mummy, don't!' Her little brother, Alan, could not be in the kindergarten photograph because his face was too bruised. A few weeks later, police found his frail body on the living room floor, his blond hair red with blood, his tiny hands bruised from trying to deflect the blows from a wooden stick with which he had been pummelled by his mother and her boyfriend for four hours.

In West Germany, an unwed mother tried several times to drown her daughter and tortured her with lighted cigarettes and boiling water for six years before the police discovered the maltreatment. In Japan, a 30-year-old mother of four threw her four-month-old baby out of a fourth-floor window. The baby started to cry in the middle of the night and when it would not stop, the mother took it out of the room. When the baby continued crying, she threw it out of the window. The baby died of extensive injuries. A mother who was quarrelling with her common-law husband while changing the nappy of her three-month-old baby hurled the infant at her husband. She missed and the baby's head crashed against the wall.

In the United States, a 31-year-old woman was accused of two counts of second-degree murder. She had scalded her two children to death with hot water 'to rid their bodies of evil spirits;' they were aged 7 and 8. In Florida, a woman was convicted of having severely beaten her 8-year-old daughter in the front of the house 'in order to exorcise the evil,' as she claimed. The judge ordered the 28-year-old mother of two not to get pregnant again or to marry a man with children while she served a 10-year probation for aggravated child abuse.

In Maine, a 29-year-old woman and her live-in boyfriend accused of shoving the woman's 4-year-old daughter into an electric oven and burning her to death carried Bibles and chanted as they were led into the court room for arraignment. An almost unbelievable instance of child abuse emerged from the indictment of a couple in the 1984 death of their 4-month-old daughter. They had told police that the baby had disappeared during the night from her crib and made an emotional plea on television for their daughter's safe return. Four days later, her beaten and raped body was found about a block away from the parents' apartment, raped, as the police ascertained, by her father and beaten to death by her mother.

In a case in which the examination of the remains of three battered children by a forensic anthropologist, Dr Ellis R. Kerley, revealed the cause of their deaths, the father had thrown the infants down the stairs until they stopped crying. He then forced his common-law wife to help him bury the bodies.

A woman whose child had been born deformed with a hare-lip and cleft palate, and who was incensed by the reproach of her husband, took out her rage on the girl, constantly pulling her hair and battering her with her fists. When the mother's brother remonstrated, she replied: 'You get a child like this, then you understand what I feel.'

In Singapore, 337 complaints of child abuse were filed in 1982. Most of the abused children were between 6 and 12 years old, and many of them had been burned with cigarettes.

Child abuse is not always physical. Maltreating children includes not only hitting or kicking but also emotional abuse, verbal abuse, constant rejection or disregard, making a child feel bad or demeaning the child.

Maltreated children usually have no way of seeking help from outside. Very often, they are too small. They have no way of communicating their fears and agonies. Often, the parents of such children cut off all contact with the outside world. Sometimes, the signs of corporal maltreatment remain unnoticed. Even when children are brought to a hospital, doctors fail to see that they have been victims of abuse.

Factors Involved in Maltreatment of Children

Violence is often directed against wives as well as children, and it often happens for the same reason. Drunkenness is one of the most common causes. People who are otherwise okay become obnoxious with alcohol. Besides alcohol, drugs are a menace to children. Drugs reduce the threshold of impulse control. When an addict runs out of drugs, he becomes impatient and takes his frustrations out on children. In the United States, one out of every ten parents has a drinking problem. Apart from physical abuse, children are under considerable emotional stress and suffer pain, anger and shame. They often have to learn 'survival skills' — such as nimbleness to get out of the way of the drunken parent, to overcome adversity and to hide the problem from their friends.

Drunkenness itself is only a symptom of deeper problems. Failure in marriage, loss of a job, financial troubles, disappointment or general boredom. Women become fed up with their rôle as housewives; they feel stuck and take out their frustrations on their children. Most of the victims of parental violence are infants under the age of three. Very often, things like refusal to eat, bed-wetting, quarrels or just play with other children become the trigger for beating up children. Children are maltreated for the flimsiest of pretexts. A father may fly into a rage because he is disturbed when watching television. Mothers may have a habit of violently scolding their children at the slightest provocation. In families in which husband and wife are at odds, both may vent their spleen on the children.

Sometimes, only one of the children of a family is subjected to abuse. It may be an unattractive, spoiled, demanding or 'bad' child, but it may also be a child unwilling to bow meekly to violence. A girl, first picked up for truancy (which is often the first symptom that something is wrong) was later caught stealing. Her father told the court sanctimoniously, 'Why, I've never had any trouble with any of my other children. Her older brother is worth 50 of her.' As it turned out, the father was a drunken brute. His chief recreation was to get drunk, go home and beat up his wife and any of the children not nimble enough to get out of his way. The girl was the only one with gumption enough to stand up to the fiendish father and her behaviour grew out of defiance to him.

It has been asserted that battered children grow up to abuse their own offspring, but the empirical evidence is inconclusive. Dianne Core, however, who founded a group called Child Watch in north-east England to campaign against child abuse, said: 'The unloved grow up to be unloving — that's why we have so many people growing up to be battering parents.' Among the parents who abuse children are some who were themselves deprived of love as children. Both parents may have had unhappy childhoods; such people seem to gravitate towards each other. Parents may be psychopaths who bash everybody, their friends, their neighbours, their children, their spouse. This type of person cannot be rehabilitated and to take away the children permanently may be the only remedy. Beating may occur when a crisis reaches a climax and the will to endure snaps.

The child becomes the scapegoat if something goes wrong, if there is a sudden increase in strain in the family. Parents may see in children qualities they hate in themselves or in their spouse. In many cases, therefore, child abuse is not an occasional occurrence but children are kicked and beaten, as it were, all year round. They may be maltreated because their parents consider them a nuisance. A 12-year-old boy told the Parisian police that his mother had kept him locked in a cupboard for nearly nine years, feeding him only bread and water twice a day. He had first been chained to a bath and was incarcerated when his mother and her boyfriend moved to a new house.

Child neglect may not necessarily be intentional. Many traffic accidents happen because parents allow children to play on busy streets carrying heavy traffic or don't take the trouble to warn them about the dangers or supervise them properly. Small children especially are unable to sense danger from approaching vehicles, they act spontaneously, running after a ball rolling into a traffic lane, or dashing out of a side street on their bike into a moving vehicle.

When children are maltreated or tortured to death, the culprits almost always are their natural parents; they are seldom foster parents or other guardians.

The health of young people is threatened by a variety of situations. The infatuation with sports may occasionally make adolescents life-long cripples. Excessive training can cause a number of disorders, including concussion of the brain, dysplasia of the hip and arthrosis, muscle fibre fissures, haematomata and marasmus of the periosteum. Young girls taken every day to ballet training by their ambitious mothers who want to realise their ballerina dreams in their daughters may ruin their bodies for life.

American courts have handled numerous cases of child neglect in which children had died because their parents, mostly for religious reasons, neglected or refused medical treatment.

Anorexia

In recent years, an illness called *anorexia nervosa,* known in the film world as 'stars' disease,' has claimed many victims. Anorexia means lack of appetite and inability to eat. Cultural pressures induce women to become so weight-conscious that dieting turns into a tragic obsession. Beauty and career success are the main motives impelling girls to dieting. Not only actresses, but also fashion models and dancers continue to starve themselves even if they are already underweight. Teenage girls become panick-stricken when the onset of puberty enlarges the curvatures of their bodies. Such girls and women under 24 are the most numerous patients. An estimated 1/100 to 1/250 teenage girls suffer from anorexia nervosa. Years ago, it was a rich women's disease but in today's 'thin-is-in' society, middle-class women also severely restrict their food intake. Because the heart becomes very inefficient, death from heart problems is frequent, but malnutrition itself can cause death, and depression related to the condition can lead to suicide. Prolonged starvation inhibits sexuality and holds off menstruation in females

Scientists reported that males make up an estimated 4 to 14 per cent of anorectics. In the Massachusetts General Hospital, 26 per cent of the male anorexia patients were homosexual, compared with 4 per cent of the females. The male patients were significantly more restricted in their sexual activity, both past and current, than females.

Some time ago, the liquid protein diet was very popular in the United States but it proved to be very dangerous. Many women literally died of malnutrition, others suffered irreparable damage to their internal organs. Diet can seriously affect future child-bearing ability.

Bulimia

Another eating disorder is *bulimia,* an abnormally voracious appetite. Victims of this disorder gorge themselves on food and then violently purge themselves by forced vomiting. Estimates put the number of bulimics in the United States at 1 million to 3 million. Bulimia is much less frequent among males than among females. Between 4 and 12 per cent of the women in the ages from 16 to 35 years may suffer from this disorder. In two studies of university students, males made up 0.4 to 0.5 per cent of the bulimics. In an interview published in *Cosmopolitan* magazine, Jane Fonda revealed that she suffered from bulimia for '23 years of agony' — from the age of 12 to 35. She overcame her craving for food when she became pregnant with her second child: 'The choice was between being a good mother and wife and being a bulimic,' she said.

Eating disorders were once thought to be strictly psychiatric problems but some researchers surmise that psychological as well as biological causes may be involved in the two diseases. A study found that anorexic women had erratic levels of vasopressin, an antidiuretic hormone which influences the body's water level.

Self-Mutilation

Self-mutilation, the deliberate infliction of injury on one's own body not for purposes of fashion or health, occurs relatively seldom and usually in three categories of individuals: people with a borderline personality disorder, psychotics and retardates. Wrist-cutting seems to be the prevalent form of self-mutilation, but people also burn themselves with cigarettes, caustic chemicals or fire, and head banging, biting and skin picking may escalate into breaking one's bones. Young adults seem most prone to self-mutilation but even children may hurt themselves intentionally trying to get attention.

Sexual Molestation of Children

A difficult problem is the sexual molestation of small children, both boys and girls. A study prepared by the Child Welfare League of America reported that 958,590 children were abused in the United States in 1984 and that one out of every seven of the cases involved sexual abuse, up from one out of ten cases in 1983. Usually the abuser is someone the victim knows and trusts — a teacher, doctor, priest, baby-sitter or the parents themselves. According to a study by Dr Gene G. Abel, director of the Sexual Behaviour Clinic at the New York State Psychiatric Institute, each of 238 child molestors was responsible for abusing an average of 68.3 young victims, more than three times the number of adult women assaulted by each rapist.

The recent trial of Mrs Virginia McMartin, principal of McMartin Pre-School at Manhattan Beach, California, has again revealed the extent of child molestation. Indicted on 208 counts involving 41 children were 77-year-old 'Miss Virginia,' and six of her collaborators, including her daughter, Peggy Buckley, her grandson, Raymond Buckley, and her grand-daughter, Peggy Ann Buckley. Pre-trial press reports said that as many as 125 children might have been sexually abused, that children were made to play naked games ('Naked movie star,' 'Twinckle' and 'Cowboys and Indians'), to pose for nude and obscene pictures, and made available against payment to paedophilic adults. Horrible threats secured the children's silence. Rabbits, doves and even a pony were slaughtered before their eyes and they were warned that they would meet the same fate if they talked. Raymond Buckley burned some bushes with a flame-thrower and threatened that he could incinerate every house in Manhattan Beach in the same way.

While in pre-trial hearings which dragged on for six months the children were persuaded to talk by a therapist using puppets, the trial itself showed the inadequacy of the present legal system for handling child abuse cases. Municipal judge Avira K. Bobb ruled that the children called as witnesses had to testify in the same room in which the defendants were present. The children sat on a raised chair, only a few feet from the defendants, their lawyers and the three prosecutors. In the examination of the first witness, a seven-year-old boy, the seven defense lawyers incessantly shouted objections to the boy's answers and tried to make him contradict himself under cross-examination. A total of thirteen children went into the witness chair and testified that they were raped, sodomised and forced to watch the slaughter of animals. All children have been subjected to savage interrogation by the defense so that the judge accused one lawyer of 'abusing' a nine-year-old boy. Child psychologists feared that the trial would traumatise the child witnesses.

For months, parents of the victims fought for the passage of a new state law permitting closed-circuit testimony by children. But the judge ruled that the statute did not apply to hearings already under way. Prosecutors had planned to call at least 28 more children but the parents of 16 of them said they would refuse to let their children testify under any circumstances, and when judge Bobb did not allow closed-circuit testimony, the prosecutors announced that the 28 children would not appear. Judge Bobb thereupon dismissed 64 of the charges against Mrs McMartin and two of her co-defendants for lack of evidence, and on the following day threw out 125 of the charges against four other defendants on the same ground. Doctors told Mrs Bobb that they found evidence of abuse in many of the children and parents were incensed at the conduct of the hearings.

When the case came to trial in January 1986, the District Attorney dropped all charges against five of the defendants because they could not be proven 'beyond a reasonable doubt.' The proceedings were only continued against two defendants, daughter Peggy Buckley and her son, Raymond Buckley. Parents were furious. They suspected a white-wash. The question whether the evidence was sufficient should have been left to the jury, they said.

In New York, allegations of sexual abuse at day-care centres spread like wild-fire in August 1984. Authorities charged that a total of 30 children, ages four to eight, had been abused at a centre run by the Puerto Rican Association for Community Affairs, and investigators examined complaints of abuse at six more city-funded day-care centres. Alleged cases of child abuse surfaced all over the country. A Senate panel was staggered by a paedophile's manual describing how to find young victims in playgrounds or through baby-sitting jobs.

In Miami, paedophiles used computer 'bulletin boards' to exchange information on children available for sex and find opportunities for the exploitation of children with anonymity.

New York state enacted legislation allowing children to testify about sex abuse by videotape rather than in person before a grand jury. The requirement that children's testimony must be corroborated will be dropped and New York city started regular on-site inspections of day-care centres. But the screening of workers in children's homes and day-care centres is hampered by legal obstacles.

Children can easily be persuaded to cooperate with molestors and are then too ashamed or afraid to talk about it with their parents. Molestors sometimes make a pact of secrecy with children and that silence can be the cause of intense mental suffering. Ann Burgess, a nursing specialist at Boston City Hospital, uses simple toys — dolls with genitals and yarn for pubic hair — to get the children to reenact the incident or asks them to sketch pictures to express what words cannot.

Psychologists distinguish two types of child molestors, fixated paedophiles — men with an attraction to young boys, and 'regressed offenders' — men with a normal heterosexual orientation who turn to young girls at a crisis point, such as a divorce or a professional setback. Frequently, regressed offenders will suddenly begin to molest their own children. Paedophilia is not an illness but a preference, like homosexuality; however, unlike homosexuality, the sexual activity is not consensual. In many cases, child molestors were themselves abused as children. They may have a genuine feeling of warmth but they may also threaten a child with harm to get what they want — which can be anything from fondling and mutual masturbation to anal or oral intercourse.

In a sensational act of revenge, Marianne Bachmeier, the mother of a girl who had been abducted and strangled, emptied a revolver into the murderer who was being tried in a German court room. It seems that she was enraged at a court procedure which had degenerated into a contest of psychiatric experts. The accused, a notorious impulsive child molestor, had been castrated at his own request. But when he met a woman willing to live with him, he wanted to regain his potency. With the consent of a woman judge entrusted with his supervision, he started a hormone treatment which had not only physiological but also psychological effects. His old passion for little girls revived and led to the fatal outcome. Miss Bachmeier was found guilty of manslaughter and sentenced to six years in prison.

This case points to some factors contributing to the sexual abuse of children. As a young unwed mother, Miss Bachmeier was not ready for the sacrifices of motherhood. A busy and sexually promiscuous woman, she did not give to her little daughter the care and love necessary for satisfying the child's need for affection and security. A child cannot be reared as an adjunct to the life of a mother living purely for her own elusive happiness. The lack of attachment made the child open to enticement. Moreover, the mother, breaking her promise, left the girl alone on the day she was murdered — the day she was to go to foster parents.

Children victimised in sex and pornography rings suffer symptoms of post-traumatic stress, such as recurrent and painful recollections of the events, nightmares, hyperalertness, insomnia and flashbacks. More often, the memories and dreams revolve around the fear that the offender will return and retaliate or carry out the threats made during the child's participation in the ring: 'I'll get you if you tell.'

Incest

Violence and threats of violence are often involved in incest between father and daughter which, in many cases, assumes the form of rape. In Japan, the most frequent type of incest is between brother and sister, followed by incest between mother and son. Excessive maternal infatuation may already appear in the sexual fondling of infants but a particular form of incest is related to Japan's so-called 'examination hell.' Young men studying for the entrance examination to high school or university, get restless or bored and mothers help them to relieve the strain by having sex with them. They may partly do it to offset their nagging and their admonitions to study harder.

In the United States, attempts have been made to discredit the taboo on incest. There is what might be called an incest lobby which asserts that incest seldom has anything to do with sexually perverse behaviour. 'Positive' incest, meaning consensual incest as distinguished from abusive incest, is said to constitute a legitimate form of sexuality.

A 17-year-old girl pumped nine rifle shots into her estranged father's head and back when he came for his weekly visit. She then called the police. 'I just killed my father,' she said. 'I can't stand it anymore. ...he does this to me every Monday night.' What her father did was rape and otherwise sexually abuse her. It began when she was 15. The jury didn't accept her claim of self-defense and, in one of those atrocious verdicts in rape cases, convicted her of first-degree manslaughter.

Robert Lee Moody killed his father who had raped two teenage daughters, had begun fondling his 11-year-old girl, had ripped his older son's head open with a screwdriver and had forced his wife into prostitution to help pay for a pleasure boat.

Shame and fear may be the main motives for keeping children who are the victims of incest from divulging their situation. In California, a 12-year-old girl refused to take the oath as a witness against her step-father who was being tried on charges that he had sexually molested her. She was found in contempt of court and spent a week in solitary confinement but said she did not want to 'further destroy the family.'

Abandoned Children

The increase in broken homes and out-of-wedlock births may be some of the factors contributing to the growing number of children living in public or private institutions. In pre-war times, poverty was the reason in about 80 per cent of the cases of abandonment of children in Japan; it now accounts for about 20 per cent while in 35 per cent of the cases, children are abandoned because they are considered a nuisance. In many cases of abandoned babies, spouses have run away from home, or the child was the outcome of an extra-marital affair. Before the war, children who were abandoned wore the best clothes their parents could afford and often, a letter was pinned to the child expressing the hope that the child would find a good foster home.

According to the Ministry of Health and Welfare, Japan had 538 institutions for children not living with families. As of July 1985, 30,245 children were cared for in those institutions, well below their capacity of 35,109 places. In addition, about 3,500 children lived with foster parents, but in about 10 per cent of the cases, the children were only temporarily entrusted to foster homes and usually for a few months. The situation in Japan is different from conditions in most western countries where between 80 to 90 per cent of unwanted children are placed in foster homes and only 10 to 20 per cent live in institutions. The reluctance of the Japanese to become foster parents has been ascribed to their fear of getting involved in something unknown, the same attitude which accounts for the low rate of adoptions and the screening of possible marriage partners. An unwanted child's history may be unverifiable — you don't know what you get.

Infanticide

After the war, many newborn babies were stuffed into dustbins, left in paper bags in coin lockers or thrown into public toilets. A newly-wed girl left a newborn baby (the second child of her lover, a university student) in the hotel room in which she had spent the wedding night with her new husband (not her lover) before departing on a honeymoon trip to Hawaii. About 200 cases of infanticide are reported each year in Japan, and unwed mothers are responsible for about 45 per cent of these cases.

A completely different form in which children meet with violent death is the so-called family suicide. This sometimes involves the entire family. The parents may murder their children and then commit suicide but the entire family may also perish together by setting fire to the house, gassing or driving a car into the sea. Seven children were killed in three separate murder-suicides on a single Sunday in February 1983. Economic difficulties are often the reason but it may also be the result of illness or the break-up of the family. A love triangle involving either husband or wife may be brought to a violent end by murder and suicide or planned suicide of everybody involved. Sometimes, a mother abandoned or betrayed by her husband may commit suicide and 'take her children along.' Many mothers who abandon or kill their children live in desperate circumstances. They may be unable to take care of themselves and nobody shows concern about their problems. They may have lovers but nobody who really loves them.

Missing Children

About a million-and-a-half children ranging in age from babies to teenagers are missing in the United States. About a million are runaways from parental authority or 'throwaways' rejected by their parents. Thousands have been kidnapped by divorced parents disputing child custody. Between 4,000 and 20,000 have been snatched by childless psychotics seeking parenthood or by baby black marketeers, paedophiles or pornographers. Under the Missing Children's Act of 1982, the Federal Bureau of Investigation cooperates in the search for lost children. Many are found mutilated, raped or strangled but others just vanish without a trace. In a California case, children testified that two girls of seven or eight and a boy of six were beaten to death for a 'snuff' movie featuring murder as sexual entertainment.

But a recent study asserted that the number of missing children had been greatly exaggerated and that, in 1985, there were only 67 actual cases of kidnapping of children in the United States. Most children who disappeared, the study said, were runaways, and many children living with one of divorced parents were reported as missing by the other.

Child Labour

A special form of child abuse is illegal child labour. Worldwide, about 200 million children are under the age of 15. The International Labour Organisation estimates that 75 million children between the ages of 8 and 15 work in the labour forces of the developing countries. The worldwide figure is much higher. About 21 per cent of all children between 10 and 15 work at least part-time. Despite international conventions and, in many countries, national laws banning child labour, children often work under extremely hazardous conditions, handling toxic chemicals, inhaling noxious fumes and carrying excessive weights. Many children are confined to illegal sweatshops or work long hours at low wages.

In its latest report, the Anti-Slavery Society stated that some 300,000 children in West Germany, 250,000 in Britain and 500,000 in Italy were working under-age for what amounted to slave wages and countless higher number of minors were enslaved in India. In many countries, abuse of children overlapped with the sex trade. The children were traded by professional organisers who supplied factories, brothels and massage parlours. Children were traded in Thailand, South Korea, Sri Lanka, the Philippines, Peru, Brazil, Senegal, Togo, Zambia and Portugal. Most children work because they must work. In many developing countries, the family can only survive if the children contribute to the family's upkeep. The physical as well as the spiritual well-being of these overworked, underfed and underpaid children is sacrificed for the survival of their families. In India, the money earned by children accounts for 23 per cent of the family income. The saddest part of the situation is that these children are sold into virtual slavery by their own parents. This happens not only in developing countries but also in Europe where Italy has the highest number of child workers. In some places, there exists a mafia-style control over clandestine employment. Children are too scared to give the name of their employers or the people who force them to work. In the West German state of Bavaria, a recent investigation uncovered 344,000 cases of violation of child labour laws.

In China, the kidnapping and sale of women and children was common before the Communist revolution and was practised to procure extra household help. It has reappeared in some provinces and occasionally, government officials and security agents are part of the racket. The price of a woman is about $250. In March 1983, 53 racketeers were arrested in Sichuan province who had sold kidnapped women for an average of $230 plus grain ration coupons. Two-thirds of the women were minors and 10 per cent were married. Little girls under 10 are brutally injured by itinerant acrobats who use them in street performances. Many children forced to work have their health ruined for life.

Child Prostitution

An ominous threat to child welfare is the increase in child prostitution. Runaways from home frequently become reluctant victims to prostitution, but sometimes girls living at home engage in prostitution and hide it from their parents. Child prostitution has become a problem throughout South America, Asia and Africa, and has appeared in Australia. In the Brazilian city of Belém, more than 15,000 young girls ply the streets, and child prostitution is rampant in Bangkok and Manila. In Manila, child prostitutes between the ages of 7 and 16 number about 20,000, and child prostitution has spread outside Manila to 13 areas, mostly cities and tourist destinations. A child prostitute in Manila earns from 100 to 600 pesos ($5 to $33) daily, but in the countryside, the rates drop to as low as 20 pesos ($1) a day. Children are sometimes sold into white slavery by their parents because of extreme poverty. In Pagsanjan, a resort town near Manila, at least 3,000 boys cater to foreign clients and a flourishing trade in young male prostitutes has developed also in other Philippine cities.

Col Patrick Montgomery, a former official of the Anti-Slavery Society, charged that foreign diplomats in London, Washington, New York and Geneva were keeping slaves and that slave girls were lent to male friends for sex. The colonel added that the police could not act because of diplomatic immunity. In Mauretania, there are about 100,000 slaves and 300,000 half-slaves. Women used for work in- and outside the house and as concubines are sold for about $3,000. Their children automatically belong to the owner and can be sold or given away.

Street Children

In addition to the millions of children working as virtual slaves, children are living by their wits as thieves, beggars, street-vendors or prostitutes in many of the world's large cities. According to the Anti-Slavery Society, street children do not show up in the labour statistics but are a 'staggering number' — estimated at 40 million in the cities of Latin America alone. Children left behind by parents migrating to industrial countries swell the ranks of the world's 'surplus' children. Impoverished rural families move to the large cities in search of work but usually their hopes fail to materialise. The father abandons his family and the mother may do the same or send the children to earn money on the streets. In Colombia, 30 per cent of all children have no known father, and in 1982, welfare institutions sheltered 32,000 abandoned children. For many abandoned children, the street gang becomes a family substitute and a protection against the outside world.

A study compiled by the Brazilian association of juvenile court judges and published in 1984 related that the number of 'street children'

— youths who make their living primarily on the streets — in Brazil had risen by over 90 per cent in three years to more than 30 million. About 25 per cent of these children had been abandoned by their parents and others turned to the streets to supplement a family income of less than $80 a month.

Children are the main victims of hunger, the lack of sanitation and medical care and the general poverty in many developing countries, particularly in the slums of the large cities. In addition to the physical misery, the lack of education and the impossiblity of obtaining any form of occupational training perpetuates the situation of hopeless destitution.

A modern form of child abuse is the large-scale displacement of children connected with political developments. Thousands of children have been brought to Communist countries for indoctrination. In recent years, large numbers of African children have been taken to Cuba, and the German Democratic Republic has built special schools for children from Angola, Ethiopia, Mozambique and Namibia. Thousands of young Ethiopians have been taken to the Soviet Union for 'training.'

In Japan, protective measures for minors are enforced under the Child Welfare Law and prefectural ordinances. They forbid the use of minors for certain kinds of occupations, for begging or some kinds of performances. The sale of alcohol, tobacco, and so forth to minors is prohibited. Violations of the child welfare legislation have been rising in recent years and amounted to 21,560 (including 15,167 girls) in 1984. Violations involving students numbered 9,944 (girls 7,195), those involving minors at work 4,766 (girls 2,735) and minors without work 6,819 (girls 5,216). Violations leading to prostitution or drug abuse are very numerous.

Child Suicide

A difficult problem is the suicide of minors. Child suicides seem to have increased almost everywhere in the world. Although their number is higher than in the past, child suicides decreased in Japan in the last two years. They accounted for 2.3 per cent of all suicides in 1984 (572 out of 24,596) and for 2.4 per cent in 1985 (557 out of 23,589). Of the minors who took their own lives in 1985, 388 were male and 169 female. By age, three boys were under ten, 57 between 10 and 14 (suicide rate, that is the number of suicides per 100,000 of the age class, 1.1), and 328 between 15 and 19 (suicide rate 7.1). Of the girls, 23 were between 10 and 14 (suicide rate 0.47), and 146 between 15 and 19 (suicide rate 3.3). The suicide rate of males, therefore, was double that of females, and this proportion obtained also in the overall suicide rates (1985: males 26.3; females 13.0). Suicides of junior high school students (192) were more numerous than those of senior high school students (159); suicides of college students numbered 262 (they include young men and women over 19). School problems were the apparent motive in 136 of the suicides of minors (boys 102, girls 34), nervous breakdown, alcoholism or other mental illness in 110 cases (boys 74, girls 36), sex relations in 63 cases (boys 38, girls 25), domestic problems in 68 cases (boys 47, girls 21), and despondency over illness in 56 cases (boys 32, girls 24). Failure in the entrance examination, despair of passing the examination, poor marks and scolding by teachers or parents for laziness or bad behaviour were some of the things that seemingly led to suicide. Below are a few cases.

A boy of 8 years hanged himself because he had been scolded by his father, and a girl of 12 did the same because she did not succeed in writing a good essay on the school's sports day. A 14-year-old girl in the second year of junior high school who had always been first in her class hanged herself because she slipped from first to second place in a mid-term exam. An 18-year-old youth electrocuted himself because he was afraid he would fail in the public university entrance examination since he had been unsuccessful in entrance examinations before. Illness, family troubles or a general feeling of malaise may be reasons for suicide. As a girl in the first year of high school wrote in a suicide note addressed to her mother: 'I am sorry. I am fed up with the world.' Three girls in the third year of junior high school jumped to their death from the top of a high-rise apartment building. The three had been friends since early childhood and there was no apparent motive for the suicide. Problems of sex relations may play a role in the suicide of adolescents but there are relatively few lovers' suicides. Recently, a 14-year-old girl threw herself in front of an oncoming train because her teacher had warned her not to associate with bad friends.

In 1985, nine cases of school bullying led to the suicide of the victims. In the beginning of February 1986, Hirofumi Shikagawa, 13, a second-year student at a Tokyo junior high school, went to Morioka (about 600 km north of Tokyo) to see his grandmother whom he had often visited in the past. When she was not home, he went back to the station and hanged himself from a hook in a toilet in a department store. He left a suicide note, scribbled on a piece of paper torn from a shopping bag, blaming two classmates for bullying him. 'I do not want to die,' he wrote, 'but it's like living in hell going on like this.' He asked the two boys to stop bullying others. The two had made him their errand boy. They were the leaders of a gang of six who made fun of Hirofumi, painted his face with markers and made him dance in the school hallway. The bullying had been going on for over eight months. The boy had pleaded with his teacher to help him; his father had twice called on the school principal and his mother had complained to the police but nobody did anything about it. Maybe the parents should have taken the matter into their own hands, confronted the torturers and punished them themselves. If teachers and parents had acted more forcefully, some of the suicides of the victims of bullying might have been prevented.

Imitation plays an important rôle in juvenile suicides. In the wake of the suicide of an 18-year-old popular singer, Yukiko Okada, who jumped to her death from a high-rise building on 8 April, 1986, a total of 25 teenagers took their own lives in the following two weeks. Over half of these suicides patterned their fatal step after Miss Okada and leaped from buildings, and many left notes stating that they were following their idol in death. Most were girls, but a boy who was a fan of the singer unsuccessfully tried to gas himself, another boy doused himself with petrol and set himself on fire, and a third-year high school student was found dead inside a parked car filled with carbon monoxide.

It is important to distinguish between the occasion of the suicide and its cause. Many suicides are preceded by a long period of incubation and sometimes attempted suicide. The younger the child, the less the realisation of the consequences of the action. In many cases, young children do not really intend to die. Frequently, suicide is committed as a cry for help rather than with a clear desire to end one's life. Children may not regard death as permanent because they have seen actors die in films or on television and later appear again. In their imagination, children see their parents standing sorrowful beside their body. Then, they will finally regret what they have done wrong and everything will be better. The suicide attempt is a desperate entreaty which says that the child or adolescent is unwilling to go on living in the same way. There have been distress signals before, ranging from increased passivity over greater aggressiveness to depression. But parents, taken up by their own troubles, ignored them.

Generally speaking, suicide is not a sign of courage but a manifestation of fear, and sometimes, a suicide attempt is an act of revenge. Suicide may be linked to masochism: the individual wipes himself out and becomes a zero. Many factors may be involved in the process leading to suicide: character, education, family, friends, occupation, financial conditions, chances for the future, home, moods, occasions for play or recreation and, particularly in the West, religious convictions, faith or the lack of it, discontent with oneself and the entire world. It may be impossible to make just one factor responsible for the suicide and a relatively trivial event may become the straw that breaks the camel's back.

It may be that during adolescence or soon thereafter, young people 'discover' death. They suddenly realise with extraordinary clarity that life does not last forever. This experience of man's mortality may upset the youthful mind and cause such an overwhelming feeling of futility that the impulse to escape the burden of life which seems a baffling riddle carries them away.

In Japan, the general attitude towards suicide may encourage young people to take the fatal last step. In the West, the tradition that suicide is a sin and its reprobation as cowardice and flight from the problems of life represents a certain deterrence. But in Japan, suicide retains an aura of romanticism and respectability (as in the case of the 47 *rōnin*, General Nogi, Yukio Mishima) and is considered an acceptable way out of a hopeless situation.

Children may have problems they cannot solve by themselves but they have nobody to ask. They have not learned to confide in others when they encounter difficulties beyond the commonplace questions of daily life. Children cannot be expected to discover by themselves how to speak about their inner life, their thoughts and feelings, moods and desires, sorrows and fears, hopes and disappointments. How to establish a functioning way of parent-child communication is the basic problem. Many children, if they could express their loneliness, would cry *Hominem non habeo* (Jo 5,7).

A German psychiatrist, Erwin Ringel, deduced from his study of suicides what he called a 'pre-suicidal syndrome.' It comprises the following indications: 1. Coarctation of the psychic sphere of life, isolation and stagnation of psychic potentialities. 2. Obstruction of aggression. Aggressiveness which cannot be deflected to the outside is directed towards one's own person. 3. Desire of death and suicidal fantasies which initially are actively sought and later become compulsive. Canadian researchers have reported a connection between suicide and hypoglycemia (low blood sugar).

Sometimes, children do not go so far as killing themselves but they flip out by getting sick. Self-destructive tendencies appear among elementary school children in the form of running in front of cars or faking suicide attempts by jumping from bridges. Pupils injure themselves when they get angry, bang their heads against the wall or stab themselves with pencils. In the United States, the Rhode Island Supreme Court upheld a lower court's dismissal of a $10 million lawsuit by a couple who claimed damages because their 13-year-old son hanged himself while trying to duplicate a stunt he had seen on Johnny Carson's 'Tonight' show.

Because of the infatuation of Japanese educators with behaviourism, each child suicide brings a barrage of editorial comment in the media blaming society in general and parents or teachers in particular for the fatality. There never is the slightest indication that, after all, the dead child's free will was involved.

For the same reason, there have been some silly court decisions, holding teachers or the educational authorities responsible for the suicide of pupils and, in an absurd disregard of the causal nexus, awarding damages to parents.

Alienation to which has been attributed a wide range of individual and social disorders, has been blamed for suicide. Freud's Oedipal conflict, the boy's subconscious hostility towards his father whom he senses to be a rival for his mother's affections (or the analogous conflict in girls) involves alienation, and in today's society, adolescents are further alienated by the frustrations and disillusionments arising from the injustices of the social order and the irrationalities of the educational system.

In modern society, man is registered as soon as he comes into this world and his name or number is carried in the files or computer memories of innumerable offices, agencies, companies, associations or unions. But human beings get lost despite this registration and accumulation of personal data which, even in the optimum case, can only bring tutelage, safe-keeping and management of the external man. The security of the welfare state which has become a hammock accommodates only man's material being but does not and cannot care for his soul. The immense administrative apparatus of modern society leaves man lonely and desolate.

John Gray, appeals director of Britain's National Children's Home, blamed the breakdown of the family for the increase in child abuse. 'The love has gone out of parenthood in many, many cases,' he said. 'And that's why it's coming to a head, ... , with the awful deaths, the muggings and the neglect. It all goes back to the home. If we don't give children love, a bit of affection and cuddling, we're not going to have a society tomorrow.'

Traffic Accidents

A considerable number of children become victims of traffic accidents. In 1984, deaths of children under 6 years of age (287) accounted for 11.1 per cent of all traffic deaths of pedestrians in Japan (2,576), and injuries to children under 6 (22,874) 27.1 per cent of all traffic injuries suffered by pedestrians (84,384). Injuries of children betwen the ages of 7 and 12 (14,687) made up 17.4 per cent of the traffic injuries of pedestrians. Many traffic deaths involved riders of bicycles and motor-cycles (2,322 out of 9,262, 25.1 per cent of all traffic deaths). Minors between the ages of 16 and 19 were particularly numerous among the cycle fatalities (bicycles 634, motor-cycles 202).

Juvenile Delinquency

While children have been the victims of violence, children have increasingly employed violence against others, particularly in home and school. There has been a sharp increase in juvenile crimes in almost all industrial countries. In Japan, juvenile delinquency reached peaks in 1951 and 1957 and again in 1983 when minors between the ages of 14 and 19 arrested because of criminal offences numbered 196,783, accounting for 44.9 per cent of all arrests of criminal offenders (438,705). The number of criminal arrests of juveniles which had increased continuously since

1977 declined in 1984 when it came to 192,665, 43.1 per cent of all criminal arrests (446,617). In addition, 55,878 juveniles under the age of 14 were taken into custody, bringing the ratio of juvenile arrests to all criminal arrests to 55.6 per cent. Minors arrested for the violation of special laws (that is laws other than the Criminal Code) numbered 38,414 (14-19: 37,543; under 14: 871). By age groups, the 14-year-olds were most numerous (52,132, 21.1 per cent), 15-year-olds numbered 51,319 (20.6 per cent), and 16-year-olds 41,058 (16.5 per cent). The largest number of arrests were for theft (190,420). The incidence of shoplifting decreased by 18.5 per cent from the previous year (1983: 81,358 cases, 1984: 66,268 cases), probably because of tighter security at department stores and supermarkets, but thefts of motor-cycles (41,504) and bicycles (30,167) were up. Arrests of minors for felonies numbered 1,905 (murder 76, robbery 690, arson 383, rape 757). Of the minors arrested for rape, 51 were 14 years old, 67 were aged 15, 134 were aged 16, 144 were aged 17 years, 193 were aged 18, and 134 were aged 19. For violent crimes, 27,140 minors were arrested (assault 6,450, infliction of bodily harm 11,594, intimidation 8,192). Of the minors arrested for criminal offenses, 118,745 (47.8 per cent) were junior high school students, 60,964 (24.5 per cent) senior high school students, 23,132 were unemployed, 22,994 were working and 14,012 were primary school pupils. Most of the juvenile offenders came from middle-class families (1982: 87 per cent of the total); only 11 per cent were from poor families and 1 per cent each from the two extremes, upper class and very poor.

A significant phenomenon in Japan has been the sharp increase in crimes committed by children in the lower age groups. About 30 years ago, the average age of minors picked up by the police for misconduct was about 18 to 19; the average sank from 16 to 17 at the beginning of the seventies and the 14- to 15-year-olds now account for the largest proportion of juvenile offenders.

The Japanese police use the term 'juvenile delinquency' for behaviour of minors violating police ordinances and otherwise socially reprehensible conduct. In 1984, 1,512,777 minors were picked up on this count. The most numerous cases of misconduct involved smoking (622,050), then late-night loitering (407,386), violence (120,049), association with criminals (85,472), drinking (41,612) and truancy (40,896).

Minors committed 1,912,614 traffic violations and thereby caused 52,712 deaths or injuries.

A glimpse into the mentality of problem children can be obtained from the following essay which a 12-year-old wrote when the class was told to write what they wanted to do before dying: 'I want to break all the window-panes in the school. When the teacher tells me to stop, I will tell him it is fun to break the glass. Then I will go to a bank and rob it. I will burn all the money I stole. I want to cut open a human body with a kitchen knife. I want to set fire to a house. I want to run over about 300 people with a car. If I could do all these things, I would have no regret before dying.'

The lack of moral restraints and the unmitigated selfishness of some young people is exemplified by the dastardly murder of five people by a college student. Two of his victims were the owner of the house in which he had rented a room and his daughter, the other three a mother and her two children living next door. The two families had been getting on his nerves, he said, because they made too much noise; so he bought a kitchen knife and stabbed them to death.

Two 14-year-old girls who had been scolded for planning to escape from a Nagoya juvenile welfare centre strangled a woman social worker sleeping in their room to get the key to the outside entrance. One of the girls had been placed in the facility after running away from home, the other had been taken into police custody for sex-related delinquency.

A 16-year-old high school student who was stopped by a policeman when riding a stolen motor-cycle without lights after midnight pulled out a knife and stabbed the policeman to death. He was afraid that his theft would be discovered.

In Yokohama, a gang of junior high school students, bored with playing video games, assaulted elderly vagrants sleeping in parks 'for the fun of seeing them run.' They beat and kicked three of the vagrants to death.

Another aspect of the mentality of minors is illustrated by the conduct of a 13-year-old junior high school student who stole a passbook from a parked car, withdrew ¥16 million from a bank and went on a month-long spree, spending money in hotels, night clubs and massage parlours. He had only ¥200,000 left when he was arrested. The boy, the second of three sons of a separated couple, had previously been arrested for juvenile delinquency and had committed a total of 162 violations of the law.

Youngsters may do strange things. A 13-year-old boy who had found five syringes in a rubbish bin of a local clinic two years ago, injected water into the arms of four younger boys. One of the victims was given injections on four, another in ten different places on both arms. Asked why he had done it, the culprit said: 'Injections are the thing I hate most. It was fun to see children crying after they were given the injections.'

A junior high school boy sneaked into a house through a bathroom window, tied the hands and legs of a ten-year-old girl with a rope, covered her mouth with masking tape and carried her to an empty house in the neighbourhood. He left a note in the girl's home demanding a ransom of ¥2 million and threatened to kill the girl unless the money was paid. The girl managed to escape unharmed three hours after being kidnapped. The boy told the police that he wanted to buy a sweater and got the kidnapping idea from an old newspaper.

Peer pressure or peer rivalry is an important factor in juvenile delinquency. Many young people just 'go along' when their friend or friends do something wrong; they do not want to lose their friend, try to show off or prove that they are not chicken. As a rule, delinquent boys and girls have fewer friends than 'well-behaved' youths. In their choice of friends, boys with problems prefer youths who smoke and like sports, cars and motor-cycles. They associate with types who wear flashy clothes and like to go out at night. Girls want friends who like shopping and with whom they can talk about human life and their problems. Well-behaved girls choose friends who like reading or sports; delinquent girls look for friends who smoke, wear gaudy clothes and go out at night.

Runaways

The number of minors running away from home has been declining. In former days, it used to be the boy who ran away to sea or wanted to; now, it's the girls who want to leave home where they can no longer communicate with parents. In recent years, the number of girls running away from home has been higher than that of boys; in 1984, girls accounted for 54.3 per cent of the runaways, 27,701 out of 51,033. The largest number of the absconders were junior high school students (20,638, of whom 10,837 were girls), senior high school students numbered 10,174 (girls 6,387) and 2,880 were primary school pupils (girls 618). One out of eight runaways (boys one out of six) comes in conflict with the law, and one out of 18 (girls one out of 11) becomes a victim of crime. In a typical case, six members of a criminal gang pried on girls who had run away from home and were loitering in Tokyo's Kabuki-cho. They hooked about 20 girls, had sex with them and then sold them to geisha houses for about ¥1.5 million each. Young gangsters strike up acquaintances with girls in coffee shops and discotheques and lure them into the sex business.

Not only runaways, but other minors, too, become victims of crime. Of the 18,108 minors hurt by criminal action in 1981, 5,515 were boys and 12,593 girls. 6,103 were attending school, 2,400 were working and 4,074 were without any occupation. Most of the girls were victims of rape or forced prostitution.

Truancy

In Japan, the number of children who refuse to go to school has been growing from year to year. In the beginning of 1986, about 40,000 children had stayed away from school for longer than 50 days without excuse. There are some privately-managed homes that take care of recalcitrant children but in most cases, the parents, after futile attempts to have the children mend their ways by persuasion or threats, let the situation drift until the children turn over a new leaf or run away from home. Japan has no special truant officers.

Violence

Very often, delinquent youths commit crimes not because they are in need but because they are looking for excitement, want money for amusement or drugs, or are left to themselves without the slightest supervision. Juvenile delinquency is not confined to runaway children. The trend to violence, vandalism and brutality is observed everywhere. In West Germany, police recently arrested a gang of juvenile criminals whose youngest member was 7 years old. The gang had committed 572 crimes such as fraud, illegal possession of arms, arson, receipt of stolen goods, rape, extortion and infliction of bodily injury; it had committed 634 burglaries of basement shops, homes and churches and about 600 thefts, including shoplifting and thefts of automobiles, motor-cycles and bicycles. About half of all thefts in West Germany department stores are committed by juveniles who steal above all expensive sports wear. Bicycle thefts by minors are frequent and parents instigate their children to steal television and radio sets.

In some places, things have become so bad that parents escort their children home from school in order to protect them from being attacked by bands of students. In western countries, older students who have failed to be moved several times often become the leaders of criminal gangs.

In Britain, gangs of children barely in their teens mistreat old men and women. What children do, cannot be considered as youthful pranks but is violence against weakness. Two girls around 13 went about knocking on doors of working-class houses. If the knock was answered by an old lady who appeared to be living alone, the girls asked for a drink of water and followed the woman into the house. While she was getting the water, one of the girls would attack her and the other would ransack the rooms for money and valuables. An old lady who had befriended schoolchildren found herself terrorised by their demands for money and unable to keep them from smashing her furniture and defacing the walls of her rooms. In a suburb, 11-year-olds ripped up the little vegetable gardens kept by retired old men and women.

School Violence

A serious problem is violence in schools. In February 1986, the Japanese Ministry of Education released a survey which showed that from 1 April to 31 October, 1985, 155,066 incidents of bullying had occurred in public schools. What the report calls bullying, is not the same as physical violence but also includes teasing, verbal abuse, cold-shouldering and ostracism.

Of the total, 96,457 cases (62.2 per cent) took place in elementary schools, 52,891 cases (34.1 per cent) happened in junior and 5,718 cases (3.7 per cent) in senior high schools. Incidents of bullying occurred in 12,968 elementary schools (52.3 per cent of the country's 24,796 public elementary schools), 7,113 junior high schools (68.8 per cent of a total of 10,346 public junior high schools) and 1,818 senior high schools (42.5 per cent of the total of 4,273). Of the cases of misbehaviour in elementary schools, 42,287 (43.8 per cent) occurred in large cities and of those in junior high schools, 25,893 (49.0 per cent) happened in urban areas but of the cases in senior high schools, 3,791 (66.3 per cent) took place in rural districts.

In the Tokyo Metropolitan area, the total number of cases of bullying during the period mentioned above amounted to 9,272 cases. Elementary schools reported 5,390 cases (58.1 per cent of the total), junior high schools 3,612 cases (39.0 per cent) and senior high schools 270 cases (2.9 per cent). Bullying occurred in 1,731 schools, 76 per cent of all public schools in the Tokyo area, a much higher incidence rate than the national average.

In the national survey, the highest number of cases for any one level was found in the sixth grade of elementary schools (11-12 year-olds; 21,394 cases, 22.2 per cent of the cases in elementary schools), followed by the first year of junior high (38.1 per cent of the junior high cases), the fifth grade of elementary (20.2 per cent) and the second year of junior high (36.4 per cent). In the Tokyo survey, too, the sixth grade of elementary schools had the highest incidence (1,477 cases; 27.4 per cent of the elementary school total), the first year of junior high school was second (1,426 cases; 39.5 per cent of the junior high total), followed by the second year of junior high (1,279 cases; 35.4 per cent) and the fifth grade of elementary school (1,221 cases; 22.7 per cent).

In elementary schools, 52.3 per cent of the victims were boys and 47.7 per cent girls; in junior high schools, boys accounted for 56.1 per cent of the sufferers and girls for 43.9 per cent.

Complaints most often mentioned by pupils of elementary schools were teasing (30.8 per cent), shutting them out from play or conversation (29.2 per cent) and physical violence (23.1 per cent). In junior high, teasing accounted for 34.3 per cent, verbal threats for 27.4 per cent and physical violence for 24.7 per cent. In senior high schools, 30.5 per cent of the complaints alleged physical violence.

The report also dealt with corporal punishment inflicted by teachers. In the April-October period of 1985, 2,815 cases of physical punishment were reported in 2,181 schools. In 1984, school officials took disciplinary action against 120 teachers (117 of them men) for excessive corporal punishment. Of these teachers, 57 were serving in junior high schools and 76 were under the age of 35.

In 1984, incidents of physical violence in schools investigated by the police numbered 1,683 cases of which 742 involved violence against teachers. In these incidents, 914 teachers were injured, 29.1 per cent of the total number of victims. Police took 7,110 delinquents into custody. Junior high schools were most seriously affected by the violence; they accounted for 1,606 cases (732 of these cases involved 904 teachers). Of the rows at junior high schools, 1,470 were cases of bullying and 57 cases of revenge for bullying; at senior high schools, bullying accounted for 343 cases and revenge for 11.

Cases of school violence investigated by the police in 1985 amounted to 5,825, more than three times the previous year's total. In connection with these cases, 1950 juveniles were taken into custody, including 85 primary school pupils. Assault and the infliction of bodily injury accounted for 60 per cent of the 638 criminal cases while 165 cases involved extortion. Nine pupils committed suicide because of school bullying while retaliation against bullies resulted in three attempts at murder and five cases of arson.

In addition to assault and battery and the infliction of bodily harm, the violence against female teachers included rape, while extortion was prominent in the violence against fellow students. Anger at being reprimanded was the main reason for the violence against teachers; dissatisfaction with school discipline and instruction and the desire to show off were other major reasons.

Of the 531 criminal offenses committed by schoolchildren and investigated by the police in 1984, 502 cases involved bullying of children by other children (assault and battery accounted for 132 cases, other physical violence for 108 and blackmail for 98 cases) while 29 offenses were committed by children who had been bullied and sought revenge. In one such incident, two high school students hammered one of their classmates to death who had tyrannised them and threw his body into a river. In another case, a junior high school student stole into the home of his tormentor and beat him to death with a baseball bat. A 14-year-old girl was abused by classmates and when she informed the teacher of the abuse, she was beaten and sexually attacked.

Tokyo police arrested two junior high school students for torturing schoolmates. The two, leaders of a gang of over ten boys, had terrorised the school, burned the back of the hands of some boys with cigarettes, burned the arm of another with a cigarette lighter, put ointment on the burn and pounded the wound with a hair brush. Their methods of torture, written up in a list found by the police, included poking hot needles under their victims' fingernails, making them eat insects and pushing them into the school's swimming pool.

A teacher was stopped on his way home by two students at the school entrance, and when one of the boys threw an iron-mesh door mat at him, the teacher took a fruit knife out of his pocket and stabbed the aggressor. The injury was not serious but the newspapers played up the incident and, with their customary bias, blamed the teacher for using a weapon. It soon transpired that the two boys were leaders of a gang of rowdies one of whom had assaulted and injured the teacher before. Violence was endemic in the school and the school authorities were apparently unable to stop it. The teacher who had recently been transferred from another school had been a one-year-old baby in Hiroshima when the city was atom-bombed in World War II, a fact the students used for making insulting remarks. Because he was physically weak and diffident, he was a favourite target of the bullies. His fellow teachers looked helplessly on when he was badgered by the students.

In the worst incidence of this kind since 1975, a student who had been drinking beat and kicked a teacher on the face and head when he intruded into a classroom where he did not belong and was told to go to his own class. The teacher fell into a coma and died six days later without having regained consciousness.

In some schools, students have become vicious, attacking anybody who is weak, schoolmates as well as teachers. In many cases, they extort money from their victims. Students whose parents are called to the school and told of the misbehaviour of their offspring usually become even more rebellious. Violence often involves kangaroo courts and hazing, and there have been a number of cases in which the victims were beaten and kicked to death by their fellow students. High school students living in a school dormitory beat and kicked a fellow student because he was 'impertinent.' The victim fell into a coma and died.

Violence and vandalism are spreading from junior high to elementary schools. Pupils hurl scissors and food at teachers, fight with pupils from other schools with chains and sticks, gamble and charge interest on money lent to fellow students for playing video games. To pay back their debts, pupils resort to stealing, particularly shoplifting. Some of the fights on school grounds have resulted in deaths. Smoking on school grounds is rampant, some pupils drink liquor and look at pornographic magazines. Sexual misbehaviour is appearing among elementary school girls.

Violence is endemic in school sports. Among the extra-curricular activities are 'clubs' for various sports which are run almost autonomously by the students (although a teacher is usually assigned as counsellor). Fundamental in the *modus operandi* of these clubs is the relationship between upper school pupils *(sempai)* and lower school pupils *(kôhai)* in which ideally the *sempai* initiate the novices into the spirit of the school, help them to adjust to the new environment and to solve their personal problems. In practice, however, the *kôhai* are often made to serve as personal valets of the *sempai,* subjected to hazing and punished if their behaviour is considered cheeky. Training sessions have turned into sadistic abuse of the victims who are not allowed to defend themselves and disciplinary action has sometimes ended with death or permanent injuries. Some years ago, a student was brutally beaten to death because he wanted to leave the club. On the other hand, the *sempai-kôhai* relationship is often carried over into adult life and provides the basis for lasting friendships and valuable connections.

Recently, the principal of a senior high school took his own life because his school had frequently been rocked by violence. A few days before he committed suicide, he submitted a letter of resignation to the prefectural board of education in which he said he wanted to step down to take responsibility for the violent incidents at the school. In a suicide note, he wrote that he was completely exhausted and desired peaceful and permanent sleep. The principal of an elementary school hanged himself because of complaints that one of his teachers had beaten pupils. Problems at work were the second highest cause of suicides of teachers in recent years.

There is a remarkable contrast in the situation in public and private junior and senior high schools. In private schools, violence seldom and vandalism never occurs. The public schools have been savaged by three waves of violence, in 1951, 1962-1963, and 1981-1983. Three reasons explain the difference. The Japan Teachers Association has no influence in private schools so that these schools can maintain discipline and give students the marks they deserve. Then, private schools can expel students (what public schools cannot) and they have no qualms about doing so. Thirdly, in private schools, students or their parents have to pay when school property is damaged, and teachers have the guts to apprehend the culprits. In public schools, teachers are afraid to intervene when pupils vandalise furniture, furnishings or buildings and nobody cares because it is public property.

Handling of School Violence

In December 1983, the Ministry of Education informed the prefectural education boards that public schools can use punishment, including suspension from school, for 'violent' problem students. Article 26 of the School Education Law provides that the local education boards can order the parents of children of 'bad character' not to send their children to school if they hinder the education of other children. But the enforcement ordinance of the Ministry of Education stipulates that punishment such as expulsion or suspension from school should not be applied to children subject to compulsory education. The principals of public junior high and elementary schools, therefore, had to put up with the misbehaviour of troublesome students and could only give oral warnings or admonitions. Anxious to placate 'progressive' critics, the ministry explained the measure as a step to protect other students' right to learn rather than as punishment for problem pupils.

Teachers have often opposed recourse to police when things got out of hand and muttered inane phrases about the responsibility of educators when discussing measures to combat the violence. But in 20 of Japan's 47 prefectures, schools have been providing police with the names of rebellious students or their photos or both in order to cope with school violence. In four prefectures, the practice covers not only high school students but also pupils in elementary schools. As usual, 'progressive' elements have expressed concern over the violation of the students' human rights.

In a survey asking 235 principals of public junior high schools their opinions on students' misbehaviour, the responses of 173 of these educators pointed out four characteristics of their conduct: telling lies without feeling guilty, being apathetic to school work, shifting responsibility to somebody else, and lack of a guilty conscience about misconduct.

Over 30 per cent of the respondents thought that misbehaviour usually starts with trendy hairdos, such as perms, unusually long or dyed hair. (Crew-cuts were obligatory before the war and still are in some private high schools and the rule for the members of the high school baseball teams.) The escalation of misbehaviour follows a certain pattern: smoking, frequent fist fights, shoplifting, frivolous relations with the opposite sex, glue-sniffing and running away from home.

Causes of School Violence

There are wide discrepancies in the perception of the causes of school violence. The Miyagi Prefectural School Board compared report cards and found out that a higher percentage of pupils causing trouble had low marks and a smaller percentage higher marks than the average. A correlation study of their marks and IQ scores showed that nearly half of the problem students were achieving less than what they could be expected to achieve. Their marks in mathematics and social studies began to decline in third grade and those in Japanese in fifth grade. But they were better at physical education in the last four years of elementary school.

In a survey on the causes of classroom violence conducted by the Aichi Prefectural Education Centre, students in senior high school rated 'teacher favouritism' as the most important reason for misbehaviour. In the opinion of the centre, parents' scolding, lack of discipline at home, teachers' indifference to student problems, classes neglecting slow learners and bad influence from friends and the social environment are other prominent factors in school violence.

The government was worried about the growing misconduct of students but obviously did not know what to do about it. Prime Minister Nakasone blamed the failure of the family and over-indulgence for the increase in juvenile delinquency. That the family has not fulfilled its task of educating its children is true, but government policies have been an important contributing factor in the breakdown of the family. Former

Education Minister Mitsuo Setoyama held the US Occupation policies responsible because, he said, they aimed at destroying all Japanese morals, traditions and customs and prevented the pre-war Japanese morality of filial piety to be inculcated. Mr Setoyama is an ardent advocate of the revision of the Constitution and one of the many conservatives who conveniently forget the excesses and atrocities of Japanese militarism and overlook that the so-called Japanese morality and filial piety were used as vehicles for chauvinistic indoctrination.

The responsibility for the failure to fill the moral and ideological void left by the defeat lies with Japan's political leaders and opinion-makers who were unable to create a new national spirit to animate the skeleton of democratic institutions. The educational policies of the Ministry of Education formulated by bureaucrats without vision and ideals must share the blame for the spiritual emptiness of the post-war era.

In the controversy on education touched off by the growing school violence, the Ministry of Education sided with the opinion blaming the post-war educational reforms initiated by the Occupation for the disastrous situation. While the measures taken by the Occupation (recommended by missions of American educators largely composed of adherents of John Dewey) were far from perfect, the actual development of Japan's school education was shaped by two opposing forces, the Ministry of Education and the Japan Teachers Union. The ministry was mainly concerned with regaining its pre-war position and subjecting education to strict bureaucratic control. The result has been a monolithic school system with inflexible curricula based on theoretical programmes without relation to the needs and capabilities of the pupils. The Japan Teachers Union's main objective was to thwart the ministry's attempt to dominate education while shaping the schools according to their egalitarian dogma and to indoctrinate their charges with the gospel of the emancipated individual.

Violence at Home

In 1984, the police investigated 1,131 cases of violence at home involving minors. Violence was directed against the mother in 701 cases and against the father in 140 cases. In 154 cases, the destruction of household property was severe. Recalcitrance against discipline or the parents' attitude was the reason in 603 cases of violence, refusal to buy things in 180 cases, admonition for bad behaviour in 152 cases, exhortation to study in 59 cases and 101 cases were without reason. That most of the outbursts involved the mother may be due to the fact that the mother is more at home and has more to do with the education of the children, but it is also connected with the tendency of rowdies to show their strength against the weak. The father often cares little about the children's education while the mother may interfere too much, is often overprotective and sometimes infatuated with the children.

Children may develop a kind of Jekyll-and-Hyde syndrome; they may be well behaved at home and be the terror of teachers and classmates at school or *vice versa*. They are obedient, polite, never talk back and are no trouble to their parents. At school, they are rebellious, insolent, pay no attention to the teacher, quarrel and cause all kinds of mischief. There are cases in which the defiance is general and others in which it is directed against one particular teacher.

It may be that parents do not allow their children to express their negative feelings at home and children seek an outlet for their repressed emotions. But it may also be a reaction to a strictly personal incompatibility, something like an instinctive mutual antipathy, just as children may have completely different relations with each of the parents. A 16-year-old boy left school because he did not want to live with his father. His mother had left the house because of the habitual drunkenness of her husband who also had ties with gangsters. The boy thought that his mother would return and that he could live with her and his younger sister if the father were no more, so he killed his father in his sleep with a baseball bat. In a quarrel between father and son over the boy's refusal to go to school, the boy stabbed his father with a steel ruler which he had sharpened. A college student who was reprimanded by his father for using the father's cash card without permission bludgeoned his father and mother to death with a metal baseball bat. A 19-year-old youth killed his grandfather by battering his head with a hammer in a quarrel over the grandfather's inheritance.

One of the factors responsible for the violence is the small size of the families. The only child receives excessive attention while he is young and gets used to having his own way. This usually comes to an end when he enters junior high school. Parents and teachers no longer let him have everything he wants and violence becomes the means of imposing his will. A 17-year-old boy became furious with his mother when she refused to buy him some stereo equipment. He tried to strangle her from behind while wringing her body with his legs. The father came to the rescue of his wife and squeezed the son's neck hard from both sides with his fists. The son lost consciousness and died. This case illustrates the tragic nature of the discord between parents and children in which the rebellion of the children provokes repression on the part of the parents which may in turn escalate into maltreatment and murder. In Nagoya, police received an anonymous telephone call telling them that a boy was chained like a dog in front of a house. The police found a 15-year-old boy with a chain around his neck sitting on a square metre of vinyl sheeting, his head and feet covered with a blanket and jumper. One end of the chain was fastened to an iron pole in the garden, the other to the fence so that the boy could not move. It appeared that the boy had a habit of running away from home. He had done so again a few days ago and had stayed away for two days. He was caught by the police stealing a motor-cycle and the father had gone to the police to pick him up. When he showed no sign of remorse, the father chained him outside the house and kept him there for 39 hours without food or drink, telling him every two hours he would be freed and fed if he would apologise. This took place in February when it is rather cold.

The incident is typical for the failure of parental education. Until the second year of junior high, the boy had been exemplary at home and at school. When he suddenly changed, the father tried to treat his rebellion with repression. But repression destroys trust, and without trust, education becomes impossible.

Among the reasons why young people run away from home is unbearable treatment on the part of the parents. A child constantly abused by a brutal, drunken father or tongue-lashed by a nagging mother may finally despair of finding a minimum of understanding and disappear. Below are some cases which show the consequences of the breakdown of the family.

A man who by hard work had succeeded in realising his dream of owning a restaurant cherished the ambition of giving his son a college education. The boy passed the entrance examination to a renowned private school and had good marks in his junior years. But in the second year of senior high, he began to skip school and his behaviour changed. He would have fits of rage and would suddenly beat his mother who always admonished him to study. His father despaired. 'If this continues, the boy will ruin the family,' he said. When the boy had again beaten his mother, the father strangled him in his sleep. It may well be that the boy felt unable to cope with the demands of an élite school and reacted violently to the excessive expectations of his parents. The mother could not overcome the loss of her son and soon afterwards took her own life.

In another case, the son's disappointed hopes caused resentment against his parents and the quarrel ended with his being killed by his father. Kenichiro wanted to go to college and entered the junior high school affiliated with a private university. But his father's business failed and the boy had to transfer to a public school. He was greatly upset by this turn of events, and in the third year of junior high, he began to play truant, refused to join in the chores the pupils had to perform and quarrelled with his classmates. His mother tried to humour him but he used physical violence against her. In the course of an altercation, the mother collapsed and had to be hospitalised. When living alone with his father, Kenichiro would sometimes become well-behaved but then his violence grew worse and in despair his father killed him.

The appearance of a new pattern of behaviour in a child should signal to parents the need to re-examine their relations with the child and the appropriateness of their own behaviour.

Disciplinary Brutality

A tale of brutality and torture emerged from the investigation into the Totsuka Junior Yacht School in Mihama. This establishment, founded by Hiroshi Totsuka, was not a boarding school in the usual sense but offered a course in yachting designed for unmanageable, mentally disturbed and autistic children. Totsuka, a yachtsman who had won a yacht race from Okinawa to San Francisco but had no educational qualifications, claimed that his two-month course cured the behavioural problems of unruly and delinquent children with a regimen of sailing and military-style discipline. But in the five years since the school opened in 1978, three students died from injuries and two students disappeared on the return voyage from a cruise to Amami Oshima, an island south of Kyushu. In June 1983, a scandal hit the headlines when Totsuka was arrested on suspicion of having beaten to death 13-year-old Makoto Ogawa. A court indicted Totsuka and two of his instructors, charging them with inflicting bodily injuries leading to death.

Parents who enrolled their children in Totsuka's school expected that the school's programme would improve their behaviour and build their character, but the methods used by Totsuka could only produce resentment and hatred. The heads of the students were shaved to the scalp, those who failed to respond quickly enough to orders received slaps, kicks or blows with wooden swords or sailboard tillers. They were thrown into the sea and their heads held under water. At dinner, the main course was served in a single dish and the students had to fight for their share. Newcomers had to sleep in cages to prevent them from escaping. In short, the violence inflicted on the students was worse than the violence it pretended to cure.

Drug Abuse

The connection of juvenile delinquency with drugs is one of the most disturbing recent developments. Teenagers held by the Japanese police in 1984 for using or possessing illegal drugs numbered 2,552 (of whom 1,010 were girls), 10.6 per cent of all arrests for the misuse of drugs. Those without work were the most numerous offenders (1,528; girls 647), followed by working minors (855, including 243 girls). Students numbered 165 (girls 120). In the eleven months from January to November 1985, the police arrested 21,788 people (of whom 3,930 were women) for the use or possession of stimulants or other illegal drugs. Teenagers held on these charges numbered 1,965, including 101 aged 14 or 15.

Students were most numerous among the minors taken into custody for sniffing paint thinner. The total number of offenders in 1984 was 46,636 (girls 9,126), of whom 17,408 were students (junior high 11,381, senior high 4,957), youths without work numbered 15,119 (girls 3,326) and working youths 14,109 (girls 1,424). Because paint thinner has become less readily available, some youths have switched to butane gas, a more dangerous substance. In the United States, typewriter correction fluids (which contain trichloral ethylene and trichloral ethane) have been inhaled by children to get a mild feeling of euphoria.

Stimulants, the young drug users claim, give them pleasant and comfortable feelings. Adolescents may first resort to drugs in order to escape the domination of their parents and the pressure of the demands of home, school and society. But the escape turns into dependency, and the unsatiable craving creates an ever growing need for money which finally leads to crime. Most boys paid for the drugs out of their earnings, most of the girls engaged in prostitution or received drugs from gangsters with whom they were living. But minors also resorted to theft and blackmail (usually of fellow students) for getting money. Of the boys, 59 per cent had no connections with gangsters but one-third of the boys and girls were involved with motor-cycle hot-rodding groups. About half of the young people using drugs came from broken homes, and 80 per cent said their parents did not know that they were taking drugs.

Students think that drugs help them study better, play music better, play football better, drive a car better, but everybody around them sees their performance deteriorating. Heroin and other drugs are more physically addictive but cocaine is the most psychologically addictive drug. A baseball player describing the impact of cocaine at the 1985 Pittsburgh drug trial testified: 'It gave me a high feeling. I felt stronger, I felt great. I felt invincible.' The thinking pattern is 'You can conquer the world.' But the feeling of total macho conceals the physiological erosion of the body and the devastation of the psyche.

Compared with western countries, Japan's drug problem appears manageable. West Germany's drug situation is one of the worst; health officials estimated that 1 million children aged 11 to 15 were regularly taking some kind of drugs. Drug addicts may number 120,000 in France, 250,000 in Italy and 40,000 in Great Britain. French police statistics showed that people under 20 constituted the largest percentage of those arrested for drug use, and some 80 per cent of the drug abusers were between 15 and 25. In 1983, deaths from drug abuse amounted to 472 in West Germany, 257 in Italy and 190 in France. Spanish police estimated that drugs were involved in 75 per cent of all crimes. In some countries, dealers are using addicted children as pushers and couriers since they cannot be prosecuted for their crimes. The Dutch Ministry of Finance has approved tax breaks for the parents of drug addicts who support their children's habits.

In the United States, drug abuse has become rampant in all strata of society and the problem seems to be most prevalent among young adults. While the use of marijuana has decreased, the number of cocaine addicts has been growing. (An estimated 20 million people had used marijuana at least once in the month preceding a 1982 survey while 4.2 million had used cocaine.) Not only has drug abuse reached epidemic proportions, drugs can be obtained everywhere, prices have dropped and new forms of drugs make drug abuse more and more dangerous. 'Designer drugs' (so called because they can be produced to meet users' tastes) started in California and spread to New York, Texas, Florida and Michigan. They are synthetic heroin, sold under names such as 'Ecstasy' and 'Eve' and far more dangerous than genuine heroin.

Cocaine which used to be very expensive has become widely available at low prices. Instead of being sniffed, it is now smoked, usually in water pipes, in a form called 'crack' or 'rock' (the conversion of sniffable cocaine crystals into a smokable 'base' is called 'freebasing'). Crack results in quick and intense intoxication which is almost instantaneously addictive. In big cities, rock houses (also known as crack houses or base houses) in the ghettos are often run by teenagers. The dealers are armed with pistols and automatic carbines and their teenage guards also carry weapons. According to a survey undertaken by the Institute of Social Research at the University of Michigan, the percentage of US high-school seniors who have tried cocaine has risen from 9 per cent in 1975 to 17.3 per cent in 1985. Of the high-school seniors who had used illicit drugs in the year preceding the survey, 49.6 per cent had used marijuana, 15.8 per cent stimulants and 13.1 per cent cocaine. Drug abuse is connected with everything from cheating and stealing to violence and sex. 'Where coke is, the girls are,' said a former young dealer. 'I had all the girls I wanted — I had all the sex I wanted.'

Typically, an adolescent's drug use proceeds in four stages. 1. Alcohol and marijuana. He learns the mood swings and chemical euphoria. 2. Quaaludes and speed. To deal with stress becomes important in addition to the mood swing. He drops out of extra-curricular activities, finds school boring and gets bad grades. Truancy increases; the youth's friends change and so does his appearance at home. His mood swings become noticeable; he leads a dual life of being one person at home and another at school. The problems associated with school and friends put increasing pressure on him. 3. Preoccupation with mood swings dominates the young drug addict who lives to get high. School and family relationships disintegrate. To support an increasingly expensive habit, he resorts to selling drugs and other illegal activities. When not high, he feels guilty and depressed and suicide comes more and more frequently into his mind. He cannot recover without treatment. 4. Burnout stage.

Adolescents between the ages of 12 and 16 are the most endangered youth group and the most prone to resort to drugs if the basic needs for which they depend on their social environment (family, friends, school, job) are not fulfilled. They crave for self-confidence, self-expression and self-fulfilment, creativeness and recognition, being accepted and being loved. They turn to alcohol or drugs to escape from difficulties in communications, disappointments, fear, anger, depression, alienation and sexual problems. The first thing parents have to do is to recognise that their child has become a drug addict and to realise that his or her attitudes and reactions are different. A drug addict experiences a special — his or her — reality and is impervious to 'reasonableness.' Parents and the other members of the family must avoid confrontation or altercation without accepting the assumptions of the addict: 'You may see it that way, but we think differently.' They should do nothing for the addict that he should do for himself, do nothing that could make life easier for him and not try to justify their conduct. The addict must experience that his drugs isolate him from his family.

Blind love is just as wrong as angry rejection. Under the influence of drugs, a young man or woman may appear more amenable or responsive than when he or she is without drugs, but if parents were to change their attitude at such a time, they would send the wrong message to the addict. They would, by showing sympathy on such occasions, reward his addiction and punish him for not taking drugs by being cool to him at other times.

Smoking Habits

A growing threat to the health of young people is smoking. A recent study of the World Health Organisation drew attention to the rise in teenage smoking which is particularly dangerous for girls. Girls are prone to health problems which do not affect boys because more and more girls use oral contraceptives. Brain and heart disorders later in life, cerebral thrombosis and haemorrhage and coronary heart disease are some of the risks.

In some countries, the percentage of adolescent girls who smoke is higher than that of boys. In Britain, a survey of the Cancer Research Campaign found that 12 per cent of the girls smoked at the age of 13 compared with 7 per cent of the boys although boys tended to experiment with cigarettes earlier. But the total number of young smokers had fallen. In 1983, 4 per cent of the boys and 2.5 per cent of the girls aged 11 and 12 said they smoked regularly; the 1975 figures were 8 per cent of the boys and 5 per cent of the girls.

In the United States in 1979, an estimated 100,000 12-year-olds were habitual cigarette smokers and more than 3.3 million teenagers now smoke regularly. At a high school in Sendai, 63 per cent of the students had smoked at one time or another, and 51 per cent smoked at least one cigarette a day. At a primary school in Niigata, 71 per cent of the boys and 6 per cent of the girls smoked once in a while.

In Italy, 55 per cent of the girls between 16 and 18 were smokers compared with 51 per cent of the boys. In Greece, the figures were 54 per cent for girls and 48 per cent for boys. Other countries were girls outsmoked boys were Belgium, the Netherlands, Denmark, Norway, Sweden, Canada, the United States and New Zealand. Teenage smoking was also on the increase in developing countries such as India, Nigeria and Ethiopia. In Uruguay, 46 per cent of both boys and girls were smokers.

Researchers blamed the increase in adolescent smoking partly on cigarette advertising which portrays smokers as sportive or seductive. Advertising is giving a very positive image of the woman smoker, showing her as feminine and sensual. Although the majority of those who engage in sports do not smoke, the ads spell out the message that a sporting life and smoking go together.

Alcoholism

Alcohol abuse by minors is also spreading and addiction may start at a very early age; 11-year-olds have been found to suffer from alcoholism. Children whose mothers have outside jobs or whose parents are divorced are particularly liable to alcohol abuse. An 11-year-old girl dependent on marijuana, speed, hash and alcohol began drinking alcohol at the age of two months when her mother put alcohol in her bottle to make her sleep.

A Japanese poll found that about 20 per cent of junior and over 50 per cent of senior high school students drank 'several times a month' and over 10 per cent of the junior and over 20 per cent of the senior high school students had some kind of alcoholic drink 'several times a week.' Apart from the frequency, 87.2 per cent of junior and 94.4 per cent of senior high school students consumed alcohol. In many cases, children had been initiated to the taste of alcoholic beverages by their parents who allowed them to sip some kind of drink on occasions such as their birthdays, the New Year holidays or Christmas. There is much peer pressure involved in drinking and young men (and increasingly also young women) who do not drink are regarded as poor sports. While 'bottoms up' for the entire party is not a Japanese custom, individuals are often made to empty their glass at a gulp when the company starts clapping and shouting *ikki, ikki* (in one breath) in unison. TV commercials associating popular movie stars and singers with alcoholic products greatly influence adolescents in their choice of drinks and in stimulating alcohol consumption.

There were about 162,500 vending machines in Japan dispensing alcoholic beverages as of the end of March 1985. Under a 'voluntary' restraint agreement (providing for a penalty of up to ¥300,000 for infringements), 134,700 shop owners belonging to the national liquor retailers organisation are supposed to switch off the machines between 11 pm and 5 am, but the ban is not strictly observed and the organisation has yet to fine any of its members for violation of the agreement.

The problem of juvenile alcoholism has become particularly serious in the Soviet Union. The average age of alcoholics was reported to have gone down five to seven years during the last decade. A third of all registered patients had been compulsive drinkers by the age of ten. In small towns in the Soviet countryside, kids of 12 or 13 could be seen sprawled in the mud clutching empty vodka bottles.

Among the factors responsible for juvenile drunkenness, two are particularly noteworthy. Children are brought up to regard drinking as a sign of manliness, and the unrelenting boredom in Soviet provincial towns with no entertainment but plentiful supplies of liquor drives teenagers to seek relief in the bottle.

In an effort to curb alcoholism, the Soviet government, in May 1985, raised the legal drinking age from 18 to 21, ordered a cut-back in vodka production, and moved the opening hour for liquor stores from 11 am to 2 pm. Members of the Communist Party can be expelled if they are found to drink too much. 'Anti-vodka' lessons have been instituted in state schools for seven-year-olds. Party chief Mikhail Gorbachev has made the campaign against alcoholism part of his drive to revive discipline. The Soviet Supreme Court announced a series of tough new penalties, above all for selling or giving alcohol to minors, home brewing, and black-marketeering in alcohol.

Punks and Hot Rodders

Violence is not the only way in which young people vent their protest against the system. On Sundays and holidays, when the streets around Harajuku leading to Tokyo's Yoyogi Park are closed to vehicular traffic, the pedestrian zone becomes the scene of a youth sub-culture which goes back to the hippies of the fifties and sixties. Behind the bushes, high school girls change into punk costumes they bring with them in paper bags and then dance to the latest rock tunes floating from portable tape recorders. Young men, also in punk outfits, show off their dance styles to the crowd of onlookers. Many young people feel frustrated and aimlessness is beginning to infect Japan's youth. While the majority still wants to climb the corporate ladder, a growing number of drop-outs has no sense of direction and aspires only to enjoy life.

A special aspect in the defiance of public order is the rôle of motor vehicles. In Japan, the young motor-cyclists in leather jackets called *kaminari-zoku* (thunder tribe) were already roaring through the streets in the 1950s. In the early 1960s, Britain had its fierce street fights between 'mods' on scooters and 'rockers' on motor-cycles. Japan's *bôsôzoku* (reckless runners) have graduated from flaunting traffic laws to unlawful assembly with weapons and gang war, to bodily injury, assault, intimidation, extortion, drug trafficking, rape, robbery, arson and murder. The extent of the challenge to the established order can be seen from the 59,585 cases of lawlessness, including 53,822 traffic law violations, committed by these gangs. Police intervened in 2,107 of their rallies, involving 101,746 youths and 43,222 vehicles (1984).

The punks and hot rodders act out the protest against the education system that produces disillusionment when high expectations cannot be fulfilled, against an employment system that condemns those not protected by the paternalism of government and big business to an inferior standard of living, and against the class system of a society that condones exploitation by the unabashed greed of politicians, bureaucrats and business tycoons. Typical of the Japanese scene is that the disreputable gangs not only imitate foreign styles in dress and behaviour but also adopted names such as 'Weathermen,' 'Black Emperor,' and 'Fascist.'

Youth Unemployment

In all advanced countries, youth unemployment constitutes an intractable problem. Born in the baby boom of the 1960s, the men and women who grew up in the economic malaise of the 1980s became a new 'lost generation.' Many are unskilled drop-outs (in Japan, drop-outs from senior high schools in the school year 1982 numbered 106,041, 2.3 per cent of the student total), many studied subjects preparing them for professions that were already overcrowded or giving them no marketable skills. In March 1983, the overall unemployment rate in the countries of the European Economic Community was 10.7 per cent, but the average was 26.4 per cent for those under 25, ranging from 14.9 per cent in West Germany to 35 per cent in the Netherlands. In the United States, the situation was particularly bleak for blacks and women. Thanks to Europe's welfare system, most of the unemployed are not hungry, but many have lost hope of ever finding a job and being able to lead a meaningful life. The social safety net does not immunise against despair or shield against the stigma of uselessness. The global recession, the death of industries such as steel and textiles, automation and the job security negotiated by the unions for their members have reduced the number of job openings while the jobless do not possess the skills for the many job openings in specialised fields.

Hackers

The computer expertise of teenagers has led to a new form of juvenile delinquency. In the United States, bright young hackers have used home computers to tap into the secret phones of the Defence Department and into computers at the Los Alamos National Laboratory, the Sloan Kettering Cancer Hospital in New York and a major bank in California. They have stolen credit card numbers and used them for charging goods and making long-distance phone calls. Groups of technology-oriented youth swap law-breaking information. In one of the computer crime cases, seven New Jersey boys ranging in age from 13 to 17 were arrested and charged with juvenile delinquency for computer theft.

Youth gangs are not limited to Japan or the advanced western countries. In Singapore, for example, school drop-outs join underworld gangs known as triads (originally Chinese secret societies) because they seek companionship, thrill and status. Most members of these gangs are thieves and petty extortionists who prey on newspaper vendors, peddlers, taxi drivers and prostitutes. In the People's Republic of China, youth problems are part of the general degeneration of the social order and self-discipline termed barbarity by the Chinese themselves. In the words of an official of the Communist Party Central Committee, 'Selfishness has become pervasive and it reflects a serious degree of alienation among the people, of estrangement of members of society from each other.' This social pathology has become a serious concern and among the initial steps taken to remedy the shortcomings were lessons in politeness for school-children. Teachers reported that some pupils did not know the words 'please' and 'thank you.'

Causes of Youth Problems

It is obviously impossible to attribute all these phenomena to a single cause and to redress the situation by a single method. There are, however, some factors that can be considered of major importance. One of them is the dissolution of the family. Children become alienated from their parents and their brothers and sisters. Parents may neglect the education and supervision of their children because they are too busy making a living. Not only in Japan but also in the West, the father may be away from morning to night. The problem can become particularly acute in families in which the mother has a job outside the family. Then, there may be parents who are incapable of taking care of their children or lack any interest in children. Sometimes, the children of super-rich parents fall into this category of deprived children who have no caring parents. They are raised by a succession of servants, disciplined inconsistently and taught to value little else but money and possessions. They are defensive, self-centred, mildly depressed, bored, shallow, uninterested in work, short on goals, values or ideals, and operating on the notion that you can buy, spend, travel or screw your way out of all frustrations.

Dr Werner Ross (Munich) thinks that much of the rebellion of today's youth is the expression of rage at not being restrained. In a permissive society, youthful aggression does not bump against the limits set by parental authority which frustrate the desire for confrontation and resistance inherent in aggressiveness.

The all-too-willing submission of young people to the leadership of their own choosing and their unquestioning sacrifices for whatever happens to be the 'cause' show their yearning for authority and guidance.

The basic problem does not lie in social or economic conditions but in the attitudes, thoughts and sentiments not only of the young generation but also of their elders. Shell's German subsidiary sponsored nine studies on youth problems. The 1981 study included post-adolescence, — the period beyond the age of 18. This period between the customary limit of adolescence and adulthood has been characterised by the intellectual and emotional tendency of this age group to remain young and to create a life-style and culture that conforms to its self-awareness and self-appreciation. However, it seems impossible to trace a profile that would be of relatively general validity. Today's youth represents too many contradictions, dissimilarities and divergent tendencies to allow broad generalisations.

Often, the thoughts, values and goals of the children develop in directions unrelated or even antagonistic to the value system of their parents so that mentally and emotionally, parents and children grow apart and the spiritual bond between them disintegrates. Adolescents may become attracted by a revolutionary ideology, the cult of power, the inebriation of terror and the illusion of domination in their attempt to smash the repressive institutions of society. The denial of the present society, the family, state and church constitutes the burden of this ideology. Young people can be won for whatever constitutes the most emotional political issue of the day: ecology, opposition to nuclear energy, armaments and nuclear war or the peace movement. Such issues lend themselves to idealisation and offer an opportunity for enthusiastic activity. Adolescents may become infatuated with the thrill of danger, the fascination of records or the excitement of risks. For a large number, the easy life devoted to pleasure and enjoyment so often depicted on TV creates unattainable dreams. The luxuries of the affluent consumer society project the hallucination of a life without effort, of hedonistic gratification, of freedom from all restraints. Post-war developments have left the illusion that everything must necessarily become bigger, better and more readily obtainable. Growth has been made the fetish not only of national economies but also of the personal fortune of every individual.

Attitudes of the Sixties

The revolutionary youth of the sixties sought the feeling of their power in the destruction of the property of others, not their own. The young people who, in May 1968, indiscriminately burned cars in the middle of Paris had providently parked their own vehicles in quiet alleys far from the mob violence. The senseless juvenile fury only creates a false self-confidence. Herostratos set fire to the temple of Diana at Ephesus in order to become famous. John W. Hinckley Jr. shot President Reagan to attract the attention of actress Jodie Forster. The young radicals who detest and attack the liberal state demand constant care and assistance in all situations from this same state and combine inane violence with utopian expectations. Fusing post-materialistic ideology with the materialistic advantages of society, they are wholly committed to the assertion that everybody is entitled to receive everything he wants.

Herbert Marcuse, the guru of the revolutionaries of the sixties, had replaced Logos by Eros as the meaning of human life and the essence of existence. His eroto-marxism which postulated gratification and fulfilment as the aim of life denounced the formally free and democratic society for having repressed man's fundamental instincts. His utopian demand for absolute freedom changed the ascetic and puritanical ardour of Marxist revolutionism into the untrammelled hedonism and wanton rage of the New Left. Marcuse dissociated himself from the extravagance of the radicals and condemned violence against individuals, but his messianic fantasies had given the student rebels of the 1960s the theoretical justification for their assault on the existing order.

The Shift to Violence

The message of happiness, love and peace which inspired the hippie movement in the 1960s and the early 1970s failed to form a new society and in the middle of the 1970s, the punk movement was spawned in the squalour of the British slums. The utopianism of the flower children was replaced by the cult of violence, destruction and hostility shouting the anger, frustration, hopelessness and defiance of the first generation that had to live with the threat of nuclear destruction. Outwardly, shaved scalps or multi-coloured hairdos, black leather jackets or dressing down in unfashionable clothes, and sporting tatoos or swastikas and the like, proclaimed the rejection of the established order. The message of punk, a youth counsellor said, is 'I don't care about me, I don't care about you, we have a hopeless society, so what's the point of going on?' The dress, the hair-styles, emblems, slogans and the defiant conduct give the satisfaction of shocking and the sense of power derived from being feared.

Psychologists have noted an abnormal increase in juvenile psychoses, particularly phobias. Many of these disorders are caused by early sexualisation and over-stimulation. Juvenile drug addiction has been explained as a reaction to the deprivation of motherly affection. Young men and women have not learned how to control and cope with their instincts, and the psychic conflicts resulting from this failure take the form of obsessions, fear and persecution complexes.

Situation in Japan

Japan's old generation still retains some of the attitudes and norms based on Confucianism, but the post-war generation is possessed by the crassest materialism which is promoted by the unashamed greediness of the ruling élite. The desire to enjoy the goods and pleasures of the affluent society creates in adolescents the need for money, and since their pocket-money is not enough to provide all the things they want, they fall into temptation to resort to illegal means. For girls, the lure of making easy money by prostitution is particularly dangerous. High-school girls have been led astray by unscrupulous people who are ready to exploit them. Such conduct is facilitated by the anonymity of the large cities but there has been organised teenage prostitution also in relatively small provincial towns. Girls who have been lured into prostitution often act as go-betweens and seduce their friends. The attempts to ensnare schoolgirls have been stimulated by the strong demand for virgins in the sex business.

Significant for everyday life in Japan is the paucity of social contacts, especially in the large cities. The family sticks to itself and does not become a bridge for socialising. Relations with neighbours are kept to a minimum. Conversation with schoolfriends is usually limited to school hours and the way to and from school. Nevertheless, to many children, school provides the only opportunity for socialising, of talking about their own affairs and of finding somebody who listens.

In 1979, the Japan Youth Research Institute undertook a comparative study of what is called 'sociality' (social-mindedness) of Japanese and American senior high school students and the basis of their social behaviour. The study distinguished four types: A: socially-minded students who are inclined towards play and amusement; B: social and diligent students who give priority to study; C: Unsociable students but intent on play and amusement; D: Unsociable and studious. The following table (percentages of students in each category) summarises the findings which indicate a lack of social attitudes in Japanese students:-

	A	B	C	D
Japanese high schools				
average	7.2	12.6	41.0	39.2
boys	6.6	10.8	39.0	43.6
girls	8.0	14.6	43.2	34.2
American high schools				
average	47.0	36.9	9.2	6.8
boys	48.1	30.5	12.8	8.5
girls	46.4	43.6	5.2	4.8

School has little attraction; instruction is often boring and largely related to memorising. While elementary school is relatively relaxed, the anticipation of examinations starts to build up pressure in junior high school and becomes dominating in senior high. Increasingly, preparation for entrance examinations overshadows the entire life and leaves no time for other interests. As mentioned above, the situation is completely reversed once a student has passed the entrance examination to a university. To enjoy life becomes the principal concern and study is reduced to the minimum required for getting passing grades. Naturally, there are wide differences in attitudes and stricter requirements depending on the kind of study (medicine, law, engineering). But pride in scholastic achievement is generally weak and the system does little to foster it.

The disappearance of Japanese politeness (which never prevailed in non-traditional settings such as public transportation) has been most complete among the young generation. Rudeness and disregard of the elementary rules of civilised behaviour are common, particularly in the metropolitan areas. It is not only a question of conduct but also of speech and literacy. One of the characteristic features of the Japanese language is the choice of words, inflection, prefixes and expressions corresponding to different situations and the variations in politeness depending on social relations. Young people seem to be ignorant of these nuances and their linguistic ability is limited to the simplest form of conversational Japanese with frequent lapses into vulgarity and crudeness. The low level of speech is parallelled by basic deficiencies in reading and above all in writing. Since comic books, the favourite reading of the young and not so young use few *kanji* (ideographs), may fail to acquire or maintain sufficient fluency in the use of Chinese characters and have to rely on *kana* (syllabic script) for reading and writing.

A recent study by Hakuhodo's Institute of Life and Living based on a poll of 1,600 18- to 20-year-olds described them as seemingly carefree, basically passive and cunning pleasure-seekers bent on self-gratification with no feelings of guilt. They possess no particular value system and despite their outward show of individualism are even more group-oriented than their elders. They borrow what others prefer, rely on fashion magazines for choosing how to dress and use how-to-do magazines for everything from preparing for examinations to love-making. They travel in packs and like to have friends along even when they date because they find it too tiring to entertain somebody on their own for an extended period of time.

Today's youth have grown up without great hardships and lack willpower, determination and resourcefulness to live up to real challenges. Although they may be clever at grasping opportunities, they have no goals except to make money and to enjoy lots of free time.

Unlike their parents, the young generation grew up in households furnished with the consumer durables considered desirable for modern living. The parental home may have been small but it provided the material comfort associated with the image of an affluent society. Since the nuclear family prevails at least in urban Japan, there is little competition for parental attention and no need to struggle for recognition. The desire to advance, the will to succeed and the pride of achievement are not prominent in the attitudes of young corporate employees who lack the sense of belonging of the old generation. To make sacrifices for the company for which they work or for 'society' is alien to their mentality. They part readily with their money when buying things they like and have little hesitation to discard things they no longer want. They are less reluctant than their elders to buy on credit and feel less concern about the future. If they save, it is more often for travel or other leisure expenditures rather than for old age or a 'rainy day.'

Attitudes of Present Generation

The likes and dislikes of West German high school students illustrate some of the attitudes of today's youth. Their positive inclinations: 36 per cent are fans of music groups, 31 per cent support the ecological movement, 23 per cent are motor-cycle fans, 18 per cent are soccer fans and 16 per cent like discos. Their antipathies: 39 per cent oppose terrorism, 33 per cent loathe nationalistic groups, 20 per cent are against nuclear power stations, 17 per cent dislike rockers, 15 per cent reject new religions, 14 per cent are at odds with the supporters of the Bundeswehr (West Germany's armed forces), and 10 per cent detest drug addicts.

A 1984 West German study found that young people wanted social security (68 per cent of 4,000 interviewees between the ages of 12 and 29) and a protected private life (62 per cent), but in addition to personal happiness, they also recognised the necessity of contributing to the good of society and 74 per cent emphasised the importance of solid occupational training. The influence of rôle models seems to be rather limited. Only 37 per cent of the 12-to-15-year-olds said that they were inspired by the example of people they wanted to emulate and the percentage dropped to 16 per cent for the 25 to 29 age group. Parents were the most important models for a quarter of the youths, friends and the media influenced about 10 per cent while teachers (6 per cent) and supervisors (4 per cent) seem to command little prestige.

The relations between parents and children become complicated when children grow up. There is a saying 'Small children, small cares, big children, big cares.' The growing generation demands greater independence but it is not in a position to stand on its own feet. Parents retain responsibility for the care and maintenance of their children while their influence on them steadily declines. If the children leave their parents after having received innumerable benefits, it is neither ingratitude nor injustice. Children owe their parents recognition and gratitude but they are not obliged to devote their lives to their parents. There is no reciprocity of duties between parents and children. St Paul already wrote: '...for the children ought not to lay up for the parents, but the parents for the children' (2 Cor 12, 14).

The maturing of the children implies a change in the attitude of the parents towards their children and of the children towards their parents. Ideally, this would mean growing confidence in the capacity of the young people to take care of their own affairs and a growing recognition of the efforts parents make to rear their children. But the most conspicuous change seems to be the increasing acuteness of the generation gap. This gap, however, is by no means the same for all generations and today, there is a marked difference in the generation clash of parents who grew up with traditional values and of parents whose attitudes were influenced by the cultural revolution of the sixties. In tradition-conscious families, parents find it difficult to grant their children more freedom. They do not want to lose their children and try to postpone as much as possible their independence. Especially if parents continued to live together only because of the children, separation would mean emptiness. But this kind of over-protection can cause rejection on the part of the children. Such parents are the target of many complaints in a Gallup Youth Survey some years ago in which teenagers took exception to the retrospective attitude of their parents. 'My parents remember their teenage years with respect to the times they lived in, and sometimes live in the past. ... They are always comparing today with when they were kids. They don't understand times are constantly changing.' — 'They are always comparing the old days to today — that things were harder then, and that we should be satisfied with what we have today.'

Children find parents with traditional attitudes overprotective, narrow-minded, overly critical and overbearing. 'They underestimate me and have a basic lack of trust in me.' 'My mother tends to treat me as if I were younger than I really am. She also tends to make decisions for me.' 'They are too grouchy, get excited too quickly.' 'They don't want to allow me to have private thoughts. They ask too many questions about my private affairs. If there is something they need to know, they should have enough faith in me that I will tell them.'

Generational Metabolism?

Konrad Lorenz considers the social conduct between the onset of puberty and the assumption of an adult rôle as phylogenetically programmed for a critical appraisal of the traditional values of the parental culture and the quest for new ideals. Even if nothing appears to change in the behaviour of adolescents, their emotional attitude towards parents, family and persons they used to respect grows cooler. While they move away from the traditional and the customary, they feel attracted by the new and the unknown, even by the things they used to fear. Probably as a result of hormonal changes, courage and aggressiveness grow. In the process of the dissociation of the young generation from the traditional rules of conduct, the love and respect formerly felt for the transmitter of the tradition becomes ambiguous and, depending on the character of the transmitter, turn into antagonism, rebellion and hatred. The adolescent finds the norms which he has been taught to observe obsolete, stupid and meaningless. Suddenly, he is ready to adopt strange customs, attitudes and patterns of behaviour. Essential for his choice is that the new traditions include ideals for which it is worth fighting. It is for this reason that adolescents join minorities which are suppressed and the victims of injustice.

Lorenz regards this phenomenon important for the evolution of mankind and submits the hypothesis that the regular temporal connection of these processes indicates a phylogenetic programme and that their contribution to the maintenance of the species and human culture consists in the removal of the obsolete and the addition of new elements of traditional behaviour which effect the continuous adjustments of culture to the constantly changing facts of the environment *(Die Rückseite des Spiegels,* S. 298).

The differentiation between generations is rather arbitrary. Actually, the propagation of mankind is continuous and a more or less uniform process. The distinction between generations is based on the changes in attitudes, value systems and living patterns resulting from the interaction with the environment, political, cultural and economic changes rather than from changes in the genetic make-up of the human beings living at a particular time. In this sense, Lorenz's theory of a phylogenetic programme seems implausible.

Intra-Family Problems of Transition

Man's long period of growth until he reaches maturity and his need for help and protection implies attachment as well as tension. Kant described the situation of the adolescent as a conflict between man in his raw natural condition and his social position. At a certain age, the natural man is already capable of procreation but in his social position he still is an adolescent or even a child. The relationship between father and son appears destined for an inevitable confrontation. Abraham in his readiness to sacrifice his son Isaac seems the archetype of the aggressive father. In his work *Totem and Taboo* (1913), Freud propounded the view that man's 'cultural' development started with the conspiracy of the sons against their aging but still tyrannical father and the ensuing parricide. Freud regarded father and son mainly as rivals but the experience of all ages puts sons in the rôles of rebels who look for more reliable guidance than the traditional norms and rules of which they, often erroneously, suspect their fathers to be the protagonists. Fathers, on the other hand, want their sons to achieve the success and social ascent which was denied to themselves, thereby aggravating the sons' defiance who do not want to be burdened with a mission for which they do not feel the slightest inclination.

The actual situation in today's family hardly fits the description of the relations between father and son prevalent in social theory. In a society in which wife and children see less and less of husband and father who returns late at night, the family usually knows very little about what father is doing. He can hardly become an example the sons can emulate and they will know little about his ideals and ambitions. Even so, the father may be influenced by his own experience when making decisions on the education and the choice of an occupation of his son.

Mothers do not want to give up their sons. They hate to see them grow into the adult world and loathe even the thought of having another woman take the son into her arms.

The Allensbach Institute of Opinion Research, however, reported that the father has again become the person children respect as authority in the German family. The institute also noted that, contrary to a widely-held belief, bad marks act on young people as a stimulus rather than a damper.

The basic problem of the relations between children who have become adults and their parents lies in the transformation of a relationship of dependency and protection into one between autonomous persons. Some adolescents are tempted to negate everything their parents stood for in order to prove that they are grown-ups. Such negativism will scarcely create an atmosphere of mutual trust and respect. While children will base their decisions on their own needs and desires, they still expect the understanding and support of their parents. To please their parents is no longer a valid motive for adults but neither should it be to offend them.

Generation Gap Among West Germany's 'Gastarbeiter'

A special case of discord between parents and children is the disagreement between the first generation of immigrants from developing countries and their children born and raised in the new country. A particularly troublesome situation exists in West Germany where the contrast between the wives of the Turkish *Gastarbeiter* who immigrated as adults and their daughters creates formidable problems. The elder women, many of whom are analphabetics, continue to live much in the same way they used to live in Turkey. They stand out by the shawl tied around their head and their long dress. They conform to the patriarchal tradition of Islam giving the husband nearly absolute control over the family. The children, who are going or went to German schools, speak fluent German which their mothers cannot understand. The girls prefer jeans and pullovers to the long garbs of their mothers. They want to live the same way German youths live, go to parties, discos and movies. They often have to do it secretly because Islamic tradition decrees a strict separation of sexes also for recreation. If there is a difference from their German counterparts, it is rejection of sexual intimacy by most Turkish girls. They want to preserve their virginity until marriage. But Islamic marriages are usually arranged by the parents who often oppose intermarriage. The clash between tradition and emancipation sometimes makes the girls sick; they have more depressions and nervous breakdowns than the German girls of the same age.

The Turkish communities have organised schools for teaching the *Qur'an* (these schools sometimes are centres of nationalistic indoctrination). Some families do not send their daughters to school — the girls have to help with the household chores, take care of their younger brothers and sisters and do the shopping — and do not allow them to go out after dark. The children are afraid that they will be sent back to Turkey if they do not obey. They often decline invitations by German friends because they might be served pork. There have been a number of cases in which Turkish girls, unable to cope with their problems, have left their homes and slipped into prostitution and drugs.

Ascendancy of Youth

Recent studies support the view that, as far as attitudes and problems are concerned, youth should be extended to include the post-adolescent years up to the age of 25. In sports, the dazzling performances of the young gymnasts from Romania and the Soviet Union won them the gold medals in the 1976 Montreal Olympics and Nadia Comaneci became the darling of the world. Youthful swimmers continued to topple world records. Single and in pairs, young men and women triumphed in figure skating and ice dancing. Youth became conspicuous also in other fields. Anatoli Karpov was hardly twenty when he captured the world chess championship. While musicians like Maurizio Pollini, Alfred Brendel and Vladimir Ashkenazy are by no means old men, their supremacy has been challenged by young pianists of whom Dimitris Sgouras was just 15. Anna-Sophie Mutter was still a child when von Karajan projected her to the pinnacle of violin virtuosity, and 14-year-old Jin Li, a pupil of Yehudi Menuhin, is having to make the transition from boy wonder to professional. Teenagers who have grown up with computers which remain a sealed book to the old generation, find this field most congenial not only for their emancipation but also as a means of making money by inventing computer games.

There often is a hiatus between the personal and social values the older generation contends or pretends to uphold and their actual behaviour which the younger generation attacks as hypocrisy. Nevertheless, despite the complaints about undue interference with their affairs, young people look to their parents for guidance and advice. They want them to take an interest in their personal problems without imposing their own views and to understand their failures without blaming them. Teenagers want to discuss sex, drugs, school and jobs without being preached to. They want information without being asked why they want it. For the decisive problems, the choice of a career and even the choice of a marriage partner, young people still want the understanding and approval of their parents. Parents remain a model in life-style and orientation, and the family is still accepted as the principal agent of education and socialisation.

The Cult of Self-Fulfilment

The 'angry' generation of the sixties protested against society, politics and the economy and exalted personal and sexual freedom. Freud had proclaimed pleasure as the purpose of life. Happiness, to the extent that it was possible at all, was only obtainable by the unrestrained emjoyment of sex. He therefore postulated man's sexual liberation and attacked religion, the inventrix of sexual taboos, as the greatest enemy of the fulfilment of sexual happiness. Culture can only be built by the restraint of instincts, but such restraints create sexual frustration.

Under the label of psychoanalysis, Freud's dogma of sexual lust as the purpose of life gained immense popularity in the United States and some European countries, especially after the Second World War. Rejecting cultural restraints and attacking the existing order under the slogan 'Make Love Not War,' the flower children of California practised free love, partner swapping and group sex. Sex and psychotropic drugs were to produce an enlargement of consciousness and transcendental life. 'Self-fulilment' was the shibboleth of a generation which — for completely unexplainable reasons — suffered from such an inferiority complex that it could bear nobody who knew more but itself knew only to reject whatever society embraced and was unable to develop attitudes that could have formed the next generation. The asocial life-style created by the 'rebels without a cause' was built on the principle 'everybody for himself and I against everybody.' The craving for a life without restraints, sex without involvement, enjoyment without duties, the pleasure of instant gratification without assuming responsibility for the consequences led to an existence filled with desire and illusion, fear and suppression, and ended in resignation, rejection and despair.

Post-War Policies and Their Problems

The basic policy of the post-war reconstruction in Europe (and less explicitly in Japan) aimed at improving the material conditions of society by economic and technological progress. This policy, however, increasingly came under attack, particularly by young people and the Greens. The stronger accent on 'post-material' values was partly responsible for the opposition to the established interests, but four lines of thought were discernible in the demands for a change of course. 1. An extreme affirmation of individual freedom rejects all restraints on self-determination — which, in its logical conclusion, leads to complete anarchy. 2. The limitations inherent in a finite world impose restrictions on a society based on material and technical expansion. The exhaustion of the world's material resources (emphasised in the Club of Rome's 'The Limits to Growth') negates the indefinite prolongation of linear expansion in the future. 3. The continuation of technical and industrial development threatens to destroy man's natural environment unless ecological considerations are given top priority and the protection of the environment is made the paramount political goal. 4. Many groups have waged a vigorous campaign against the use of nuclear energy. They condemn not only nuclear weapons, but also the so-called peaceful use of atomic energy and point out that there is no technology which can claim to be free of risks.

Because the established parties are neither willing nor able to make the improvement of the quality of life their over-riding policy goal, the advocates of the new course have often taken uncompromising ideological positions. Although the dangers from uncontrolled economic and technical development are real, the scenario of a world catastrophe can hardly serve as a rational argument. The attitude of making an albeit legitimate concern the sole and absolute objective of political action and to assert this interest by violence and terror is inadmissible in a democratic society.

While expressing concern for the ecology, many of the anti-authoritarian protesters were demolishing human society. They were opposed to the existing public order without any goal of their own, and their chief characteristic was the intransigence, irrationality and utopianism of their rejection of institutions, norms and values. They only had scorn for people who appealed to reality against their repudiation of technology and their opposition to the construction of airports and power plants (conventional and nuclear), to armaments and anti-terror legislation. At the root of their attitudes lay a frightful lack of security. This generation 'has been taught that there are problems, but not how they are solved' (Manfred Rommel, son of Field-Marshal Erwin Rommel and mayor of Stuttgart).

The worst fears come from dangers that seem unavoidable and unconquerable. Man needs the confidence that problems can be solved. There is a tendency in the media to emphasise the unusual, the sensational, the negative. The reason is simple. Journalistically, the ordinary is not interesting. Readers and viewers are captivated by the extraordinary, and the extraordinary is mostly negative: crimes, wars, revolutions. Shortcomings and breakdowns in the social order account for a disproportionally large share of the news and create the impression that society is on the brink of ruin. Nevertheless, today's situation hardly inspires confidence in society. Fear, suspicion and anxiety are much more in evidence than assurance and hopefulness: anxiety about nuclear war and the survival of mankind, anxiety about the environment, anxiety about employment. The present state of affairs makes it difficult for adolescents to look bravely to the future and difficult for adults to tell the young generation to expect more from life than disappointments and failures.

The protagonists of nihilism constitute a small although vociferous group. The vast majority of today's youth is definitely 'privatistic.' They want personal freedom and affluence, the right kind of a well-paid job, a nice home and plenty of leisure.

The lure of pleasure and affluence is particularly tempting for students studying away from home. For quite a few, to earn money by part-time jobs becomes more important than study. While boys often have to be content with menial jobs such as dishwashing, girls, especially those with good looks and pleasant manners, can make a lot of money as bar hostesses, Turkish bath attendants, or artists' models, at least in times of economic booms. Naturally, such pursuits have their 'professional' risks, including prostitution, VD, unwanted pregnancies and sometimes murder.

Alienation from the Public Order

The mentality of affluence breeds complacency, and the absorption in one's personal well-being entails a lack of interest in public affairs which, however, is occasionally turned into disgust and anger by the corruption, incompetence and impudence of politicians and officials. Almost everywhere, leaders have lost their credibility because they are not inspired by their convictions but swayed by opportunism. Parents and educators failed to present models in whom the young generation could believe and those posing as leaders in the world at large seldom are shining examples of selfless idealism.

It is hard to see how, under such conditions, the young generation can be brought back to a positive attitude towards society and the affirmation of civic responsibility. The pluralistic relativisation of the validity of all systems makes the entire tradition a museum piece. All authority is regarded as authoritarian. Youth is looking for its future in a society without fathers and the ballast of tradition. But they are dejected by a motherless society when motherliness is dissolved by emancipation.

The modern state and its organs have failed dismally in creating an image of the public order that could attract youthful enthusiasm and elicit their cooperation for solving the problems of society. The ethos of today's state does not extend beyond the economy. Despite its affluence, modern society is pauperised and shabby. Cultural achievements appeal only to snobbish cliques. It is not surprising that young people feel no sympathy for the emotionally empty public institutions and look for meaning, security and belonging elsewhere. The attractiveness of dissident movements derives from their opposition to the establishment rather than from their positive goals but the fact remains that there is a dearth of causes and organisations able to mobilise youthful enthusiasm for contributing to the renewal of society.

In the modern state, war has become the only event that can galvanise the nation into action; in peace-time, sports and amusement must cover up the emptiness of the public order. It would be unjust to blame the family or the school for the alienation of the young generation from the existing order and its infatuation with the illusions of perfect justice and eternal peace. In an attempt to save Singapore from becoming a 'nation of thieves,' the Singapore government decided to make religion a compulsory subject in schools. In the West, one of the effects of the loss of religion has been that the feeling of personal guilt has become generalised into social inadequacies and structural violence. As Senator Daniel Patrick Moynihan said: 'Society becomes guilty until proven innocent.'

There are people who think that youth problems have been over-emphasised and that youth is being given too much attention. Recently, Helmut Kohl, West Germany's chancellor, was asked, 'Do you have the impression that this kind of demonstration is a political need of youth and the population?' To which Dr Kohl replied: 'First of all, I object to the fact that for all political questions, we always have to ask, will this meet the needs of youth? Why should people aged 70 have fewer requirements than those aged 17?'

Infatuation with Esoteric Cults

One of the phenomena related to the rejection of the present society by young people has been the quest of new personal values in esoteric cults and non-traditional religions. Young men and women sat at the feet of assorted gurus, trekked to sundry Shangri-las, or joined organisations that promised something different. Prominent among the sects that attracted young people was the Holy Spirit Association for the Unification of the World Christianity founded in 1954 by the Reverend Sun Myung Moon. Parents complained that their children completely changed after they joined the sect. They gave up jobs and school, left their parents and often disappeared. Parents charged that their children were being brainwashed and forced into working for the organisation. They particularly opposed the mass weddings arranged by the sect in which the officals of the sect picked believers not even knowing each other to be married in order 'to produce sinless children.'

When children did not listen to the pleas of their parents urging them to leave the organisation, parents sometimes had them kidnapped, brought home by force and 'deprogrammed' in order to rid them of the convictions with which they had been indoctrinated under captive conditions. This procedure created the anti-cult deprogrammer whose intensive grilling of allegedly brain-washed devotees made him a kind of 'gun for hire' for restoring misled children to their families. But the American Civil Liberty Union attacked their methods as kidnapping and rights violations and recently, the US Supreme Court let stand a federal appeals court decision permitting a 'Moonie' to pursue a suit against his parents and 31 others he linked to his captivity for 35 days in efforts to get him to deny his religious beliefs.

On the other hand, a British court turned down the application of the British branch of the sect for a writ of *habeas corpus* to force the parents of a girl who, the sect claimed, was detained against her will and subjected to 'deprogramming,' to say where their daughter was. The court held that parents are under no obligation to disclose to others who have no authority to demand the whereabouts of members of their family. The sect also lost a libel suit against Britain's *Daily Mail* which, in an article headlined 'The Church That Breaks Up Families,' claimed that the Unification Church was a 'bogus organisation, masquerading as a Christian church whose objectives in reality were political and commercial. The appeal court refused to set aside the verdict.

The moral, legal and social problems posed by such cases involve the age-old antinomy of freedom and authority. The most basic requirement for solving these problems is to distinguish between thought and action. Freedom of thought and freedom of religion are rights which must be recognised also in minors. The recognition of these rights implies that nobody should be forced to do something which is against his conscience (the basis of the exemption of 'conscientious objectors' from military duty involving the use of arms). But nobody has an unlimited right to follow his conscience in his outward conduct. In his actions, everybody is bound by the precepts or prohibitions of the law. Nobody can commit murder or arson because his conscience commands him to do those things. A teenager has the right to believe in any new religion but he has no right to leave his family without the consent of his parents or guardian. If he runs away, he can be brought back, not by force or kidnapping but by appealing to the courts. In countries where minors need the consent of their parents for getting married, they have no right to get married against their parents will but they cannot be forced to marry the mates chosen for them by their parents. In many such cases, the open conflict is the result of a lack of understanding and trust which has made it possible for such a confrontation to develop.

7

Adoption

Purposes of Adoption

ADOPTION MEANS TO ESTABLISH a parent-child relationship between persons who have no such relationship either in fact or in law. A person becomes the child of somebody who is not his or her parent and the parent makes somebody his or her child who is not so related to him or her. Adoption is practically a worldwide institution found already in many old societies. Because the continuity of the male line was considered important for political, religious, social or economic reasons, the person adopted used to be male and often adult.

The purpose and significance of adoption have undergone a certain change. Adoption has shifted from a system serving the interests of the family to a system satisfying the wants of the parents and further to an arrangement meeting the needs of the child. In the patriarchal family, the head of the house who had no son adopted a male who would become his heir and assume the leadership of the house. When the large family was replaced by the nuclear family, adoption enabled a childless couple to obtain what nature had denied them. An adopted child would provide both additional labour for the household and support for the parents in old age. In modern times, the emphasis is on giving the child parents who will provide a home, care for the child's health, upbringing and education and bestow on it the affection a child needs for an emotionally stable development.

Adoption, therefore, can answer several purposes which are by no means exclusive. Inheritance can still be a major consideration, and although modern law and practice aim at promoting the child's welfare, the adopter is not required to act from purely unselfish and altruistic motives. Adoption admits many personal considerations and the desire to continue the family line or to secure rights to inheritance do not necessarily conflict with the welfare of the child.

Adoption assumed large proportions after World War I which, on the one hand, left vast numbers of children homeless and, on the other, deprived many families of their own children. The problem of children without families has been growing since World War II with the sad increase in the number of displaced persons and refugees and the growing poverty in many developing countries. In the West, the sharp increase in the number of unwed mothers has enlarged the pool of children available for adoption.

Legal Requirements

In most countries, the adoption of adults is permitted but legal provisions are generally formulated in terms of child adoption. The adopter must usually be an adult. The consent of the child to be adopted is required if it is older (commonly over 12 or 14 years of age). An investigation of the suitability of the prospective home according to criteria stated in the governing law is often prescribed, and a probationary period of residence in the adoptive home can be stipulated. Usually, the law lays down that only a married couple can adopt a child, but in the United States, a few agencies have accepted applications by single adults. A major problem in the United States is placement across religious and ethnic lines.

Regulations have been made to protect children against exploitation and violations of their dignity. Adoption of older children involves difficulties. People are ready to adopt a new-born infant but reluctant to adopt children in the 5- to 12-year-old age group. This is understandable because couples adopting a child want to bring it up as their own and older children will retain memories of their early childhood. For the children, to be reared in a family is usually better than to grow up in an institution, but it is impossible to exclude all risks. Nobody can make a definite judgement on the genetic inheritance of the child and the attitude of the adoptive parents. Even apart from illness, death or divorce, nobody can predict how relations between the adopting parents and the adopted child will develop.

The old German law required that the adopter had no children of his own, was at least 50 years old and 18 years older than the adopted child. This requirement of a minimum age of 50 years (from which dispensation could be given) was completely wrong. Naturally, it was meant to protect against too drastic changes in the fortunes of the adopter but it created a great obstacle to the development of an emotionally strong relationship between parent and child and increased the risk that the parent would die before the child grew up. In the new law (Adoptionsgesetz of 2 July, 1976), therefore, the minimum age of the adopter has been fixed at 25 (in some cases 21) years. The provision that the adopter should have no natural children of his or her own may be appropriate in most cases but may not always work in the best interest of the parties involved (for example, the problem of an only child).

Japanese Law

According to Japanese law, only an adult can adopt (Civil Code, Art.

972). Adoption of a lineal ascendant or somebody older than the adopter is not allowed (Art. 793). For the adoption of a minor (under 20 years of age), permission of the Family Court is required but such permission is not needed if the person to be adopted is the lineal descendant of the adopter or his (her) spouse (such as a child from a previous marriage; Art. 798). For the adoption of a child under 15 years of age, the consent of his legal guardian is required (Art. 797). If the person to be adopted is married, his or her spouse must also be adopted; this is not necessary if one of the spouses of a married couple adopts a child of the other spouse (Art. 795).

Effects of Adoption

The adopted person obtains the status of a legitimate child (Art. 809) and acquires the family name of the adopter (Art. 810). Marriage between the adopted person, his (her) spouse and lineal descendants as well as their spouses on the one side and the adopter as well as his (her) lineal descendants on the other side is prohibited, even after the termination of the adoption (Art. 737).

The adoption becomes legally effective with the acceptance of the notification for entry into the family register (Art. 799). It is invalid if the parties did not intend the adoption (for example, if there has been an error in the person) or if it is not notified; it can be declared invalid if it contravenes legal requirements (Art. 802-808). The adoption can be dissolved by mutual consent; if the adopted child is below the age of 15, the consent of the person who will become his legal representative is required (Art. 811, Par. 1 & 2). If the adopting parents divorce, one of the divorcing parties must agree to assume parental rights over the adopted child (Art. 811, Par. 3). After the death of the adopting parents, the adopted child can apply to the Family Court for permission to cancel the adoption (Art. 811, Par. 6). If the adoption is rescinded, the adopted child regains his (her) former family name (Art. 816).

As explained above, the adoption of a man in order to marry a daughter of the family (usually a family without a son, *muko yôshi*) is not mentioned in the post-war law as a special form of adoption but is still possible. There is a legal provision concerning adoption by Japanese living abroad (notification to Japanese embassy or consulate, Art. 801), but nothing about the adoption of Japanese by foreigners. According to Japanese law, the requirements for adoption are governed by the laws of the home country of the parties concerned, but the legal effects of the adoption and its dissolution depend on the law of the adopting parent(s) (Law Governing the Application of Laws, Art. 19). This means that the Japanese authorities will recognise an adoption made in accordance with the law of the homeland of the adopter but can do nothing to make an adoption valid if the adopter is an alien living in Japan. According to the provisions of the conflict of laws as recognised in the United States, adoption is generally governed by the law of the place of the court which has jurisdiction over the domicile of the adoptive parents, or the child to be adopted, or both. But in Japan, the legal effect of an adoption depends on the entry into the family register, the same as for marriage, and since an alien cannot have a family register, he cannot adopt by Japanese legal procedures.

Among Japanese, the adopted person acquires the family name of the adopter, which is effected by transferring him from the family register of his natural parent(s) to that of the adoptive parents. Again, since a foreigner has no family register, no transfer is possible if a foreigner adopts a Japanese child; there will only be an annotation in the family register of the natural parent(s) that the child has been adopted, but his official family name will not change.

Not only unwanted babies are put up for adoption, but orphans, children whose parents died (for example, in an accident), disappeared or divorced, or children of parents who cannot cope are also offered for adoption. For an unwed mother opposed to abortion, private placement is often a less painful and legal way of giving up her baby than entrusting it to an institution. Arrangements are made with the adopting couple through a lawyer generally before the baby is born.

Illegitimate Children

The Japanese family register creates difficult problems for the adoption of illegitimate children. As mentioned above, an illegitimate child is entered into the family register of the mother (which virtually makes it impossible for the mother to get married except to the father of the child). If such a child is adopted, it is entered into the family register of the adoptive parents as 'adopted child,' and the fact of its illegitimacy remains obvious from the family register of the mother. People who adopt a small child and bring it up as their own do not want the child to know the facts of his or her birth until the child is mature enough to cope with them. Therefore, some people who adopted children had them registered as their natural children — which cannot be done without falsifying official documents. Some years ago, Dr Noboru Kikuta, a gynaecologist in Ichinomaki (Miyagi Prefecture), created a great stir when he announced that he had, over many years, arranged for the adoption of children of unwed mothers and reported the children as the natural children of the adopting parents. No mention of the birth, therefore, appeared in the family register of the real mother. Many women would rather have an abortion or kill the child than live as an unwed mother. What he had done, the doctor said, he had done in order to save the children's lives. To hide the fact of adoption can be helpful because people are prejudiced against adopted children and foster parents. The present adoption system, he remarked, and the family registration law should be blamed for the prevalence of infanticide. If anything should be condemned, it was the system and the law. Dr Kikuta was suspended from medical practice for six months and his suit to have the suspension cancelled was dismissed.

A revision of the Civil Code prompted by Dr Kikuta's criticism of the present system and proposed by the Legislative Council would permit the registration of an adopted child in the same way as a real child in the family register, making the adopting parents the only legal parents and severing the child's legal ties with its biological parents. But the names of the real parents would be entered in the family register separately in order to prevent consanguinous marriages. Only children under six years of age or who have been reared by the adoptive parents before they reached this age could be adopted under this system. The children could not inherit from their real parents nor would they be obliged to support them. Under the present system which would also remain in effect (the adopting parents could opt for either of the two systems) children can inherit from both their real and their adoptive parents and may also be obliged to support them.

The main objection against Dr Kikuta's procedure was that it involved the chance of marriage between brothers and sisters. Actually, however, the registration of an adopted child as the natural child of the adoptive parents has been possible in the state of New York since 1915, and has been introduced in some other states, in the Soviet Union, France and Uruguay. Under the British Children's Act passed in 1975, adopted persons over 18 may apply for access to the original records of their birth and be given the address of their natural parents. In the United States, only Alabama, Kansas and Pennsylvania allow an adult adoptee to receive his original birth certificate (which contains the names of his natural parents). Other states have set up 'mutual-consent registries' in which any adopted child or natural parent can enter his name. After both parties have registered, a meeting of the parties can be arranged. New York and California require the consent of the adoptive parents for registering children placed before 1984. Some states permit agencies that handled the adoptions to act as go-betweens in helping adoptees search for their real parents.

In June 1983, the US Supreme Court decided that the mere fact of being the natural father does not give a man the right to interfere with the adoption of a child born out of wedlock.

Foster Parents

In addition to the adoption system, there is a system of foster parents in which children are not adopted but reared in a family. The system intends to make it possible for children to be brought up in a family instead of in an institution which decreases the burden on public institutions. In Japan, the regulations require that a foster-care mother should be between 25 and 55 years of age and that one parent must not work outside the home. The family should have at least two 10-mat rooms (the traditional straw mat — *tatami* — measures 3' x 6' or 1.6525 sq. m.). Children placed in foster homes range in age from two to eighteen, and a monetary allowance is paid to private institutions and homes accepting foster children.

Baby Trade

In the United States, a large demand for adoptable babies exists because there are many couples unable to have children of their own. Because of the shortage, a black market has developed, particularly for white babies. Prices for the infants are haggled over like bargaining for a used car, with the baby often going to the highest bidder without regard to the kind of person who is doing the bidding. Adoption agencies are very active, and international rings dealing in babies sell babies from all over the world in the United States while American babies are sold in Mexico and other Latin American countries. Latin American babies are illegally adopted and smuggled to the United States and Europe. A baby abandoned or sold for $50 in Colombia or Ecuador can fetch $3,000 in Turin, Brussels or Paris, but prostitutes in European capitals are also selling their babies.

A Reuters' survey of legal and illegal adoptions revealed that you can buy a baby in the United States with no questions asked. The price could be up to $25,000. In Peru, illegal adoptions were estimated at 4,000 in 1982 and 1983; in Ecuador, tribal Indian children were adopted by American and European families for use as unpaid servants. In the Dominican Republic, police arrested five people involved in a ring which had exported 100 children to North America at the price of $10,000 a piece.

Sicilian police exposed a child adoption racket in which childless couples paid up to $12,000 for children of anonymous Yugoslav mothers who received $1,200. An official at a registry in western Sicily became suspicious when a midwife reported the birth of the first child to a woman aged 40. He checked previous birth certificates signed by the same midwife and discovered that a surprising number of births were first-time babies of women approaching middle age.

The baby trade flourishes partly because legal adoptions are hampered by red tape and are often delayed for years. The black market in some Latin American countries exists because the route to legal adoptions lies through mountains of paperwork and can take up to two years. Black market operators have been known to provide a child within 24 hours. In Bolivia, for example, adoptive couples must have a medical certificate stating that they are sterile and must show that they are psychologically suitable and financially solvent.

Illegal adoptions are often from women who refuse abortions but cannot afford to keep their children. A pregnant woman would be smuggled in from Mexico, enter a hospital posing as the wife of the adoptive father and be sent home after the birth with a small payment.

Baby Stealing

Taiwan police rounded up a gang of baby snatchers who stole at least 35 babies all over Taiwan and sold them, for an average price of $5,000, to families in Australia, Switzerland, Finland, France, Italy, the United States and Thailand. The sales were handled through a trading company which used 'order forms' but did not properly identify the babies' parents or provide documentation showing the parents' agreement to the adoption.

A London newspaper alleged that a Calcutta-based welfare organisation, the International Mission of Hope, was selling babies for adoption by overseas foster parents. Indian newspapers took up the charge. The West Bengal government instituted an inquiry which exonerated the agency. The mission had sent nearly 500 children abroad and charged adopting parents about $4,000 per child of which the largest part, $3,700, was spent on arranging the adoption and the rest used for the upkeep of the mission which took care of about 50 infants. The incident drew attention to the enormous problems of thousands of babies abandoned by mothers too poor to look after them and the inadequacy of the social services as well as the lacunae in the adoption legislation.

South Korea, India and Colombia are the major donor nations to Sweden where 1,464 foreign babies were adopted in 1983. Sweden's National Board for Inter-Country Adoptions estimates that fewer than 7 per cent of foreign adoptions are in any way illegal.

Indonesia laid down stricter regulations for the adoption of Indonesian children. Foreigners wanting to adopt an Indonesian child must have lived in the country for at least three years and must produce a medical certificate to the effect that they are incapable of producing children due to health reasons.

In the United States, arrangements for adoption before birth are legal in all states except Minnesota, Connecticut and Delaware. The problems involved in the arrangements are about the same as those complicating contracts with 'surrogate mothers.'

Many public and private agencies are looking for foster parents for the children under their care. A London institution is said to have been successful in 'marketing' its children. It advertised them by displaying their pictures in shop windows.

Children are sometimes simply just sold -- without any consideration as regards adoption. Usually, the reason is simple: the parents need money. Recently, an indigent couple were arrested in Fort Myers, Florida, for selling their two sons for $300 each so they could pay their rent. The two families who bought the children were charged with receiving a child for pay. A woman sold her three-year-old daughter to her neighbour because she wanted money for moving in with her boyfriend.

Some women realise in later life what they have lost by giving up their children for adoption. They think that they have been manipulated into agreeing to an adoption and blame society's bias in condemning the pregnancy of unmarried women.

Under the pressure of circumstances, young unmarried mothers find adoption an acceptable option for getting out of an awkward situation. As mature women, they may feel the void they have created, particularly if they cannot have other children. The anguish of infertility is aggravated by the remembrance of the child they have given away.

8

Inheritance

INHERITANCE PRESUPPOSES a system of private property as well as economic conditions under which individuals or families possess things that continue to exist and to be useful after the death of the owner. Among primitive people, the personal belongings of a deceased may be destroyed so as to protect the survivors from being haunted by his spirit. In many civilisations, victuals, utensils, weapons, treasure, slaves or wives were buried with the dead or burned to provide for his needs in the other world. But the distribution of the possessions of a deceased among his relatives or friends has also started at an early age.

Meaning of Inheritance

The restriction of inheritance to property applies only to the legal system. In a wider sense, inheritance also includes social position, political status, influence, reputation, ways of thinking and behaviour, values and principles, goals and ideals, preferences and aversions, truths and errors, expectations and prejudices. In modern society, children may have built up their own positions by the time their father dies but the social position of the father or mother may help children to gain their own social position which, therefore, is often influenced by that of their family. Social classes consist of families and class attitudes are largely transmitted by the family, the main reason why leftist education tries to eliminate the educational influence of the family.

In a society in which the large family, the 'house,' constitutes the prevailing form of family organisation, the family property and therefore inheritance is of fundamental importance. In today's society, the lack of property seems to be a more urgent problem than its devolution, but it has almost become yesterday's problem. The western world started its history as a predominantly agricultural society and property, above all ownership of land, was one of its basic institutions. A peasant's existence may be threatened by natural disasters, by droughts, floods or storms, by epidemics or wars, but as long as he can stay on the land he is able to survive. The conditions under which he and his family can maintain the occupation of the land are of vital importance.

Common Ownership

Group ownership of land is found in many societies and has persisted into modern times in India and other parts of Asia as well as in Africa. Common ownership, particularly of pastures and woods, was prominent in the development of many Teutonic and Slavic peoples in Europe. But common ownership of land, let alone of all goods, never was universal and individual ownership of land prevailed, as, for example, in the German settlement of the regions east of the Elbe in the tenth to the thirteenth century and in the European settlements in the Americas, South Africa, Australia and other parts of the world in modern times. Collective forms of ownership and cultivation of land have been introduced, partly with disappointing results, in the Soviet Union (kolkhozy), the People's Republic of China (communes) and Israel (kibbutzim).

With the development of the cities, the basic factors in the rise of a money economy, labour and technology, reduced the importance of land. Labour and work imply toil and exertion but labour is also something specifically human because it is almost always more than brute physical force and can serve as a means for man's self-realisation. It was through the industrial revolution that mass demand for labour emerged, and for today's family, work and the security of employment are much more important than property. Without work and employment, the family will have no property to transmit. For man's personal development and the function of the family, 'social' inheritance, a child's upbringing and education, is of far greater importance than the property which may become his by inheritance. This does not mean that inheritance has no longer any significance. Shôkichi Uehara, former president of Taisho Seiyaku, Japan's leading pharmaceutical firm, who died in March 1983, left an estate valued at ¥67 billion. With the greater economic affluence, inheritance has gained in importance also for middle-class families. The rise in house ownership, in particular, has made inheritance a difficult problem, and the increase in one-child families has had the effect that husband as well as wife may inherit a home.

But the 'sacredness of property,' which played such an important rôle in the debates over socialism (communism) in the nineteenth century, hardly appears to be of much consequence today. Even less essential is the relation of the right of succession to political power and status which was prominent in the Middle Ages when family law was public law and the basis of the distribution of power. In feudal society, and wherever succession implied succession to power, the son (and where the Salic law did not apply, the daughter) inherited from his father title, power and property, mainly real estate, the land and the people. As long as property remained the principal foundation and premise of power, property conferred status and the law of succession served to protect status together with property. These implications are largely irrelevant to today's world;

nevertheless, the system of private ownership remains one of the distinctive features of the so-called capitalistic economies, and private ownership is intimately connected with the West's family system.

Meaning of Ownership

Ownership concerns primarily the use of material things. In the use of things, two forms can be distinguished, the actual use of things which may be a one-time act and include their consumption, and the permanent appropriation of things. Ownership only bcomes meaningful if man's relations to things pass from a state of mere fact to a state of law. Man's use of the things of nature, and even their permanent appropriation, is a purely physical phenomenon as long as this relation between man and thing lacks social significance. It is only when the relation between man and things is considered relevant for the public order and regarded as a legal relation that the notion of ownership can apply. ('Legal' does not mean based on a law ordained by a law-giver but rights and duties that are recognised and enforced by a community.) With the development of culture, the things of nature become means of the formation of culture which is a social phenomenon connected with the formation of a public order.

Theory of Ownership

There are large differences not only in the actual systems of ownership but also in its theoretical understanding. In the scholastic theory of property, the point of departure is the 'natural' destination of external things to serve man. In theistic terms, this means that God created all things for man, a point of view which reflects the mandate related in the biblical account of man's creation: 'Be fruitful and multiply, and fill the earth and subdue it, and rule over the fishes of the sea, and the fowls of the air, and all living creatures that move upon the earth' (Gen. 1, 28). This basic relationship excludes property rights but implies that a particular individual is free to use a particular thing. It is a general ordainment of the universe to the human race which has often been called 'negative communism' because the 'community of things' is to serve the 'community of men.'

A similar view underlay a maxim often found in the works of Roman jurists which reflected Stoic thinking: *iure naturae sunt omnia communia omnibus* (by the law of nature, all things are common to all). According to the scholastic theory, any property system that disregards or contravenes this basic ordainment of things is unjust. From which it was concluded that in case of extreme necessity, the basic ordainment of things takes precedence over the disposition of positive law. Somebody in the gravest danger of losing something of greater value than property can take (or accept from others taking it for him) so much of the property of others as is necessary to escape this danger, and the owner of the property has the duty to allow this taking of his property. If the danger ceases and the property is still left, it has to be given back. (This principle is often stated in the practical example that a man can take whatever he needs if he is about to die of hunger.

Expressed in terms of law, 'negative communism' means that all men have the same right to use all things but that nobody has any ownership right. Because there is no title to property, all things would be *res nullius* (things belonging to nobody) but everybody would have the right to appropriate things for his actual use — *ius primi occupantis* is the counterpart to *res nullius*. Before international treaties and national pillage interfered with international law, all things in the oceans were considered *res nullius* as were wild animals everywhere.

The actual use of a thing would not negate 'negative communism' but its appropriation would remove the thing from the totality of the things available to all men and thus raise the question of the legitimacy of ownership. The question of ownership, therefore, arises when somebody says 'This is mine.' Nobody knows when and how this first happened but it certainly happened sometime, somewhere, and may have involved food, clothing, tools, weapons or ornaments. It seems less likely that it started with land, but it is in land that the difference between two forms of ownership became clearly recognisable, that is to say, collective ownership and private ownership. In collective ownership (which is not the same as 'negative communism'), the owner is not an individual but a group, which may be a clan (possibly prior to the family), a tribe, village, an association or the state. Private ownership is not identical with ownership by an individual. In today's property system, ownership by a family or a company is private ownership, and many property rights of public bodies are not collective but private rights.

Communism

Pierre Joseph Proudhon (1809-1865) put the question: *Qu'est-ce que la propriété?* (What is Property? — the title of one of his books) and answered: *C'est le vol* (It's theft). He was by no means the first to negate the legitimacy of private ownership. The moral censure of opulence led many Christian sects not only to advocate poverty as a religious ideal but to declare riches and even property as such as contrary to Christ's teaching. The idea of 'negative communism' dominates the patristic literature from Clemens of Alexandria to Isidore of Seville, and the assertion that private property is the result of sin is often found until the beginning of the Middle Ages. The scholastic theologians proposed various solutions to the theoretical justification of private property, but the problem of the actual distribution of wealth is still with us despite several revolutions and worldwide upheavals that so far seem to have generated only more iniquity.

Legitimacy of Private Property According to St Thomas Acquinas

St Thomas Aquinas treats the question of the legitimacy of private property in two steps. He first (S. theol. 2-2, q. 66, a.1) inquires whether the possession of external things is natural for man and explains that external things can be considered with regard to their nature, and in this sense, they are not subject to man's power but only to divine power. Then, things can be considered according to their use, and in this way, man has a 'natural dominion' over external things. 'Use' includes the usefulness inherent in things as well as making use of them, and 'man' stands for the human race. A right understanding *(secundum rationem)* discloses the dominance of man because things are made in such a way that man can use them. Elaborating his thought, St Thomas explains that God in his providence ordained some things to the corporal sustenance of man and that therefore man has a natural dominion over things with respect to the power of using them.

This first step applies to the appropriation of things possible under a system of 'negative communism' but says nothing about individual ownership. The second article, therefore, poses the question whether it is allowed for somebody to possess some thing as his own. With regard to external things, St Thomas says, two things have to be taken into account, first, the power to procure and dispense (distribute) things and, second, the use of external things. To possess things as one's own is lawful as far as the power of procurement and distribution is concerned, and St Thomas gives three reasons: 1. Everybody is more concerned with procuring something over which he alone can dispose than something which is common to all. 2. By letting everybody have power over things for himself, human affairs are treated with more order. 3. In this way, a more peaceful situation is preserved among men.

As for the use of external things, however, man should consider external things not as his own but as common. In the ordinary way of speaking, this sounds somewhat puzzling because to procure and dispose of things certainly implies using them. But what St Thomas means here is that the institution of private property has to respect the ordainment of all things for the use of mankind. A property system that makes the access of some people to the use of external things impossible is against the natural order of things. In a further elaboration, St Thomas explains that common ownership is said to be an institution of natural law not in the sense that natural law commands that all things be owned in common and nothing be owned as one's own (that is, positive communism), but because separate (or private) ownership is not based on natural law but on human convention which pertains to positive law. Therefore, private property is not against natural law but has been added to natural law as an invention of human reason (meaning that men have found it more reasonable to have private property, and the reasons are the three given above: greater efficiency, better order, and more peace in handling external things). Some scholastic theologians speculated that the institution of private property would have been unnecessary if mankind had remained in the state of original innocence and thus come to the conclusion that it is on account of man's depravity that private property has become necessary, but neo-scholastic authors generally try to defend private property as somehow based on natural law although they recognise that the actual property systems have been established by positive law.

On the whole, the arguments of St Thomas and the theologians who followed in his footsteps show that private property is a useful arrangement since man as a social being must live in harmony with his fellow men, but since every actual system of private ownership is devised by men under particular historical conditions, every system has its limitations and drawbacks. One of the basic shortcomings of every system is the impossibility of ensuring compliance with the proviso that the ordination of all things to serve mankind (and hence the possibility of every human being to avail himself of material things to sustain his life) is left intact. Private ownership certainly appeals to man's acquisitiveness and is an incentive to work, but in a money economy, there are no inherent limitations to the accumulation of wealth and no checks to its unequal distribution even to an extent incompatible with the basic equality of all human beings. There is no compelling reasons why the right of private ownership should extend to all kinds of property, nor does it seem reasonable that an owner should have the right to do with his property whatever he pleases.

There was a famous controversy regarding this last point occasioned by an expression in the French Civil Code. Article 544 of the Code said: *La propriété est le pouvoir de jouir et de disposer des choses de la manière la plus absolue.* This gave the impression that ownership confers an absolute right over things only subject to limitations imposed by positive law (the Code provides, *pourvu qu'on n'en fasse pas un usage prohibé par la loi ou les règlements),* but such an assertion is basically incorrect and was probably not intended by the authors of the Code. The passage referred to above was obviously drafted in view of Article 17 of the *Declaration des Droits de l'Homme* which proclaimed that the right of ownership was *inviolable et sacré.* This article was not meant to assert something like absolute sovereignty over things but that ownership was not subject to the old feudal rights and particularly the right of eminent domain as understood in the eighteenth century. Ownership cannot mean a right which includes the negation of the basic ordainment of things to serve mankind. There can be differences of opinion about the merits of different ways of using things but the destruction of property in order to enhance the (market) value of the rest seems hardly consistent with the meaning of property.

Political Signficance of Private Property

Property has been called a necessary condition of human freedom.

Without economic independence, man cannot guard his freedom. But in today's economy, economic independence is the exception and economic dependence the rule, and man must rely on the public order and the protection of personal liberty provided by law. Unfortunately, some of the institutions and agencies originally intended to protect the freedom of economically dependent individuals (for example, labour unions) have become instruments of oppression. In today's economy, property has little significance for the protection of liberty, although wealth is extremely important for power.

As mentioned above, relatively few individuals can provide for their families because they own property, and the same holds true for contingencies such as accidents or illness as well as old age and death. In today's economy, the property left behind by the breadwinner can take care of the needs of his surviving dependents only in relatively few families. There is neither a 'natural' obligation nor a 'natural' right to provide for one's offspring through the accumulation of property and the transmission of this property. On the other hand, it seems 'equitable' that parents can leave their property to their children, and although this is not necessarily the only consideration relevant to the law of inheritance, it should not be completely neglected. In an economy in which property formed the foundation of independence and freedom, continuity of ownership was important for the preservation of the family, its stability and its ability to fulfil the functions of a 'community of life.' Providing for the future was an integral part of the tasks of the family as a 'community of successive generations.' The modern family is not rooted in the soil and its mobility and atomisation relegate provision for the future to a hypothetical rôle. In the law of inheritance, therefore, emphasis shifted from securing the economic foundation of the family to an equitable distribution of the assets among the individual members of the family.

The system of inheritance has been attacked because it furthers the accumulation of wealth in a few hands. There is some truth in that assertion but private fortunes are of less importance today than they used to be, and the modern state inhibits the growth of individual wealth by progressive taxation, particularly the progressive taxation of estates (although these measures are not always very effective). The importance of individual fortunes is overshadowed by the enormous conglomerations of wealth (and thereby of economic and political power) in corporate form. Furthermore, there are hardly any acceptable alternatives to inheritance. To let everybody grab a dead man's possessions on a first-come, first-served basis would be incompatible with an orderly society, and to let the state take over everything would aggrandise the state's power which already is far too pervasive for a free society.

In western countries, two systems serve the transfer of the property of the decedent to his survivors, intestate succession in which the decedent's property is distributed to his relatives in an order fixed by law, and the disposition of the property by last will and testament. The rules incorporated in these systems determine to what extent a property owner can choose to whom his property will go, in particular, whether he can leave it to a single individual.

Testamentary Disposition of Property

The freedom to dispose of one's property has often been limited just as ownership itself has been limited. In Rome, the right to dispose of property by testament went through various stages. It was fully recognised in the first century AD and reached its mature form in Justinian's *Corpus Iuris* in the sixth century which became the model for continental Europe in the Middle Ages. Originally, the Roman testament had to start with the institution of the heir *(heredis institutio)*; every disposition preceding this designation was invalid. For this designation, a set formula was to be used *(Titius heres esto)*, but in the times of the Antonine emperors, *Titium heredem esse iubeo* had also become valid. In later times, *mancipatio*, that is, purchase, became one of the forms of making a will; the testator acted like a vendor, and the heir as a purchaser *(familiae emptor)*, buying the whole estate of the former.

The freedom of testation incorporated in the Roman law system was diametrically opposed to the old German law based on the idea of the 'natural' heir *(der Erbe wird geboren und nicht erkoren)*. Inheritance has often been regulated by custom. In the German region of Franconia, the eldest son became owner of the farm but the right to brew beer (which was connected with almost all larger farms) was inherited by the eldest daughter.

Limitations on Freedom of Testation

The freedom of testation has often been limited for what were called 'reasons of public policy.' A conspicuous example was the rule against perpetuities in English law barring limitations that would make a property unalienable for a longer period than a life or lives in being, and 21 years beyond. A more recent tendency restricts the circle of people who can inherit from a person who died intestate. Under the English Administration of Estates Act of 1925, this circle was limited to grandparents, uncles and sisters of the decedent. Among the Germanic peoples, land was controlled by the kinship groups, and later, feudal rules left no place for disposition by will.

In modern law, two tendencies appeared. Proceeding from the premise implied in Roman law that the entire estate is the property of the deceased, the property is, on principle, subject to the free disposition of the testator, and his freedom is only limited in favour of certain persons for reasons of equity (German and Japanese codes). The other view considers the property of the deceased as property of the family or related to the family and therefore restricts the freedom of disposal to a certain portion of the property. Hence, the freedom of the testator to disinherit his surviving spouse, children or other heirs has been limited. A testator who is survived by descendants, parents or (in some countries) brothers, sisters or even more distant relatives cannot dispose of what is called the 'reserved portion' of his estate. The size of this share depends on the number and the degree of nearness of the surviving 'forced heirs.'

In English law, the interest of dower guaranteed a life estate to the widow in the real estate of the predeceased husband, and a widower was entitled to curtsy, a life-rent in his wife's immovable property. These rights disappeared in England but were preserved in the majority of the states in the United States. Under this system, each spouse had an 'estate' in the realty of the other spouse, a portion of which continued beyond the death of one spouse until the death of the surviving spouse. The system has been abolished, for example, in New York state because it was a great nuisance in the conveyance of real property without providing adequate protection.

Some American states have adopted the so-called community property system which also exists in numerous European and Latin-American countries. The community property generally consists of the property acquired during the marriage by the gainful activities of either spouse, and the surviving spouse is entitled to one-half of the community property. In the German and Scandinavian systems, the assets of husband and wife remain separate, but upon the termination of the marriage, the property acquired in the course of the marriage is distributed among them. In France, community property law applies unless it has been expressly contracted out by the parties to the marriage.

In the Soviet Union, a compulsory share of two-thirds of his intestate share is guaranteed to each minor child of the decedent and to any of the following who are unable to work: the decedent's children, spouse, parents, brothers, sisters and incapacitated persons who were dependent upon the decedent for at least one year prior to his death.

Primogeniture

The question of undivided inheritance was of special importance in feudal times in Europe when primogeniture was the prevailing form of inheritance for land. But other forms have also been in use, such as secundogeniture (certain lands went to the second son), tertiogeniture and, under Nazi law, a system of ultimogeniture existed for farms. Primogeniture prevented agricultural holdings from becoming too small which happened in France under the strict system of partition introduced by the Code Civil. An amendment now makes it possible to postpone at least temporarily the physical partition of a farmstead and certain other small holdings. In continental Europe, the *fideicommissum* of late Roman law was used by the nobility to preserve their estates intact while their political power enabled them to procure lucrative positions in church, army and the ever-growing bureaucracy for their younger sons. Otherwise, the reception of Roman law introduced the freedom of testation which contributed to the dissolution of the family, particularly the rural family. The modern codes do not recognise the family as a subject of rights which makes family property impossible. Due to the individualistic character of the law, farm property was divided over and over again, and the shrinking size of the farms made them economically inefficient and reduced the social status of the rural population. In Japan, the small size of most farms has made farming largely a secondary occupation, and for most farmers, wages constitute the largest part of their income (in fiscal 1980, wage income accounted for 78.9 per cent, and income from farming for only 21.1 per cent of the income of the average rural household).

Last Will and Testament

The usual way in which a person lays down what shall be done with his or her possessions in the event of his or her death is by the practice of 'last will and testament.' The term 'will' as an expression of the final disposition of one's property is confined to English law, whereas the term 'testament' derives from Roman civil law and is used in continental jurisprudence. Last will and testament means an instrument embracing equally real and personal property, constituting a legal declaration whereby a person makes a disposition of his property to take effect after his death. Since it is a unilateral disposition (not a contract), it can always be revoked or amended. The juridical construction of a will involves the difficulty that it only takes effect at the moment of the testator's death or precisely when he is no longer capable of any human action.

A will must take the form of an instrument in writing. A nuncupative (orally declared) will is exceptionally admitted in some jurisdictions in emergency situations, such as those of a soldier on active war duty, a sailor on board ship, or a person finding himself in immediate danger of death.

The main forms of wills found in today's legal systems are 1. the witnessed will; 2. the unwitnessed holographic will; 3. the notarial will. The witnessed will is an instrument which may be typed or printed or written by anyone subscribed by the testator whose signature must be attested by two or three witnesses who must also sign their names to the instrument. This form prevails throughout the United States and in the common-law parts of the British Commonwealth. The holographic will which is recognised in most civil-law countries and in many states in the South and West of the United States requires an instrument written entirely and exclusively in the testator's own handwriting. It must include the date, indicate the place of execution and be signed by the testator. Witnesses are not required. The notarial will is in use in most civil-law countries. The testator either dictates his provisions to the notary (a member of the legal profession not to be confused with the notary-public in the United States) or hands him an instrument declaring that it contains his will.

Intestate Succession

A person is said to die intestate if he dies without making a will or without leaving anything to testify what his wishes or intentions were with respect to the disposition of his property. In this case, succession takes place according to the rules laid down in law and the estate is distributed to the persons and in the order prescribed by law. There has been no uniformity in the selection of the groups to which the property is allotted in the case of intestate succession. In the past, one of the most prominent tendencies was to keep property, particularly real estate, within the bloodline. The Roman emperor Justinian regulated intestate succession by new legislation (novella) which distinguished four classes of relatives and this regulation has greatly influenced Anglo-American law. These classes were as follows: 1. descendants of the decedent; 2. ascendants of the decedent, his full-blood brothers and sisters and the children of such brothers and sisters; 3. the decedent's half-brothers and half-blood sisters and the children of such brothers and sisters; 4. the other collaterals of the decedent related to him in the nearest grade of consanguinity.

No person in a more remote class was to succeed as long as the decedent was survived by a member of a prior class. The surviving spouse stood outside the four classes of relatives. He or she was to succeed only if there was no blood relative at all. As long as any blood relative, no matter how remote, could be found, the family wealth was not to be diverted from the bloodline. But a widow's needs were ordinarily taken care of by the dowry which, given to the husband by the bride's family at the time of the marriage, was to be hers after the husband's death. For the exceptional case of a 'poor widow,' that is, a widow without dowry, a share in the estate was provided.

German law regulated succession by so-called *parentelae* — lines of descendants and ascendants. The first parentela comprises all lineal descendants of the decedent, the second, the parents of the decedent and their desendants, the third, the decedent's grandparents and their descendants, and so on. In each parentela, heirs of the first degree (generation) are entitled to equal shares, and a deceased is represented by his (her) descendants among whom his (her) share is divided. As long as there are descendants of the first parentela, no property passes to the second parentela, and the same applies to the other parentelae. The spouse is not included in this scheme but is assigned a certain portion of the inheritance apart from it.

Legal Portion

In modern legislation, the main concern has been the protection of the interests of the surviving spouse and children and to prevent what was regarded as an arbitrary disposal of the property. The provision of a legal portion is one of the methods used for this purpose. The legal portion cannot be changed by testamentary disposition except in certain cases (such as, an attempt at the life of the testator, maltreatment, and so forth).

Illegitimate and Adopted Children

Illegitimate children have been given inheritance rights also with regard to their father's property in the Scandinavian countries, the German Federal Republic, in several Latin American countries, in the countries of Eastern Europe, in England and Wales, Scotland and in some states of the United States. The new Greek Family Law made the inheritance rights of illegitimate children the same as those of legitimate offspring. In West Germany, an illegitimate child can ask for an anticipatory settlement of his claim against the father in the period from his 21st to his 27th year of age (BGB, Art. 1934d). This regulation intends to provide the child with a 'head start' capital.

The common law rule that illegitimate children are not entitled to inherit from their natural fathers was held to violate the equal protection clause of the 14th Amendment by the Rhode Island Supreme Court. A child born out of wedlock may inherit from his father if he is able to prove by clear and convincing evidence that he is the child of the individual he claims to be his father, the court ruled. Under common law, an illegitimate child had the right to inherit from his/her mother but could only inherit from the father if the parents married and the father acknowledged the child as his own.

Laws on inheritance of adopted children differ considerably. As a general rule, the child may inherit from the adoptive parents and they from him, but in German law, adoption does not create a right of inheritance for the adopting parents — for obvious reasons. Inheritance of the child from his natural parents, once commonplace, is increasingly prohibited, except in case of adoption by step-parents. There has been a trend to broaden the right of an adopted child to inherit from relatives of the adoptive parents.

Personal Assets

The growing complexity of the economy has created problems that could not be foreseen when the present law of inheritance was formulated. In today's law of inheritance, only rights pertaining to personal assets making up the estate of an individual are capable of transmission by inheritance. Since a corporation cannot die, it cannot be a testator, and although it cannot be an heir, it can be a legatee. Purely personal rights do not pass by inheritance but personal assets may include a great variety of present and future rights, corporeal property, claims, interests in organisations, enterprises, patents, trade marks and other industrial property, rights to royalties and other literary property. To preserve a family enterprise, a complex arrangement of testamentary dispositions,

Elderly people may bequeath their property to an institution or agency in exchange for the promise to take care of them in their old age while divorce and remarriage complicate the traditional inheritance system.

For jurisprudence, inheritance involves a few theoretical problems to which no satisfactory solution has been found. In intestate succession, a considerable time may elapse before the estate is settled and during this period, the ownership is, so to speak, in limbo: the old owner is dead and no longer capable of any rights; the new owner is not yet fixed so that there is only a potential or prospective owner or owners. For some forms of disposing of one's property in the event of death, a more or less acceptable jurisprudential explanation can be offered. The *donatio mortis causa,* a gift to take effect when the donor shall no longer exist, can be explained as a gift among the living with a suspensive or resolutive condition, and a similar arrangement is the hereditary contract recognised in German law. There are legal arrangements which take effect upon the death of a person which do not involve rights or dipositions of the deceased (for example, insurance).

Japanese Law on Inheritance

The law of inheritance is enormously complex and cannot be summarised in a few pages. Below are some of the most important provisions of the Japanese law on inheritance.

In the case of intestate succession, a system combining features of the Justinian and the parentela systems explained above is used. Relatives in the same degree of relationship to the deceased are entitled to equal shares of the inheritance, and as long as a member of a prior class survives, nobody in a more remote class has any claim to the inheritance. Until 1962, the classes of heirs were defined as follows: 1. lineal descendants; 2. lineal ascendants; 3. brothers and sisters. In 1962, the designation of the heirs in the first class was changed from 'lineal descendants' to 'children' (Civil Code, Art. 887, Par. 1). The effect of the change was that grandchildren and later generations no longer have an independent right to inheritance and can only inherit if they take the place of a child who has died or has otherwise lost his right to inherit (Art. 887, Par. 2 & 3). If, therefore, the decedent had children, the inheritance will be divided on the basis of the number of children, and if all children had died at the time the inheritance takes place and all heirs are grandchildren, they will not receive equal shares (as would be the case in a strict parentela system) but grandchildren will receive the parental share.

The share of an illegitimate child is only half that of a legitimate child, and the same is the case for the shares of half-brothers and half-sisters (Art. 900, Nr. 4). The draft of the revision of the inheritance law had contained a provision making the rights of illegitimate children the same as those of legitimate children, but the proposal met stiff resistance from the Liberal-Democratic Party and was dropped.

A presumptive heir is disqualified from inheriting if he has been punished for killing or attempting to kill the inheritee or an heir of a higher rank, if he knew of the intention to kill the inheritee and failed to reveal or denounce the plot, if he tried by deceit or coercion to influence the making of a will or falsified, altered or destroyed a will. A presumptive heir is cut off if he maltreated or gravely insulted the inheritee or for other serious misbehaviour. Because the inheritance takes place the moment the inheritee dies (Art. 882), only those living at that time can become heirs, but the law provides that a child already conceived at the time of death is considered as having been born unless it is still-born (Art. 886).

An adopted child has the same right to inherit as a natural child. If an adopted child married a real child (mukoiri kekkon), both husband and wife are entitled to an equal share in the inheritance. But no duplication of title is recognised. If an illegitimate child has been adopted, it inherits only as an adopted child (its right as an illegitimate child becomes extinct). If the elder brother has adopted a younger brother, the younger brother loses his right to inherit as brother.

If there are no children, the inheritance goes to the parents, but there is no substitution for parents because in the absence of parents, the inheritance goes to brothers and sisters. For those, the rules of substitution are the same as for children (Art. 889, Par. 2).

'The spouse always becomes heir' (Art. 890). There is no problem if the spouse is entered in the family register at the time of the death of the inheritee, but in the case of a nai-en relationship, the situation is difficult. There is no general rule that a nai-en relationship will be treated as a regular marriage. The law provides that the family court can recognise the rights of somebody who has shared the household of the decedent and has taken care of him or has had some other special relationship with him (Art. 958-3). Mere cohabitation, irrespective of its length, is not enough to support such a claim but if cohabitation was preceded by a marriage ceremony and the parties were considered husband and wife and only failed to register the marriage, the claim will generally be recognised. The *nai-en* relationship may involve some problems such as to differentiate between a *nai-en* spouse and a concubine, or the case of a man who lives apart from his wife without a divorce and cohabits with another woman. Also problematic is the inheritance in case spouses agreed to divorce but failed to register the divorce. A moot point in the present law is the absence of substitution between spouses. If the husband dies before his parents, the wife is not entitled to inherit from the husband's parents — which is not inequitable if there are children who take the place of the father but seems unfair if there are no children (naturally, this is the necessary result of the Justinian principle of inheritance based on blood relationship). Spouses who cannot solve their problems will usually divorce, but it is also possible to disinherit each other. A divorced spouse is not entitled to a share in the inheritance.

Inheritance does not require a special legal qualification so that, generally speaking, foreigners can become heirs of Japanese. But there are cases in which ownership is restricted to Japanese (cf. Alien Land Law, Art. 1; Mining Industry Law, Art. 17) so that the foreign wife of a Japanese who retained her foreign nationality would be unable to inherit that part of the property of her husband.

As mentioned above, special provisions regulate the inheritance of family tables, religious articles and family tombs (Art. 897, Par. 1).

The entire estate of the decedent with all rights and duties is the object of the inheritance with the exception of strictly personal rights. According to a decision of the Supreme Court, the right to compensation of the victim of a traffic accident passes to his heirs even if no claim has been filed.

The heir or heirs must declare within three months after being informed of the inheritance whether they accept it, either unconditionally or with reservations, or reject it.

There are two kinds of apportionment of the inheritance fixed by law. The first is the partition in case of intestate succession (or if the testator's will is invalid), the second by the assignment of legal portions which the testator cannot change. In case of intestate succession, the surviving spouse is entitled to one-half and the children to the other half of the estate (prior to the revision of the law which went into effect on 1 January, 1981, the children received two-thirds and the surviving spouse one-third). In case spouse and ascendants are the heirs, the spouse receives two-thirds and the ascendants one-third. If the inheritance is divided among spouse and brothers and sisters, the spouse is entitled to three-quarters, brothers and sisters to one-quarter.

In case spouse and children are the heirs, the legal portion is one-half each for the spouse and the children. If the spouse and lineal ascendants are the heirs, the legal portion of the spouse is two-thirds, that of the ascendants one-third. For spouse and brothers and sisters, the spouse is entitled to three-quarters, brothers and sisters to one-quarter. Renunciation of the legal portion prior to the inheritance is only valid if it is sanctioned by the family court. The renunciation of one co-heir does not affect the rights of the other co-heirs (Art. 1043).

If one (or possibly several) of the joint heirs has made a particular contribution to the creation or increase of the estate of the deceased, this individual can be given a larger share of the inheritance commensurate with his (her) contribution either by agreement of the joint heirs or by the adjudgement of the family court (Art. 904-2). This system, which also went into effect on 1 January, 1981, is meant to apply if the partition according to the common rules of inheritance would be unfair. A wife who has contributed to the estate of the husband by her work can claim such preferential treatment but the system cannot be used by a wife who has 'only' performed ordinary household chores (the increase in the share of the spouse in case of intestate succession or in the legal portion was designed to remunerate the contribution of the housewife). Neither can the partner in a nai-en relationship invoke these provisions to claim a share in the inheritance.

A person full fifteen years old is capable of making a will (Art. 961). The law recognises three ordinary forms of wills: holographic will (Art. 968), notarial will (Art. 969) and secret will (Art. 970). Special forms are the will of a person in extremis (Art. 976), the will of a person in quarantine (Art. 977), the will of a person on board ship (Art. 978), and the will of a shipwrecked person (Art. 979).

The law makes it possible to give the surviving spouse economic security so that a wife has not to rely on the children after the death of her husband. Even if there are children, the wife can be left three-quarters of the estate by will. If, however, a family enterprise is not organised as a joint-stock company, it may be difficult to preserve it intact.

According to a survey of the Prime Minister's Office, about 80 per cent of old people owning property would leave their property to the eldest son or any other child willing to take care of them in their old age. About twice as many men as women would prefer to leave their possessions to their eldest son while twice as many women as men would divide them equally among all children. About one in five is in favour of the arrangement to leave his or her estate to a local entity in exchange for the promise to take care of them in their old age. A majority of old people (52.3 per cent) would not leave their property to children who would not look after them in their old age.

The principle of equal shares for all children introduced after World War II did not find ready acceptance in rural districts. Theoretically, equal inheritance means equal shares in value and does not require actual division of the land but most Japanese farms are small and the land used to be the only object of substantial value parents could bequeath their children. It was usual that the land and the other properties necessary for cultivation were left to the eldest son while the other children waived their right of inheritance or were given funds to start a business while girls were given a bridal trousseau. In former years, the management of the farm became rather difficult when the other children were compensated with money but the enormous increase in rural wealth (thanks to the government's policy of retaining the war-time rice control system under which the government buys up almost the entire rice crop at prices considerably higher — in 1986 by a factor of 8 — than world market prices) has solved this difficulty. Moreover, full-time farmers account for only 14.3 per cent of Japan's farm households (1985: 4,376,000 households) while another 17.7 per cent are engaged in agriculture as their main occupation but derive income also from other work; for 68.0 per cent of all farm households, agriculture is only a secondary occupation.

The rural custom preserved some of the features of the feudal family system. The position of the head of the house was passed on from father to son and from generation to generation. The heir of the house *(katoku, atome)* had a privileged status. As a rule, the eldest son became heir and succeeded to the property of the house which had been owned under the father's name. The younger sons and the daughters had no right to inherit anything of the house property. But the inequality of rights was accompanied by unequal duties. The eldest son was responsible for the support of the parents as well as his younger brothers and sisters.

For most Japanese families, the inheritance tax is no heavy burden. According to the existing taxation system, all liabilities of the deceased and the funeral costs can be subtracted from the estate. Religious articles are tax-exempt. Of life insurance payments, ¥2.5 million multiplied by the number of heirs and ¥2 million of retirement allowances paid on account of the death multiplied by the number of heirs are tax-exempt. A basic allowance of ¥20 million plus ¥4 million for each legal heir can be deducted for minor children and for handicapped children. The inheritance tax is calculated on the basis of the legal order of succession and the amount thus calculated is allocated in proportion to the share in the estate actually received by each heir. The share of the surviving spouse is tax-exempt if it does not exceed one-half of the estate. The tax rate varies according to the taxable amount and ranges from 10 per cent for amounts under ¥1 million to 75 per cent for amounts exceeding ¥500 million but there are certain offsets and allowances. Generally speaking, the Japanese inheritance tax is not used as a means for the redistribution of property but as a relatively minor source of fiscal revenue.